P9-AOU-521

915
Hil

95134

Hill.
The Indian sub-
    continent.

Date Due

The Library
Nazareth College of Rochester, N. Y.

THE INDIAN SUB-CONTINENT

Rockliff New Project Illustrated Geographies

by P. R. HEATON, B.SC., F.R.G.S.

Headmaster, Holmshill Secondary School, Boreham Wood

CANADA

"A beautifully produced book containing all any pupil would need to know about Canada – and much more which makes it fascinating reading." *Teachers' World.* "Likely to have an appeal, not only to children for whom it was intended, but to adults wishing to know more of Canada, for whom the text is refreshingly free from unexpressive text-book English." *The Schoolmaster.* "The first of a promising series. It would be hard to praise it too highly." *The Librarian.* "Detailed but not boring, and although written for lower secondary, many of the seniors of the secondary will be glad to have access to them." *Scottish Journal of Education.*

Fully illustrated, bound in cloth   21s. net

CANADA – Practical Book

A book of illustrative models to make from scrap material to accompany the study of Canada.

Demy 4to, card covers   10s. 6d.

ANTARCTICA

"Could be placed with advantage in the libraries of both primary and secondary schools." *National Froebel Foundation Bulletin.* "Stimulating and full of interest." *The Independent School.* "Abundant and well-chosen photographs illustrate a stimulating text." *School Library Association Journal.*

Fully illustrated, bound in cloth   8s. 6d. net

AUSTRALASIA *In Preparation*

THE ROCKLIFF NEW PROJECT
ILLUSTRATED GEOGRAPHY

THE
INDIAN SUB-CONTINENT

by

JOHN HILL
B.Sc. (Econ).

MAPS AND DRAWINGS BY CHARLES GREEN

BARRIE & ROCKLIFF
LONDON

NAZARETH COLLEGE LIBRARY
DISCARDED

© JOHN HILL 1963
FIRST PUBLISHED 1963 BY
BARRIE AND ROCKLIFF (BARRIE BOOKS LTD.)
2 CLEMENT'S INN, LONDON WC2

PRINTED IN GREAT BRITAIN BY
THE TEMPLAR PRESS
WARSTONE LANE
BIRMINGHAM

95134

DISCARDED

CONTENTS

PREFACE

This book is about the Indian Sub-continent – that large region in which lie the Commonwealth nations of India, Pakistan and Ceylon, together with small independent states in the Himalayas. It is a vast, roughly triangular patch of the world's surface which has always held the imaginations of kings, soldiers, empire-builders, traders and adventurers. Here live peoples of different races, religions, customs and habits; of widely different environments from the icy Himalayas to the suffocating jungles of Kerala. Here is a contrast of modern and ancient; ruined temples, stand near power stations and factories. Here is the clash of poverty and wealth; families live on fifteen shillings a week in the shadows of princes' palaces.

In this book you will learn of the people, their past and present, their livelihoods, their fascinating customs; of industries producing everything from cars to canned curries; of primitive Stone Age tribes; of wild animals, and many other things.

But to give an adequate picture of this vast land within a single book is impossible. The book is intended as a base from which you start your own individual projects and as a spur to further studies.

The question which then arises is what are you individually to do? The answer will depend very much on yourself. Whatever arouses your personal interests should be pursued by reading some of the very many books about the Sub-continent, including selected articles in encyclopaedias. Such books are in your nearest Public Library or can be ordered for your own school use. The books should not be the school textbooks – this is your textbook – but should be about travel, animals, products, dress, peoples, etc. These books are not by any standards dull reading. How can they be when they tell of hunting tigers, of living with primitive tribes, building dams and cutting canals, climbing the world's highest mountains? Those of you who read such books as *The Ascent of Everest* and *Man Eaters of Kumaon* will realise this.

Your researches should be recorded in your notebook so that they can be written up as a final essay or report and illustrated with your own drawings.

As well as books you can use travel brochures, tourist guides, booklets and posters. These mines of information can be got by writing a polite letter to the Indian, Pakistan and Ceylon Commissions in London explaining that you are studying their countries in school and would appreciate information and booklets. You will be surprised at the generous response. These offices also have film libraries that can be used by schools. Among other sources, keep a watch on television and radio programmes.

Much of the material should be carefully handled so that later pupils can have the benefit of your initiative. But much can be used straight away in major group projects. Your geography room will have facilities for display. The pictures and maps could be worked up into a Form wall-display, with pupils' essays and descriptions accompanying the illustrations. A note here: compose the texts yourselves but try to have them typewritten as this looks better and is easier to read than hand-writing.

But there are things to do with your hands. This book contains many drawings and pictures especially selected to help you make models of boats, houses, tools, etc. With a little patience and imagination, models can be made from materials as common as drinking straws, match boxes, cardboard, raffia, etc. What you model is a matter of your own choice and your teacher's permission. An exciting project in which every member of the form can do some specialised task, is to make a large scale model of a village. There are a number of drawings and illustrations in this book to guide you. The choice of individual topics is wide. Girls might like to work on the varied and beautiful dress of Indian women, but boys will find the hunting weapons of a tribe more interesting. One with a mechanical bent might like to study the workings of a major dam like Bakhra; another interested in art would move towards Indian painting or the wall carvings of a temple.

From this introduction you will gather that *The Indian Sub-continent* is a starting point for a great number of adventures in learning. Study it well and from it select your own particular interest. The countries offer opportunities for many and varied adventures, but one last word of advice. Whatever topic you choose for specialist study, it should be followed as far as time and space will allow.

INTRODUCTION

AN HISTORICAL BACKGROUND

RACES OF THE SUB-CONTINENT

THE Indian sub-continent is populated by a great diversity of races, cultures and languages; there are more than 170 minor and fifteen major languages in the Indian Union alone. The following are the main racial stocks of the sub-continent.

1 *Negroid:* These, the first people to live in India, came from Africa and bore a close resemblance to the people of that continent. Few traces of this race remain on the Indian mainland today, but the Andaman Islanders belong to this group.

2 *Australoid:* This group is closely related to the aborigines of Australia and has a culture not much more advanced than theirs. The Veddhas of Ceylon and the tribes of central India are survivals of these primitive people.

3 *Dravidians:* Some time before 3500 B.C. these people, coming from Asia Minor, brought the first advanced civilisation to India. They settled in the fertile Indus valley and built large and prosperous cities like Mohenjo-daro. The coming of the Aryans and, perhaps, excessive flooding of the river Indus, caused the downfall of the Dravidians in the north. Today they are found mainly in southern India and make up 20% of the Union's total population.

4 *Aryans:* The migration of these people into India from the Middle East established Hinduism in the sub-continent. The Aryans produced the great literature of Hinduism, the *Vedas*, the *Upanishads*, the *Gita* and the heroic epic of the *Ramayana*. They came in from the north-west and pushed the less advanced Dravidians to the south. The Aryans did not mix with the peoples they encountered in the new land, but assimilated them into their society as low, servant castes or 'out-castes'. These Aryans were pastoralists and brought an advanced culture to India. They invented the decimal system, made great discoveries in medicine and astrology and gave India her village society.

5 *Muslims:* Peoples belonging to this great religious group entered India in waves between the eighth and eighteenth centuries. India first met Islam through the Arab traders, but later Afghans and the Moguls invaded India to set up states of varying permanency. The Mogul Empire which centred upon Delhi brought the first unity to the heart of India.

The pattern of these great migrations is clear. Each invading people aimed at the fertile northern plains where agriculture was easy. They defeated and displaced the existing peoples by superior arms and techniques and drove them into less favourable areas; the Dravidians pushed the early tribes into the jungles of central India where the natural environment was so difficult that they have remained primarily primitive hunters, collectors and hoe cultivators; the Aryans drove the Dravidians from the wide fertile plains to the Deccan. Because each fresh migration aimed at the fertile northern plains, the Deccan and south became places of refuge for the vanquished.

INDIA AND THE WEST:
ANCIENT AND CLASSICAL TIMES

TRADE in spices, ivory, peacocks, gems and rare woods brought about the earliest contact between India and the Mediterranean civilisations. The Phoenicians took their ships as far as the west coast of India to trade for these goods. In 1000 B.C. King Solomon's ships visited Ophir, now thought to have been where the small village of Puvar stands in Kerala. They were seeking

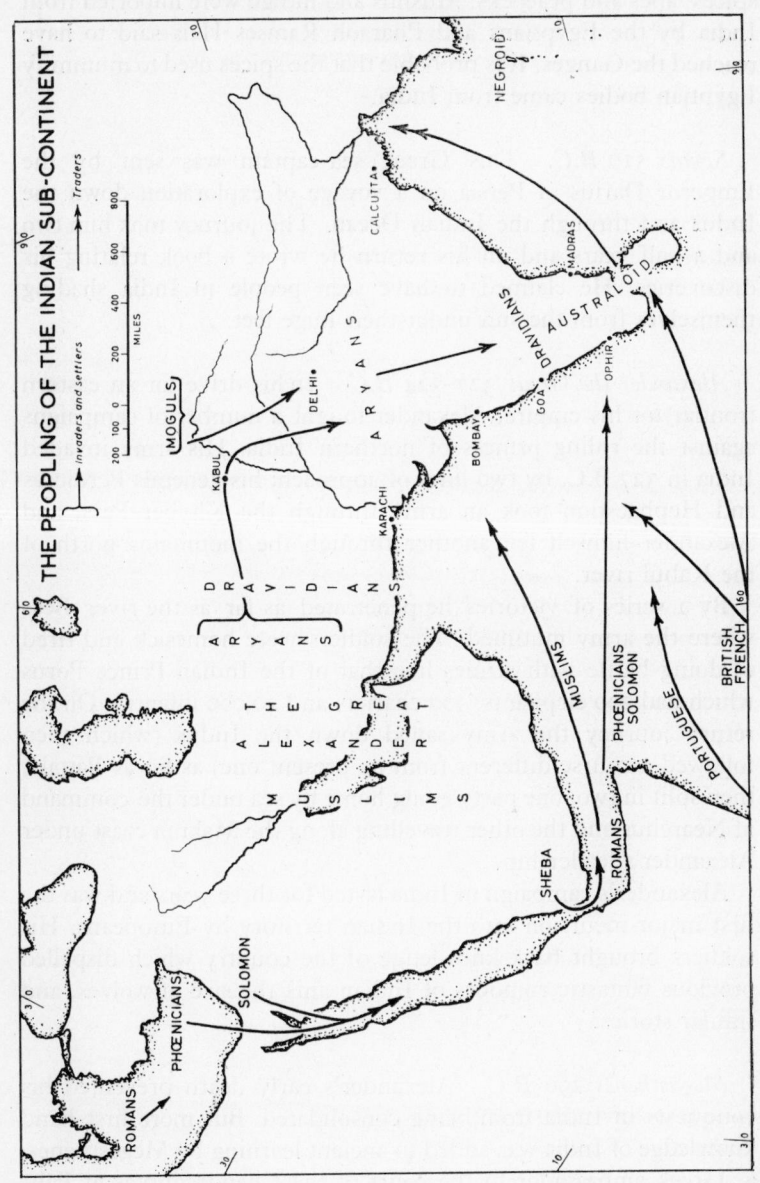

spices, apes and peacocks. Muslins and indigo were imported from India by the Egyptians and Pharaoh Ramses II is said to have reached the Ganges. It is probable that the spices used to mummify Egyptian bodies came from India.

Scylax 510 *B.C.* This Greek sea-captain was sent by the Emperor Darius of Persia on a voyage of exploration down the Indus and through the Indian Ocean. The journey took him two and a half years and on his return he wrote a book relating his discoveries. He claimed to have seen people in India shading themselves from the sun under their huge feet.

Alexander the Great 327–324 *B.C.* In his drive for an eastern frontier for his empire, Alexander fought a number of campaigns against the ruling princes of northern India. His army invaded India in 327 B.C. by two lines of approach; his generals Perdiccas and Hephaestion took an army through the Khyber Pass, and Alexander himself led another through the mountains north of the Kabul river.

By a series of victories he penetrated as far as the river Beas where the army mutinied. The soldiers were homesick and tired of doing battle with armies like that of the Indian Prince Porus which had 200 elephants, 300 chariots and 30,000 infantry. On the return journey the army sailed down the Indus (which then followed a course different from its present one) as far as Pattala, then split in two, one party going home by sea under the command of Nearchus and the other travelling along the Makran coast under Alexander's leadership.

Alexander's campaign in India lasted for three years and was the first major incursion into the Indian territory by Europeans. His soldiers brought back knowledge of the country which dispelled previous fantastic rumours of Indian ants the size of wolves, and similar stories.

Megasthenes 290 *B.C.* Alexander's early death prevented his conquests in India from being consolidated. But more first-hand knowledge of India was added to ancient learning by Megasthenes, a Greek ambassador to the court of the Chandraguptas at Pali-bothra. This area had never before been visited by the Greeks and

4

Megasthenes made detailed studies of the customs of the people of the Indo-Gangetic plains, and of the monsoon.

Eudoxus 120 *B.C.* With the help of an Indian whose ship had been carried to the shores of Africa, Eudoxus reached India to trade in luxury goods. He was the first Greek to make the journey by sea.

Hippalus A.D. 45 The use of the monsoon winds to eliminate the long coastal voyage to India had long been known by Arab seamen. In A.D. 45 the trader Hippalus broke the Arabs' monopoly by discovering the monsoon winds when he sailed from Cape Fartak to the Indus. His object was to trade in luxury goods that were in great demand by the Roman nobility.

The Romans With the rise of the rich Roman Empire, trade with the East became more important and profitable than it had ever been before. From A.D. 60 to 160 knowledge of India increased, but was often inaccurate.

Vast quantities of pepper, cinnamon, ginger, tortoise-shell and precious stones were imported into the Empire from India. Roman merchants in great numbers were to be found dwelling and going about their business in the towns of western India. Pepper was the most prized item of trade. In exchange the Romans sent wines, and trained soldiers as personal guards for the Indian princes. They also sent out bullion in the form of Imperial coins, and hoards of Roman denarii have been found near Coimbatore where the main trade road crossed south India.

Roman ships plied their way to Cranganore, Kalyan, Barbarikon and Broach Gujarat, and carried archers as a protection against the pirates of the Indian Ocean. In return, embassies from India brought expensive presents to Rome for Augustus. So great was this trade between India and Rome that Pliny regretted the drain on Roman bullion.

With Roman trade and Alexander's wars, knowledge of India was considerable. But in the eighth century the forces of Islam overran the Middle East and the Mediterranean. All trade fell into the hands of the Muslims and Europe had to wait for nearly seven centuries before India and the East became once more open to her.

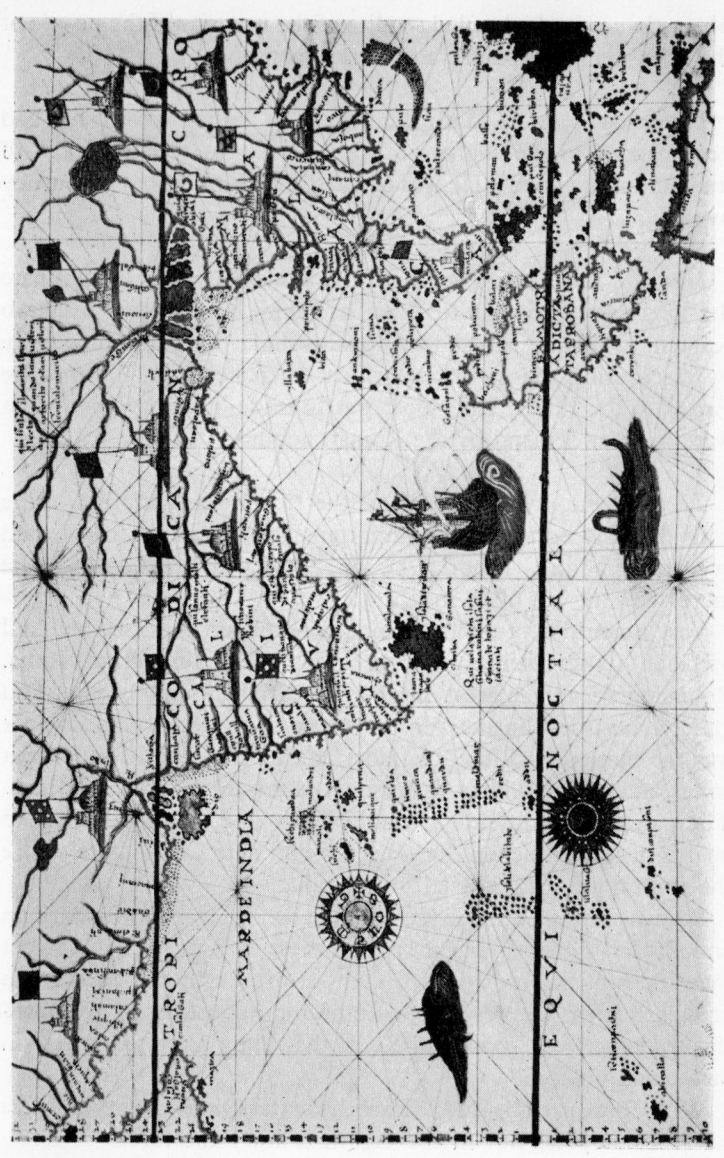

The Portuguese Empire of the East at its greatest. This map, drawn in 1578, shows the principal Portuguese bases in the East—From a print in the British Museum

With the forces of Islam barring the land routes to the East, the quest for a sea route began. From 1415 onwards Portuguese mariners, inspired by Prince Henry the Navigator and a great hatred for Islam, took the lead in exploration. The coast of Africa was charted by stages, and in July 1497 Vasco da Gama, ordered by his king to reach the Malabar coast which had been visited by Pero de Covilhao in 1488, sailed from Lisbon commanding a fleet of four ships. On 20th May 1498 da Gama's vessels anchored off Calicut (Kozhikode). Here a mixed reception awaited the Portuguese captain. The Indian ruler welcomed him, but the Moors and Arabs were hostile. "May the devil take you", he was told. Not stopping at this they hatched a plot to murder him, from which he barely managed to escape. But this attempt on his life left him with a grudge and when, in 1502, he captured a large company of Muslims off the Indian coast he had their ears, hands and noses cut off.

When the fleet returned to Lisbon in July 1499, it was found that the profits of the expedition exceeded the costs sixtyfold.

The ruler of Calicut refused Pedro Cabral permission to found a Portuguese settlement in his domain when Cabral arrived there in 1500. Sailing farther south along the coast Cabral came to Cochin, a better harbour ruled by a Hindu raja who was an enemy of the ruler of Calicut. This raja allowed Cabral to found a colony and by 1507 the Portuguese had fortified Cochin.

All the charts made on these voyages were held by the Portuguese king to be great state secrets, and the penalty of death awaited any person convicted of trying to pass them to foreign agents.

In February 1509 the Portuguese fleet defeated the Muslim forces at Diu. Within a year they had occupied Goa which was to be the first territory in India ruled by Europeans. Portuguese dominance increased rapidly after this. By 1540 they had established themselves at Damao, at Diu, at Goa on the west coast, at San Thome (site of Madras), Hooghly and Chittagong on the east coast, and in Ceylon. Besides these large settlements there were also smaller colonies at places in the south like Tuticorin,

Calicut in the sixteenth century from a book publish

where the Portuguese base consisted of a small hut and one man who was called "Captain Major of the Fishery Coast".

Weakness soon crept into the administration of Portuguese holdings in India. After the Portuguese and Spanish crowns were united, the Dutch, sworn enemies of the Spanish, ravaged Portuguese ports in the East. From 1580 the power of the Portuguese in the East began to wane rapidly, and soon other European nations were to struggle for the monopoly lost by the Portuguese.

BRITISH AND FRENCH IN INDIA

In 1526 Baber, a Muslim chieftain, and his followers poured through the Khyber Pass into northern India. He founded the great Mogul Empire which was to rule and unify most of India

.EBERRI.
PORIVM.

1573 — From a print in the British Museum

for nearly two centuries. So long as emperors like Akbar sat in the seat of government, all Europeans confined their interest to commerce and settled at ports with his permission only.

Since da Gama first landed on Indian soil the Emperor had favoured the Portuguese. But the riches that poured into Europe awoke the interest of other nations. In London in the year 1600 the East India Trading Company was formed. It sent a number of trading fleets to the East, one of which showed a profit of 234%. In March 1607 the Third Voyage sailed from London. On 24th August 1608 one of the ships, *Hector*, anchored off Surat and flew the English flag in India for the first time. William Hawkins was on this ship and in 1609 he left Surat for Agra, the great Emperor's capital. He took with him a bodyguard of fifty Pathans. The

9

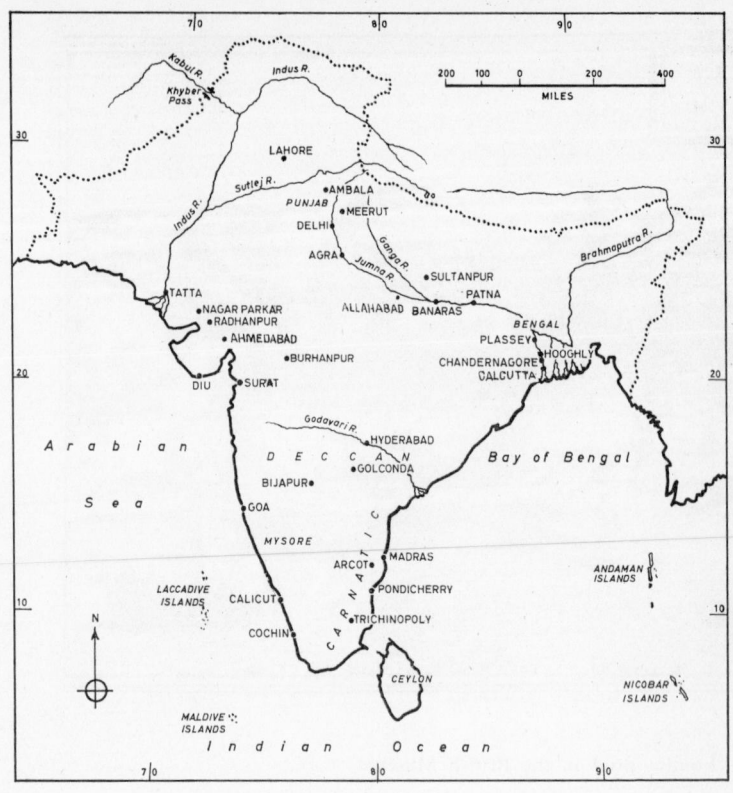

Map of the main places referred to in this chapter

Great Mogul was impressed with the newcomer, besides being rather tired of the Portuguese, and promised him that the English would be permitted to set up a factory at Surat. 'Factories' were depots or agencies where the English merchants bought spices when the price was low to store them until the Company's ships came next.

The Portuguese took alarm at the growing danger to their monopoly and attacked the English ships in Swally Roads off Surat. Despite heavy odds against him, Captain Best beat the Portuguese, and the Emperor, impressed by the victory, allowed the English to found their trading station at Surat. In 1615 the Portuguese again fought the English ships at Surat—and were beaten again. From 1615 to 1618 the Emperor Jehangir entertained Sir Thomas Roe as King James I's ambassador. Roe did much to bring Jehangir to look kindly upon the English. Portugal, having lost the favour of the Emperor, was now a spent force in India. In 1635 the English were granted the right to trade with the ports on the west coast of India.

The East India Company also expanded elsewhere. Francis Day, one of its servants, obtained land on the Coromandel coast and here built Fort St. George, at Madras.

In Bengal, too, the Nawab had let the English establish a factory at Hooghly, but he would not allow them to fortify it. Soon the Nawab grew tired of them and attacked their post. They retreated to Calcutta and here Job Charnock built defences. Twice the English were driven from Calcutta, but they returned in 1690 to stay. Eight years later the fort of St. William was built to defend the factory at Calcutta.

In 1674 the French also settled in India. It was in this year that the French East India Company was established at a strongly fortified factory at Pondicherry. Several other stations were opened by them.

In 1707 the last Mogul Emperor, Aurungzeb, died and the force that had held India together for 200 years was gone. Wild Marathas rushed into Delhi and central India and Afghan invaders stormed in from the north-west. Disputes arose over thrones and civil wars broke out. Such anarchy made the position of the European trading posts precarious.

In 1741 Dupleix arrived as Governor of French posts in India. He immediately summed up the position and saw that he might oust the British and win India for France by taking advantage of the confused situation. His plan was for the French to set up puppet rulers. The British were thus forced to support rival claimants to the thrones. Dupleix put his puppets on the thrones of the Carnatic and Hyderabad and thus gained control of south India. In 1746 the French took Madras. In 1751 Robert Clive, who started as a clerk with the East India Company, took Arcot, the capital of the Deccan, and forced the French to abandon their siege of Trichinopoly. Clive thus dashed the hopes of France and the ambitions of Dupleix.

Robert Clive. Copy of the portrait by Nathaniel Dance

After defeating the French in the south, the British faced a crisis in Bengal. The Nawab, Suraja Dowlah, took Calcutta and imprisoned 146 English prisoners in a small room. Overnight 123 of these died in this "Black Hole". Clive hurried to Bengal, drove the Nawab from Calcutta and also took the French post at Chandernagore. The next year (1757), Clive, with a very small force, defeated the massed armies of the Nawab at Plassey and set a British puppet on the throne, Mir Jaffier. British victory over the French in the south was completed when Sir Eyre Coote starved the French garrison at Pondicherry into surrender.

EUROPEAN TRAVELLERS IN INDIA

Whilst the great powers were struggling for trading advantages, individual travellers, inspired by a lust for knowledge or, in the case of missionaries, a desire to save souls, penetrated into many parts of the interior of India. The following accounts are selected from those of a long list of enterprising men.

Ludovico di Vartheme, 1502–9 After travelling through the Middle East, di Vartheme reached Diu and Ormuz. From here he visited much of the west coast, the Deccan and the Coromandel coast. On his return he published a book telling of his experiences.

Ralph Fitch, 1583–91 The ship *Tiger* sailed from London in February 1583, carrying Fitch, John Newberry, William Leedes and James Story. When these travellers landed at Ormuz they were arrested by the Portuguese who transported them to Goa. Here they escaped their captors and fled across India on a journey that took them to Fathepur Sikri *via* Bijapur, Golconda, Burhanpur and Agra. At Fathepur they parted company. Leedes, a jeweller by trade, remained at Fathepur in the service of the Mogul Emperor.

Fitch pressed on and sailed down the Ganges stopping at cities like Allahabad, Banaras and Patna on the way. He saw much of Cooch Bihar and East Bengal before continuing his wanderings to Malacca. In April 1591 Fitch arrived back in London after an absence of nine years during which he saw more of India than any other European living then.

William Hawkins, 1608–13 The East India Company sent its third expedition to India under the command of Hawkins. On landing at Surat he faced the hostility of the Portuguese, and on 1st February 1609 he journeyed to Agra where he remained the guest of Emperor Jehangir who gave him a daily allowance of 100 rupees (£10). But the Portuguese were persistent and Hawkins was forced to flee from Agra in 1611. He died before he could reach England again.

William Finch Finch was a member of Hawkins's party, but while his leader resided at the Emperor's court at Agra, Finch made a number of journeys from that city. He visited Bayana to buy indigo for the East India Company. Then he went to Lahore by

13

way of Delhi, Ambala and Sultanpur. During the seven months that he was in Lahore he gathered information about the surrounding country, and especially about the trade routes to Kabul.

Nicholas Withington, 1613–16   From Surat in 1613, Withington journeyed to Ahmedabad and thence to Cambay and Sarkhej. His next journey was to Tatta *via* Radhanpur and Nagar Parkar. On the way his caravan was molested by brigands who killed all the Indian merchants but spared the Europeans. Withington was freed and returned to Surat. He set out again on 7th June 1614 for Agra, and from this city he went on various excursions through the surrounding country.

Thomas Coryat, 1612–17   Coryat travelled to India by land at a cost of twopence per day. He visited Lahore, Delhi and Agra and followed the Emperor to Ajmer. From Ajmer he went to Hardwar and Mandu, where he died.

Antonio de Andrade   In 1624 de Andrade left India searching for a group of Christians who were thought to live in Tibet. His journey took him through much of the untraversed country of north India and he was the first European to climb the Himalayas. From Delhi he went through Hardwar to Garhwal and then through the Mana Pass and the upper Sutlej valley into Tibet. He returned to India, but in 1625 set off again with a band of brother priests to found a mission in Tibet. This mission lasted for sixteen years.

Stephen Cacella and John Cabral, 1626   These two men explored much of the eastern Himalayas during their expedition to Shigatse. They visited Cooch Bihar and Bhutan. Cabral's route on his return journey took him through Nepal.

Hippolyte Desideri, 1716   On his journey to Lhasa, which he reached in 1716, Desideri went through the Pir Panjal Pass to Srinagar in Kashmir. From here he followed the valleys of the Indus and Brahmaputra.

George Bogel, 1775–83   On his various missions to Tibet for Warren Hastings and the East India Company, Bogel traversed Bhutan and the middle course of the Brahmaputra a number of times, bringing back with him fresh information of new places.

14

MAKING AN EMPIRE

The story of how the British won their empire in India has been too often told for it to merit more than a brief final survey here. After Clive had crushed the French, the English East India Company had free rein in India. It increased its territory by conquest and treaty. Many Indian rulers asked its protection and patronage; others were deposed for cruelty or oppression and replaced by friends of the Company; still others challenged or attacked the Company and were eventually defeated.

Tipu Sultan challenged the British from Mysore, but he was defeated and killed as his capital fell in 1799. The help he expected from the French never came.

The Marathas troubled both the Company itself and its allies. They were finally defeated in the Third Maratha War in 1818.

The Punjab fell to the Company in 1849 after the brave and powerful Sikhs had been defeated in the Second Sikh War.

But all was not going well in other ways. In 1857 the sepoys (native troops) in the Company army mutinied and murdered their officers and civilians at Meerut. The mutiny spread over north India. Discontent for various reasons was the cause; but it was precipitated because of religion. The sepoys were issued with cartridges that had to have their paper torn off with the teeth before loading. It was rumoured amongst the Hindu sepoys that the grease on the cartridges was from the cow, the sacred Hindu animal, and amongst the Muslim sepoys that it was from the pig, an animal despised by the Muslims.

The great mutiny was quelled, but it killed the Company. The rule of India passed to the British Government and in 1876 Queen Victoria was proclaimed Empress of India.

INDEPENDENCE

Religious differences between Muslims and Hindus, resentment against British domination, and periods of unrest all contributed to the fall of the Indian Empire. Gandhi and his policy of passive resistance gained much sympathy for the demands of Indians for freedom. In 1945 a Labour Government was returned to power in Britain. Two years later it passed the Indian Independence Act which recognised and gave birth to the two nations, Hindu India and Muslim Pakistan. Great civil disturbances followed, refugees fled from the one new state to the other and religious riots led to thousands of deaths. But the countries settled down, and today India and Pakistan take their place as sovereign republics within the Commonwealth.

Ceylon is in the same position as Canada or Australia, having a Governor-General representing the British Crown. Ceylon never has been ruled from Delhi and so, historically, has never been a part of India.

HOW INDIA WAS MAPPED

It can hardly be said, in the face of its dense population and ancient civilisations, that the Indian sub-continent was ever actually discovered, but much of it was first explored scientifically under British rule. The mapping of the sub-continent and much scientific exploration are chiefly due to officers of the British Army, men like Captain James Rennell and William Lambton.

Native rulers of the Indian states had produced maps of their domains, but these were confined to roads, villages and field measurements for they were needed only to help in assessing the princes' taxes. Much of India's coastline was charted from ships, but the interior was known only from reports and sketch-maps, usually very inaccurate, brought back by adventurers and travellers untrained in the skills of the surveyor.

When Bengal became a British province the first real attempt at mapping the country was made. In 1767 Clive, its Governor, appointed Captain James Rennell as Surveyor-General of Bengal with the duty of mapping British territory. Rennell took to the field and during the next ten years produced surveys along the main routes and rivers of the province. These, when put together, formed the first map of Bengal. Rennell used instruments of the simplest kind: on his traverses he took a magnetic compass and a perambulator which is a large wheel of known circumference with a revolution-counting attachment. Further afield, parties of British troops sent on military expeditions took bearings and measured distances on their marches.

In 1801 the first comprehensive survey of India was planned and started by William Lambton, another Army officer. He selected his base line near the city of Madras, measured it accurately and using a theodolite mapped much of south and central India by a series of great triangles. Lambton's achievement is astonishing considering that his huge theodolite weighed nearly 1,000 lb. and had to be carried to hill-tops, over rivers and set up on the roofs of high buildings. Lambton died in 1823, still working in the field, but his successor, George Everest, after whom the mountain is named, continued his work. India was completely mapped by the Great Triangulation Survey by the end of the nineteenth century.

If the glory of planning the grand scheme goes to men such as these, the credit for filling in the details on the maps must go to the hundreds of plane-tabling parties that worked through India in the last century. The early days of mapping in India were perilous and difficult ones; the heat, forest dangers, contact with diseases, working in elephant grass 10 ft. high and camping out for weeks at a time all took their toll on British and Indians alike. The plane-tabling parties were mobile units consisting of a trained Indian "tabler", a group of about five labouring helpers and a bullock cart for carrying food, instruments, tents and personal equipment. These small bands took to the country in November, after the rains, and worked until the onset of the very hot weather in April. The rest of the year was spent in making fair copies of their field-maps and planning the next expedition.

At the selected base point, the plane-tabler set his table and took his sightings through his alidade or clinometer whilst one of his labourers held a large umbrella over him to ward off the hot rays of the sun. Much of the measuring of distances with the chain was done by the leader of the labour gang. He often remembered all the measurements in his head ready to give to the surveyor on return to camp. In this way, the Indian plane-tablers produced their maps, on a scale of 1 in. to 1 mile, working at the rate of 30 to 40 sq. miles surveyed in a month.

In the 1860's when the mapping of the Indian sub-continent was near completion, the Survey of India, established in 1867, spread its interest beyond the frontiers of its territory into other parts of central Asia. Little was known of Tibet and the Chinese authorities there were set on keeping it that way. They would allow no Europeans or persons connected with them across the Himalayan

Still the work of making the maps of India more accurate goes on. Here a plane-tabler is working, shaded from the hot sun

borders. But an experiment in "spying" was tried with great success.

A Kumaun schoolmaster, Pandit Nain Singh by name, was sent to Tibet disguised as a Buddhist monk with instructions to make measurements and take bearings on his journey, which was to take him to Lhasa if possible. He crossed the frontier, his resemblance to the Mongolians securing him this passage, and travelled with a caravan to Lhasa where he stayed for some time before returning to India. Constantly on his journey he was surveying in secret.

In his lama's prayer-wheel there was a magnetic compass instead of the usual scroll of prayers, and his string of holy beads had only 100 instead of the usual 108. He counted his paces on the journey, on this string. The information Singh brought back from Tibet allowed fairly accurate maps to be made, and his "survey-cum-spy" expedition led to many others in the latter half of the century. Many of the "pundits", as these spies were called, returned but many others never came back.

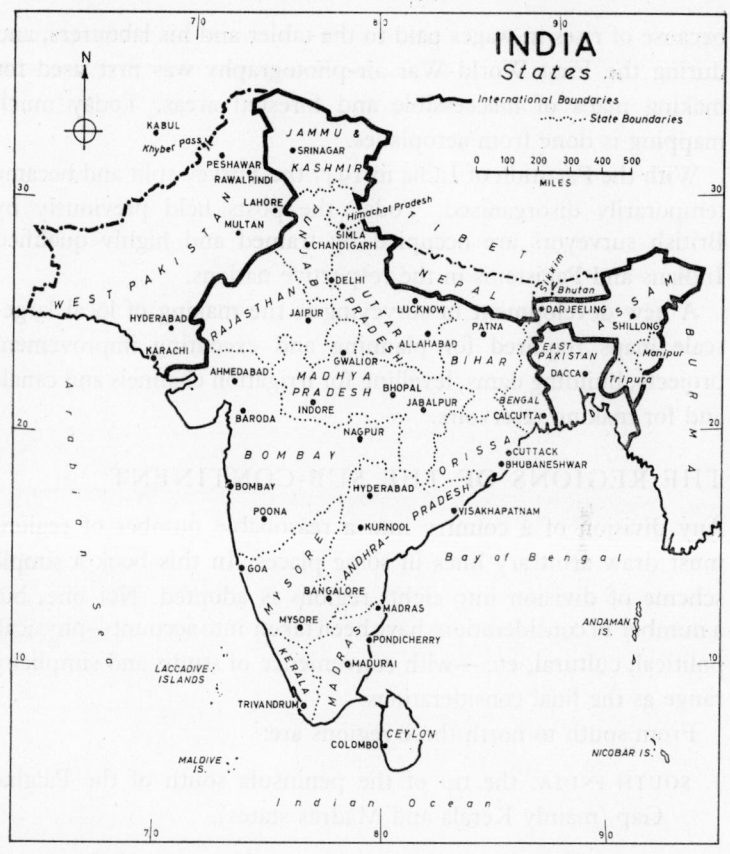

INDIA
States

International Boundaries
State Boundaries

0   100   200   300   400   500
MILES

Similar difficulties were experienced by the surveyors of the North West Frontier region. It was only in the present century that the home of the Pathans was mapped with some accuracy. Soon after the First World War Chiragh Shah set off to map part of the tribal territory; at his first camp he was fired upon by hillmen. Royal Air Force fighters were sent to give him cover from the air, but by then he was staying in the home of the Pathan chief as an honoured guest. Not all such stories ended so happily.

From 1905 to 1939 the Survey of India was fully occupied on a new survey project of India. Plane-tabling became very expensive because of rises in wages paid to the tabler and his labourers, and during the First World War air-photography was first used for making maps of inaccessible and forested areas. Today much mapping is done from aeroplanes.

With the Partition of India in 1947 the Survey split and became temporarily disorganised. Today the posts held previously by British surveyors are occupied by trained and highly qualified Indians and Pakistanis in the respective nations.

A new development in surveying is the making of local large-scale maps required for planning and executing improvement projects, building dams, levelling for irrigation channels and canals and for making reservoirs.

THE REGIONS OF THE SUB-CONTINENT

Any division of a country into a reasonable number of regions must draw arbitrary lines in some places. In this book a simple scheme of division into eight regions is adopted. Not one, but a number of considerations have been taken into account—physical, political, cultural, etc.—with convenience of study and simplicity range as the final considerations.

From south to north these regions are:

1. SOUTH INDIA: the tip of the peninsula south of the Palghat Gap (mainly Kerala and Madras states).

2. CENTRAL INDIA: mainly Mysore, the Deccan and the central mountains, including the Thar Desert. There are many possible sub-regions here, but the whole has been taken as the ancient upland and plateau core of peninsular India.

3. WESTERN INDIA: the coastal plain below the Western Ghats, including the Rann of Kutch and Kathiawar.

4. EASTERN INDIA: the coastal plain between the Eastern Ghats, and the Bay of Bengal, including the deltas, in Orissa and Andhra Pradesh states.

5. GANGES PLAIN: a physical region bounded by the edges of the alluvium.

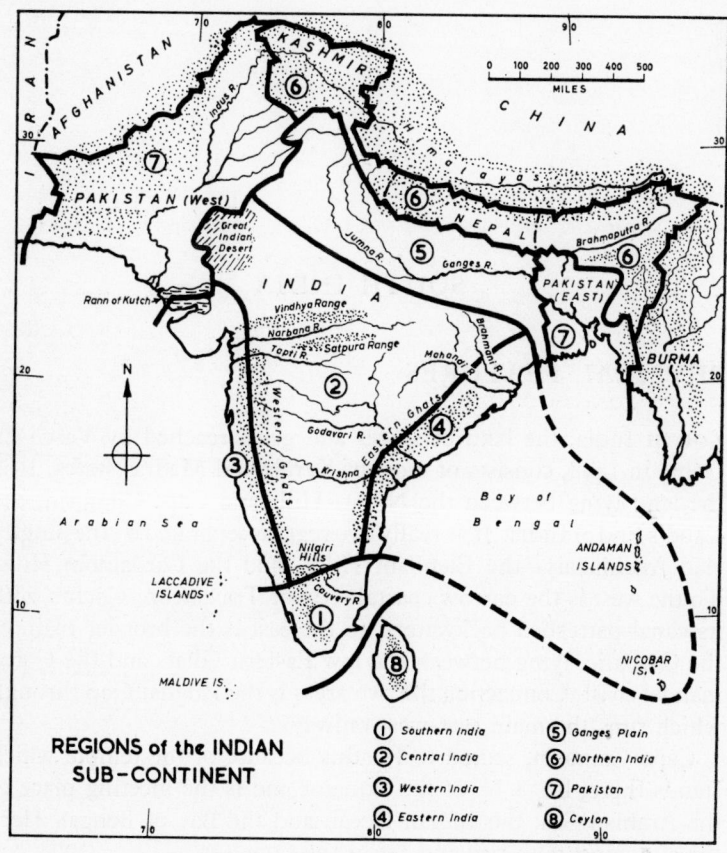

REGIONS of the INDIAN SUB-CONTINENT

① Southern India
② Central India
③ Western India
④ Eastern India
⑤ Ganges Plain
⑥ Northern India
⑦ Pakistan
⑧ Ceylon

6. NORTHERN INDIA: the Himalayas and associated highlands. Assam has been included here for the main interest is in the hills, not in the Brahmaputra valley.

7. PAKISTAN: political region.

8. CEYLON: an obvious island region.

I

SOUTH INDIA

PHYSICAL FEATURES

SOUTH India, the land of spices and gems reached by Vasco da Gama in 1498, consists of most of Kerala and Madras states. It is the land lying between the Nilgiri Hills and Cape Comorin, the Land's End of India. It is really two regions separated by the jungle-clad Anaimalais—the Elephant Hills—and the Cardamom Hills. To the west is the narrow coastal strip of Travancore-Cochin with its canal-patterned backwaters; to the east is the broader plain of the Carnatic, lying between the low Eastern Ghats and the Coromandel coast. Connecting the two areas is the Palghat Gap through which runs the main east-west railway.

Cape Comorin, sacred to Hindus because of the temple which stands there, lies 8°N. of the Equator and is the meeting place of the Arabian Sea, the Indian Ocean and the Bay of Bengal. Here the sun appears to rise and set in the same sea.

Travancore-Cochin has a very high rainfall, three-quarters of which falls between June and September when the South-West Monsoon brings its dark rain-clouds across the Arabian Sea. Nearly 200 ins. fall on the hills of Kerala state. Rainfall decreases from north to south; the port of Kozhikode receives 119 ins. a year, but further south Trivandrum has only 64 ins. Temperatures rarely rise above 90°F. and rarely fall below 70°F., making the air hot and humid. Days are relatively cool and the weather fine in December and January. These are the most pleasant months for Europeans in Travancore-Cochin.

This tropical monsoon climate makes Kerala a green and lush land with luxuriant jungle on the hills and widespread growth of

SOUTHERN INDIA

Irrigation by modern canals		+ + + +	Railways
		— · — · —	State Bdys.
Rivers		Hill Ranges	

colourful forest orchids, bamboo, palms, mangoes, jack and bread-fruit trees. The creeper-latticed jungle areas are the haunt of the leopard, tiger, panther, elephant, bison and the Nilgiri ibex, an attractive wild goat. Teak, sandalwood and eucalyptus grow around the hill-stations of the Nilgiris in Madras, and tourists take advantage of the lower temperatures (rarely exceeding 60°F. even in the hot season) and less humid air.

The winds of the South-West Monsoon have shed their rains by the time they have crossed the Cardamom Hills. The Madras coastal plain, therefore, is a very dry and dusty country except between the months of October and December. It is then that the

23

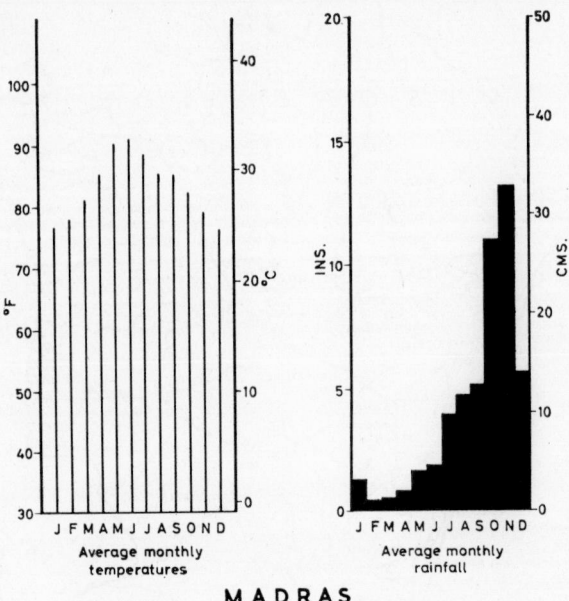

Average monthly
temperatures

Average monthly
rainfall

MADRAS

North-East Monsoon, following on the heels of the retreating
South-West Monsoon, brings the area its chief rains from the Bay
of Bengal. The official date for the beginning of the North-East
Monsoon is 15th October. The land is so hard and dry during the
hot season (March-May) that groundnuts, harvested at that time,
have to be dug with crow-bars. All but the largest rivers are dry
for nine months of the year.

There is a saying that the city of Madras has three climates—
hot, hotter and hottest! This reflects the fact that average temperatures there reach almost 100°F., and so irrigation is necessary to
grow crops. Weirs, called "anicuts", tap the larger east-flowing
rivers to take the precious waters to parched lands.

THE PEOPLE

The people of south India are descendants of the Dravidians who
ruled the land in centuries past and built the striking gopuram
temples that attract pilgrims and tourists to the cities. They speak

A dancer from the
Malabar coast

the two main languages of Tamil in Madras state and Malayalam in Kerala state. Proud of their unique traditions and culture, the people of south India have strongly resisted the spread of Hindi as the common language. Languages are taught in schools in the following order: first the local language (Tamil or Malayalam), second Hindi and third English.

Fertile land and ample rainfall or irrigation potential over most of south India have given it a large population. Compared with an average density of 287 persons per square mile for the whole of India, Kerala has 903 persons per square mile and Madras 598. Only areas of thick jungle and certain dry tracts of Madras are thinly populated. Such pressure on the land means that the people, mainly small cultivators ("ryots"), are poor and generally underfed. Because of the hot and humid climate the white cotton loincloth ("dhoti") is worn as it is airy and easily washed. Houses are designed to keep out the heat.

South India is almost entirely Hindu country with the main features of Hinduism—festivals and caste.

Madurai, "City of Festivals", was once the capital of the Pandi-yan civilisation and is now a temple city popular with tourists. Of its many temples of the distinctive south Indian style, the most spectacular is that of Meenakshi, the fish-eyed goddess. It is a wonderful sight at night when lit by the torches of worshippers. In it there are groups of hollow stone pillars, the "musical pillars", that give off notes when struck.

Just outside Madurai are some rocks called Elephant, Serpent and Crocodile. They resemble these animals in shape and Tamil legend gives their origin. Centuries ago magicians of the rival Jain religion sent an elephant, a serpent and a crocodile, each one hundred times normal size, to destroy the city and force its peoples to Jainism. But Siva, a great god, came to the rescue of the faithful people of Madurai and turned the monsters to stone.

Near Mahabalipuram to the south of Madras city is the Hill of the Sacred Kites. About 500 ft. high, the hill is topped by a small shrine. Every day just before noon, two kites, held sacred because they are thought to be saints, arrive on the hillock to be fed from the hands of a priest.

South India is a stronghold of the rigid Hindu caste system. Hindu society is divided into classes called castes.* A person is born into a caste and cannot move upwards from it with ease. The highest caste, the Brahmins, are priests and landowners. At the other end of the scale are the 55 millions of the "unscheduled castes", commonly known as the "untouchables", but called by that great humanitarian Gandhi "harijans", meaning "the children of God". Depressed and poor, the harijans suffered great disabili-ties; they were forbidden to approach a Brahmin lest they pollute him, they were not allowed to draw water from the village well nor enter parts of the village reserved for the higher castes. In some places they were not allowed to sleep on a bed. The Nayadis, a tribe of hunters living in the forests of Travancore, polluted higher castes at a distance of 72 ft. As late as 1932 an example of "unsee-ability" was known in Cochin of a caste of harijans who were not allowed to move from their huts by day lest a member of a higher caste saw them and became polluted.

*A list of some of the main castes of south India appears at the end of this chapter.

Mahatma Gandhi

An interesting group of the Madurai area is the Kallan caste of thieves. It is possible that they are the descendants of soldiers of a defeated Tamil army. The house-breaking section of the caste (there are also cattle-stealers) are employed as nightwatchmen in Madurai, for a Kallan will never steal from a house in which there is a fellow Kallan.

Village plans are largely governed by the caste system. Each caste occupies a street named after it. The harijan's quarters are on the outskirts or even form a separate village, and are the poorest. Untouchables were debarred from entering the temple and did the scavenging tasks of the village.

In an effort to carry out the section of its Constitution declaring basic human rights, the Indian Government passed the Untouchability (Offences) Act in 1955. This laid down severe penalties for persons practising untouchability towards the harijans, but ancient customs die hard and in remote villages in the south the worst features of the caste system are still accepted—even by the harijans themselves.

Strict Hindus are vegetarians. It is therefore an unusual experience to smell meat cooking in country districts of

27

south India, but one can do so in the villages of the Christian fishermen. The Christians of south India number about $2\frac{1}{2}$ million, and half of them are Roman Catholics. They are a poor people and make their living mainly by fishing. Small silver crosses are painted on the bows of their canoes as a sign of their faith.

Christianity came to India before the arrival of the Portuguese. Tradition relates that St. Thomas the Apostle landed near to Kodungalloor on the Kerala coast in A.D. 52. Before he died at Mylapore, where his tomb may still be seen, he built seven churches and made converts to Christianity especially among the lower Hindu castes. In 1947 archaeologists found in the dense jungle near Kottayam the remains of a church thought to be one of the seven. When the Portuguese first arrived in the fifteenth century they were surprised to find the Christian community. The first Roman Catholic church was begun in 1503 and dedicated to St. Francis of Assisi. Kerala, until recently ruled by the only Communist state government in India, owes much to the work of the Christian mission schools. They laid the foundation for Kerala to become the most literate state in the Indian Union.

THE HILL TRIBES

On the rolling grassland of the high plateau of the Nilgiris, the "Blue Mountains", live the Todas. The origin of these pastoralists is a puzzle, for their light skin and fine features make them a striking contrast to other hill peoples. It has been suggested that they are descendants of soldiers from Alexander's army. Their religion precludes manual labour as degrading and their only work is caring for the herds of buffalo that graze on the downland. Religion also makes them vegetarians with a diet of rice, butter, milk, raspberries, curried orchids, nettles, thistles and vegetables. To greet the rising sun they press their thumbs to their noses and spread wide their fingers.

'On', the Toda god, created the Toda to serve the buffalo not the buffalo to serve the Toda. According to legend, 'On' conjured 1,600 buffaloes from a hole in the mountainside. Clinging to the tail of the last animal appeared the first Toda.

A Portuguese priest called Ferreiri made early contact with the Todas in 1602. Today, this once numerous and wealthy tribe has

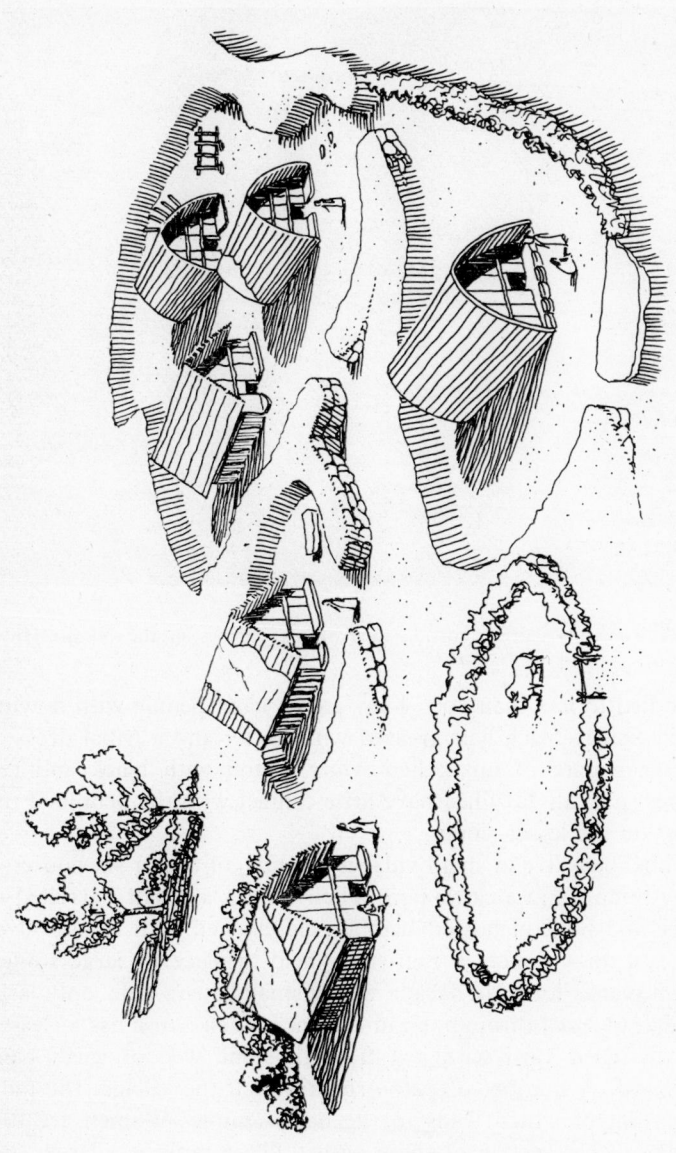

Toda village

Toda women squatting outside their strange homes in the Nilgiri Hills

dwindled to less than 500. They are an aloof people with flowing beards, curly black hair greased with butter and a tribal dress of a large square of unstitched white cotton with black and red stripes (putkulis*). They have little contact with the people of the forest on the lower slopes.

The Todas live in small villages (munds) of five or six houses, a dairy-temple and a cattle pen. Their houses are half-barrelled in shape and built of bowed bamboo closely tied with rattan. Over this is a thick thatch of ragi-straw held in place by large stones. Wood planks form the façade with a small square hole, only large enough to crawl through, as an entrance. Each house has a cleared and flattened yard with a 3 ft. high stone wall or earth bank surround. A number of paths run through the village, the most important of which leads to the dairy-temple. Women are forbidden to use certain of these paths. The temple is a larger and more striking version of the dwelling houses. Here the priest

* Rancid Butter is appled to the putkulis to act as a preservative.

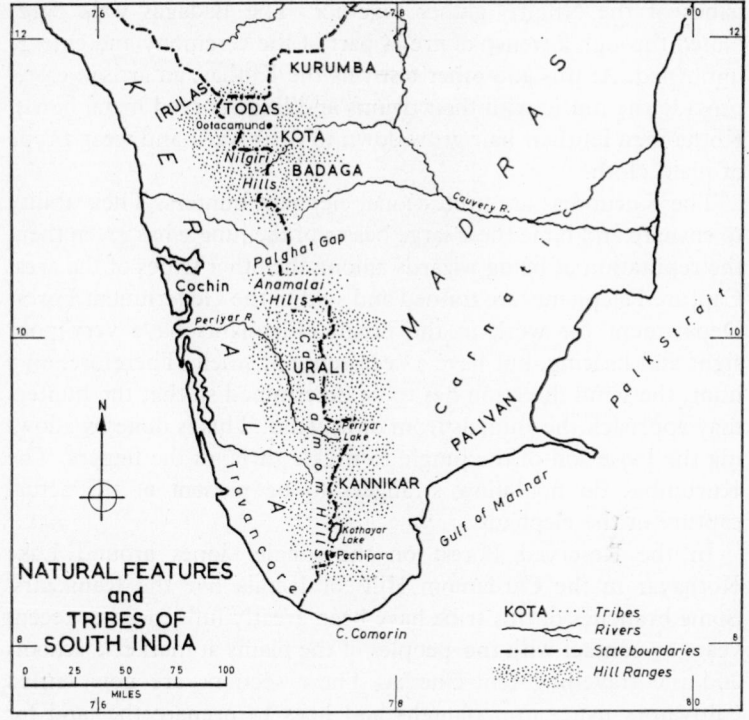

NATURAL FEATURES
and
TRIBES OF
SOUTH INDIA

KOTA ····· Tribes
Rivers
State boundaries
Hill Ranges

turns the buffalo milk into "ghi", the sacred clear butter, by pouring it from one container to another until it solidifies. Ghi plays an essential part in every Toda festival whether it be the opening of a new cattle pen or a funeral.

The Todas cremate their dead accompanied by the sacrifice of buffaloes, whose spirits follow that of the dead person into Paradise which lies beyond a high peak in the Nilgiris called Mukerti. Few buffaloes are sacrificed today, but in the past when the tribe was richer and owned more buffaloes, up to one hundred animals would be used in the ceremony.

Certain other tribes living on the lower forested slopes of the Nilgiris are of interest. On the hillsides and in the valleys the Badagas, who are cultivators, terrace the soil for growing paddi (rice). In most respects the Badagas differ little from the people of the plains. At the festival of Kali, the goddess of death, the hill

31

tribes of the Nilgiris gather together. The Badagas walk bare-footed through a trench of fire as part of the ceremony and emerge unburned. At this and other festivals the Kothas, an artisan caste, provide the music with their drums and large curved metal horns. Kotha men let their hair grow down to their waist and wear a type of plaid cloth.

The Kurumbas are professional elephant hunters. Their ability to ensnare and tame these large beasts of the jungle has given them the reputation of being wizards among the other tribes of the area. Captured elephants are trained and sold to the Government Forest Department for work in the jungle. Elephants have very poor sight and hearing, but have a keen sense of smell. Therefore, on a hunt, the wind direction has to be determined so that the hunters may approach the animals from downwind. This is done by allow-ing the loose soil of the jungle to trickle through the fingers. The Kurumbas do not allow strangers to be present at the actual capture of the elephant.

In the Reserved Forest on the jungle slopes around Lake Kothayar in the Cardamom Hills of Kerala live the Kanikkars. Some branches of this tribe have been greatly influenced in recent years by contact with the peoples of the plains at markets, schools and the travelling tent-cinema. These sections are now settled cultivators using iron ploughs and hoes to prepare the land for paddi crops, but many of the Kanikkars still live the old life. The primitive Kanikkar village, built far away from elephant tracks, consists of bamboo huts with roofs of plaited leaves. Some huts stand above the ground on poles so as to keep away from prowling tigers. Other dwellings are mere shelters built in the forked branches of trees, often 50 ft. above the ground. Access to these tree-homes is by a bamboo ladder which is raised at night. The remote Kanikkars are mainly jungle hunters and collectors, but they do grow cassava,* sugar cane, hemp and cereals in jungle clearings near the village as shifting cultivators. Bananas, roots, wild berries, fish and animals are also eaten. The pellet-bow, a sling bent by two strands joined together by a leather square, is used to stone prey; fish are caught in wickerwork traps and rats in bamboo traps. The large field rats are a favourite delicacy among Kanikkars who also eat tiger, tortoise, owls and wild pigs.

*Cassava: sweet potatoes.

Like some Kanikkars, the Uralis build their huts above the ground as protection from wild animals

As this is the dampest region of south India, fire is important to the Kanikkars. It is produced by a fire-drill or an ingenious device of a hollow bamboo section containing a white powder and pebbles. By shaking this up and down friction is produced by the clashing pebbles and ignites the powder. Fire not only heats food, but it also frightens off wild animals and dries the atmosphere. So humid is the air that matches will not strike and strangers find it difficult to breathe.

The Kanikkars can shape neither metal nor stone. Until cheap cotton came to them by trade they dressed in cloth made from the bark of trees. The "kokara" is their only interesting invention.

It is a musical instrument made from split bamboo with notches cut across the split. A stick is rubbed across these producing a scraping sound. Hatchets, hoes and other tools are obtained by trading at markets in small towns like Pechiparra. The Kanikkars exchange or sell bananas, tapioca, chillies, coconuts, honey and wax in the presence of a Forest Department agent who ensures that they get a fair deal from the trader.

The Ullatans of Kerala are famous for their ability to catch crocodiles with iron hooks enclosed in bait. Another tribe, the Pandarams, collect honey and beeswax to trade for salt. These jungle products often have to be collected from holes in a cliff. The Pandaram is let down the face on creeper ropes and dislodges the comb with a stick.

Other of the many south Indian hill peoples have become cultivators and Hindu castes of the lowest orders.

THE VILLAGE

India is a land of 560,000 villages housing 300 million people, some 85% of her population. Mahatma Gandhi, the great Indian reformer said ". . . if the village perishes India will perish also". The character of the Indian village varies from area to area as it depends upon a number of factors including shape of the land, climate, water supply, history and religion.

A "Tank" Village in Madras Province Scanty, irregular rainfall and the need for irrigation have produced a village with the houses grouped around the "tank", which is an artificial lake. Tanks are made by building earthen dams across streams. This holds up the water which flows in the stream during the rains and stores it for irrigating paddi fields (rice-plots), gardens and orchards in the dry season. Besides irrigation, tanks are used for washing clothes, cattle watering, cooking and, if no wells exist, for drinking —a habit which spreads intestinal diseases. Often they contain fish.

Stone-lined sacred tanks surrounded by temple buildings are found in most cities of Madras. Hindus believe that every twelve years the Ganges, the sacred river of north India, wells up into the tank at Kumbakonam, and in 1921 three-quarters of a million pilgrims washed their sins away in it. Even the village tanks are used for bathing and every sincere Hindu chants the following prayer when going through the rites of purification:

May the waters of the Ganga, the Jumna, the Godavari, the Saraswati, the Narbada, the Sindhu and the Cauvery mingle in the waters here and now.

The water tank is the nucleus of the village around which are grouped the houses, and these are collected into caste blocks so that there are often two distinct districts in a village, one of higher castes and the other of the lower castes and casteless. Always there is an open space where the travelling players give their shadow-plays and puppet shows. Richer villagers have houses of brick or stone with tiled roofs. Walls are often decorated with whitewash designs of animals or gods. In this part of the village live the Brahmins. They serve in the temple nearby, possibly dedicated to Ganesa, the elephant-headed son of the great god Siva, and the god of Prosperity. The small cultivators who farm the paddi and millet plots surrounding the village make their house walls of mud which is cheap and keeps the interior cool. Roofs are thatched with rice straw, palmyra leaves or bamboo stalks.

The pariah "cheri", the sub-village of lower caste people and scavengers, is on the outskirts of the village proper. Here there are no streets, only footworn paths, and the condition of the cheri is squalid and poor. Houses are made from palm leaves woven over a framework of sticks. Floors are of bare earth and interiors are dark. The cheri has its own temple, perhaps to Desamma, the goddess of smallpox.

Each house has a yard or garden, its size depending upon the social standing of the occupant. In it are grown bananas, mangoes, coconuts and vegetables such as chillies, brinjals and drumsticks* which help to feed the family. Cultivated land surrounds the village. Rice is grown on "wet" land which is irrigated and therefore situated near the tank. There are two paddi crops: the "kar" crop is harvested in October and the "samba", which is the main crop, in January. "Dry" land, unirrigated and depending entirely upon rainfall, supports crops of millet and groundnuts.

*CHILLIES: a type of pepper pod. They are used to make very hot flavourings especially in curries. BRINJALS and DRUMSTICKS: pear-shaped vegetables, somewhat similar to each other.

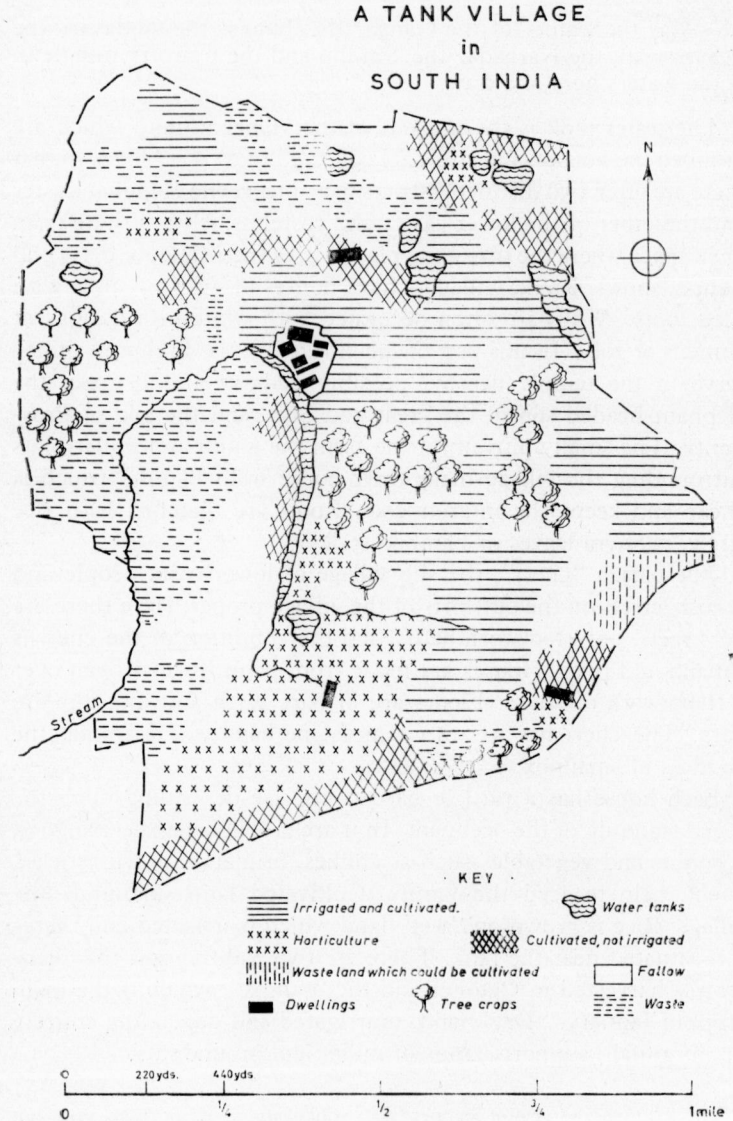

A TANK VILLAGE
in
SOUTH INDIA

N

· KEY ·

≡≡≡ Irrigated and cultivated.

XXXXX Horticulture
XXXXX

▒▒▒ Waste land which could be cultivated

■■ Dwellings

🌳 Tree crops

🌊 Water tanks

▓▓▓ Cultivated, not irrigated

☐ Fallow

▤▤ Waste

Stream

0 220yds. 440yds

0   1/4   1/2   3/4   1mile

36

The Tank village illustrated opposite has a total population of 980 people – 600 males and 380 females. Of these, 800 are Caste Hindus and live in the main village. Others live in three smaller settlements out in the fields. There are 9 temples still in use, 5 of which are in the main settlement. There are also 3 ruined temples in the fields.

Area	640 acres approximately, 400 acres of which are cultivated
Natural Vegetation	scrub, with some cactus and thornbush on waste
Soil	generally poor sandy soil, clay on the better cultivated areas
Irrigation	5 Diesel pumps, 21 shadis, 15 bucket-and-buffalo
Crops	Grain – paddi occupies one third of all irrigated area and is the main crop, – ragi (millet), cholam (great millet)
	Pulses – black gram, green gram (lentils or chickpeas with black or green seeds)
	Oil Seeds – gingelly (a plant rather like mustard, the seeds of which are pressed for oil. Used in popadums)
	Vegetables – brinjals, lady's fingers, pumpkins, chillies
	Fruit trees – mango, citrus fruits, palmyra palm (toddy), coconut palm, casurina (plum like fruit)
	Indigo – grown for dyestuffs
Cattle	450 bulls and bullocks
	150 cows
	135 bull and cow buffaloes
	100 goats
	4 donkeys
Implements	53 wooden ploughs, 5 new iron ploughs for hard, dry land
	1 tractor
	10 carts
Fuel	cattle dung

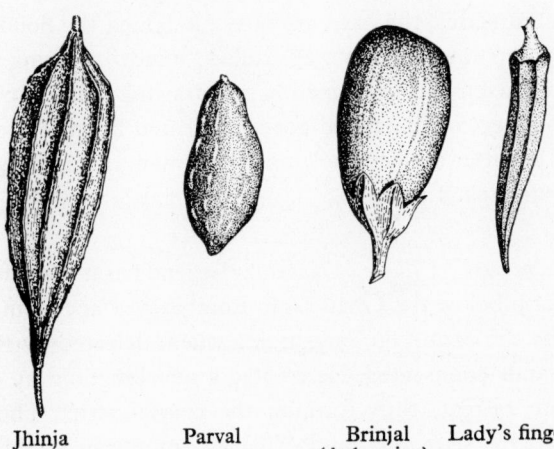

Jhinja   Parval   Brinjal   Lady's finger
(Aubergine)

37

A view of the backwaters, the natural highways of Kerala's coastal fringe

Domestic animals wander about the village. When the paddi fields have to be prepared for transplanting the young rice plants from the nurseries, the oxen are busy ploughing the flooded fields which are separated by low walls called "bunds". During the slack season the oxen are used mainly for drawing water from wells. Large numbers of sheep and goats are reared because the climate is dry. The latter are kept to supply field manure and only the low castes drink goat's milk.

A "Backwater" Village of Kerala   Legend has it that the narrow coastal strip below the Ghats from Bombay to Cape Comorin was created by the demi-god Parasurama when, defeated by Rama, he had his lands confiscated. He created a new kingdom by ordering the sea to retreat, thus forming the coastal strip. The Kerala section of this strip is a land of canals, mud banks and lagoons

These country-craft, the wallams, are loading and unloading their
cargoes at Alleppey

called the "backwaters". Here the chief factor which decides the
site of a village is not a constant water supply for irrigation, but
sufficient dry land above the shallow lagoons to build upon. The
village is scattered and is no more than a line of houses strung

along the palm-fringed embankments just a few feet above the water. With such a ribbon development, caste separation is not as clear as in Madras, but nevertheless, there is a centre of village life, usually the bazaar or temple. Land is often reclaimed in the form of islands. At a shallow place in the lagoon a ryot (peasant) encloses an area with a wall. By filling this in with sand he raises an island upon which he builds his hut and plants coconuts.

Houses are separated by yards or gardens. In the north-west corner of the yard is a grove where the family worships snakes. With the poor the yard is merely a cleared area. Richer villagers have coconuts, bananas, sweet potatoes, lemon grass* and vegetables growing in their gardens, and have outhouses in their yards.

Within the individual dwelling lives the undivided family. The living places of the relatives are grouped around a central courtyard in a four-sided house. The Malayalam word for this house is "nalupura", meaning four houses.

Only the more prosperous build their houses of stone or brick walls. Lower-caste houses are made of bamboo and plaited palm leaves or occasionally low mud walls with thatched roofs. A coconut leaf is split down the centre and the fronds are woven into each other to form an efficient covering called "kadjan". Tile roofing is, by custom, confined to the houses of Brahmins and higher castes. Because of the heavy monsoon rainfall the house roofs slope steeply to allow quick run-off. Gable corners turn upwards to form an attractive shaped roof similar to the Chinese style. Every house has a well to supply drinking water. Because of the low level of the land these wells are quickly and easily dug and are never empty.

All transport between villages in the backwaters is water-borne along the lagoons and canals. Children travel to school, women visit neighbours and shop by boat. They either catch the water-bus, a diesel-driven launch, or they have their own canoes dug out from coconut tree-trunks. "Wallams", large barge-like boats covered amidships with a roof of kadjan, carry cargoes of coconut husks and coir† along the canal highroads to Alleppey, the centre of the coir industry.

*LEMON GRASS: a grass from which oil is taken—used mainly for making soap.

†COIR: coconut fibre.

Rice is grown on the polders* and gives two crops per year. Poor people of Kerala live mainly on tapioca, a "dry" crop which grows on soils too poor for rice. It is boiled and eaten in the form of a white pulp. A diet of tapioca is low in proteins and vitamin A and causes gastric and duodenal ulcers, complaints that are common in Kerala. Small supplies of proteins are obtained from fish, vegetables and fruits. Hook-worms and elephantiasis, also known as Cochin-leg, are other common disabilities.

During the four days of the harvest festival or Onam Festival (August or September), the backwater village feasts, sings and dances. Gifts are exchanged, magnificently decorated elephants parade through the streets and fireworks are let off. The climax of the festival comes with the Vallomkali, the boat race in which racing boats manned by a hundred oarsmen compete to the rhythm of drums and cymbals.

FISHING

Scattered along the coast of south India, from Madras in the east to Kozhikode in the west, are hundreds of small fishing villages peopled by robust, hardy and weather-beaten men. Their skill in fishing and knowledge of the habits of fish are based upon ages of tradition passed on from father to son. They are a poor people. Fluctuations in catches, like the complete failure of the sardine shoals off the west coast in 1941–42, cause great hardship and privation. But still their diet of fish ensures them a larger supply of vitamins than the ryot can get.

Fishing in south India is still a "cottage" industry, carried on with tackle and in boats that have changed little over the centuries. In an effort to increase efficiency and catches the Kerala and Madras governments have established centres at Cochin and Tuticorin. At these twenty fishermen students at a time are given six months' intensive training in modern fishing methods. More and more boats are being fitted with engines. On the shores of Kerala Chinese fishing machines are used. These are baited nets hung from large bamboo frames to form an inverted cone. The nets are lowered into the shallow water and left there for a period. A

*POLDERS: reclaimed lagoons and swamps.

The unique Chinese fishing machines of the Kerala coast

light is fitted to the central rod at night to attract the fish. The nets are quickly raised leaving the fish trapped in the bottom of the cone. Prawns are caught in the lagoons of the backwaters.

Sea-fishing is confined to within the 10-fathom limit, less than 6 miles from the shore. Boats, fitted with food and water, are launched from the beach when the tide has risen. At the fishing grounds sails are furled and the nets lowered. When the tide turns again the catch is hauled aboard and the boats make for home on the shoreward current of water.

Styles of fishing boats vary with localities. On the Coromandel coast where the sea is rough, boats have to be able to withstand the buffeting of the surf. The most common type here is the "catamaran", which in Tamil means "tied trees". It is a non-rigid boat made of three carefully chosen and shaped logs lashed together. Usually the centre log, the stoutest, is set just below the level of the others to form a shallow keel. Rowing rails are added. Catamarans are propelled by oars and a triangular sail often held

Beaching a catamaran

by a human mast. Variations of the catamaran are to be found. For instance, the "kola maram" of the Cape Calimere coast is a much larger craft of seven logs. It is used for sailing 25 miles offshore to catch the flying fish that appear between July and August. Another common east coast boat is the "masula". Non-rigid again, it consists of planks sewn together with coir rope and has no framework. Caulking is done with dry straw. Beaching the catamarans on the surf-battered coast of Madras is an art. Near the shore the sail is reefed and a large breaker chosen upon which to ride. Paddling furiously, the crew guide the boat on to the beach surf, jump from it and pull it abreast of the waves.

The shore surf of the Arabian Sea coast is much less severe than that of the Bay of Bengal. Therefore boats can be made more rigid and the most common type is the dug-out canoe. A tree trunk is scooped out leaving the keel portion thicker than the rest to give it stability. "Odam" canoes, from 32 to 40 ft. long, are large enough to operate boat-seines. The smaller "thome"

A Masula. Its stitched sides are strong enough to resist the big breakers of the eastern coast. The boats are repaired and resewn once a year

canoe, from 28 to 32 ft. long, is used for drift-net and gill-net fishing.

Mackerel and oil-sardines make up the largest catches on the Kerala coast. Tellicherry, Cochin and Kozhikode are the chief centres of the mackerel fisheries. From September to February is the busy season when shoals are large; after March activity decreases until fishing stops completely during the monsoon season. Pickled mackerel are exported to Ceylon. Sardines are pressed for their oil, and the guano* is used as fertiliser in the coconut groves and coffee plantations of the hills. On the Comorin coast are found perches, pomfrets, sharks and rays. Mackerel and sardines do not appear in great numbers on the Coromandel coast, but are replaced by horse-mackerel and herrings. Sharks and rays, fished for with long lines and revolving chain hooks, are caught for their oil and for their flesh which is edible when dried. Pomfrets are caught by a very clever device. Palm leaves, tied at intervals to an anchored line, encourage the fish to shelter beneath them.

*GUANO: waste material or manure.

44

Men in four catamarans raise the bag-net, called "mada valai", from the sea floor thus enmeshing the fish. Off Negapatam and Cuddalore flying fish appear in the months of June, July and August. The Gulf of Mannar and Palk Bay shores are wealthy in pearl-oyster and chank beds. Chank (conch) shells are used for making bangles locally and in Calcutta. A large, well-shaped shell will fetch as much as Rs. 5,000.* These shells are fished for by the Paravans, a Roman Catholic group, who dive to the beds. This fishing is now under State control.

The nets used vary with the area and the fish caught. All are made by hand, the smaller of cotton and the larger of hemp, and they are preserved with a bark preparation. The "rampan" shore-seine of the Malabar coast is a long wall of net with floats on the top and stone sinkers at the base. One end is left with a party of men on the shore. Canoes take the other end and play out the net in a semi-circular shape so that they return with the second end to the shore. The two parties of men draw in the net which holds shoals of mackerel or sardines. Catches are landed and auctioned on the beach. Fish to be sold are put into baskets and carried by coolies on bicycles to the local markets. They have to move fast as fish putrefy quickly in the hot climate. Within an hour fresh fish from the catch can be bought at a market 5 miles from the coast. Fish are also cured either by sun-drying on mats for two or three days, or salt-cured in leaf-lined pits. The governments of Madras and Kerala are encouraging the fishermen to bring their catches to curing yards, but they are still reluctant to do this. The Madras government has installed a cold storage plant at Mangalore.

Fishing in south India is not without its occupational hazards. Sharks are always dangerous; dolphins often leap from the sea to stab at the fishermen with their many-toothed beaks and sword-fish have been known to spear boats. Poisonous sea-snakes enmeshed in nets are also dangerous as Gilbert Slater observed near the city of Madras:

". . . I watched with my wife fishermen pulling their net on to the beach. They warned us not to come near and handled the net very cautiously in emptying it. There were several snakes in

*1 rupee = 1s. 6d., or 21 U.S. cents. This high price would be for a rare type of conch believed to bring good luck.

45

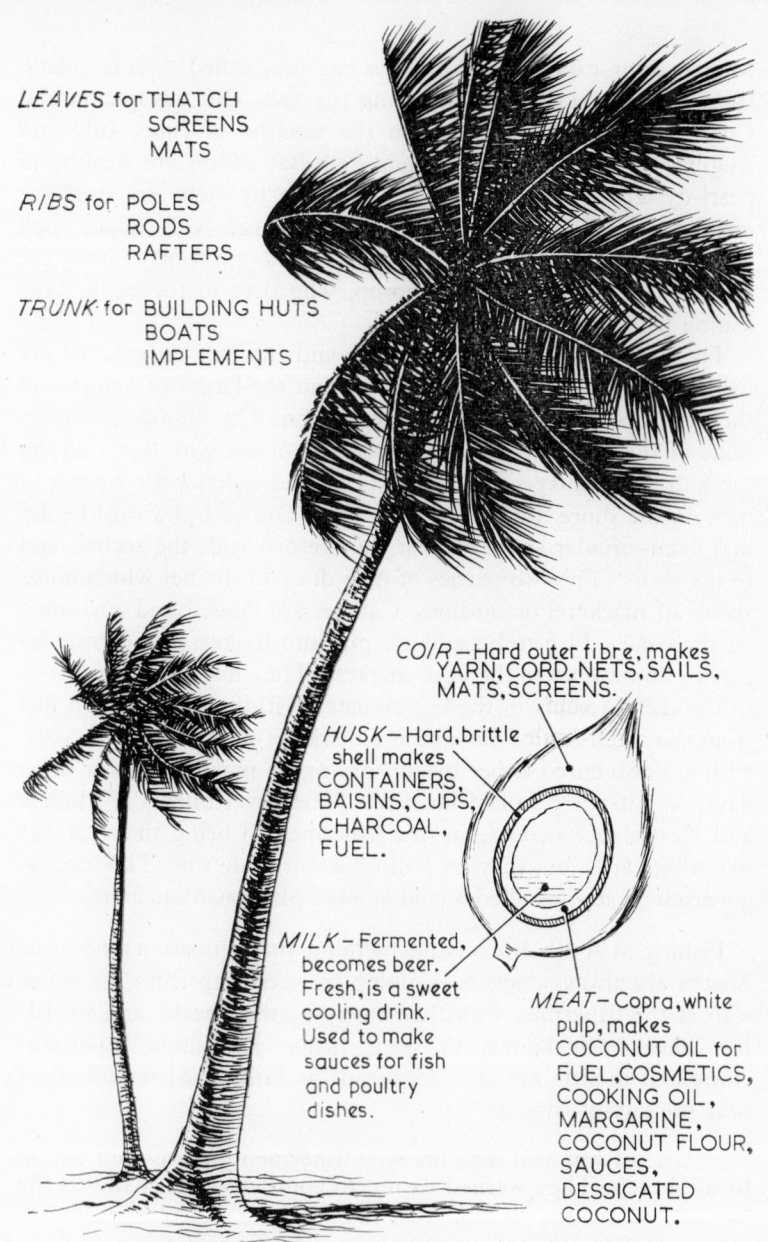

LEAVES for THATCH
         SCREENS
         MATS

RIBS for POLES
      RODS
      RAFTERS

TRUNK for BUILDING HUTS
        BOATS
        IMPLEMENTS

COIR – Hard outer fibre, makes YARN, CORD, NETS, SAILS, MATS, SCREENS.

HUSK – Hard, brittle shell makes CONTAINERS, BAISINS, CUPS, CHARCOAL, FUEL.

MILK – Fermented, becomes beer. Fresh, is a sweet cooling drink. Used to make sauces for fish and poultry dishes.

MEAT – Copra, white pulp, makes COCONUT OIL for FUEL, COSMETICS, COOKING OIL, MARGARINE, COCONUT FLOUR, SAUCES, DESSICATED COCONUT.

The coconut, the tree of life

46

the catch, and the task of seizing them one at a time by the neck and dashing them on the sand to dislocate their backbones was allocated to a boy, on the assumption, as I suppose, that if he were bitten the loss of his life would matter less than that of a man."*

COCONUT PALMS

Over one million acres in Kerala state are devoted to growing the coconut palm, yielding more than 70% of India's total coconut production of 4 million tons each year. The coconut is the basis of life in Kerala, and for centuries the people have tended the trees that thrive in the tropical climate and backwaters. "Kalpavriksha", the wish-granting tree, is the Malayalam name for the coconut palm. It is well deserved for every part of the tree has its uses. A mature palm will reach 40 ft. in height and will live for eighty years. It will bear a monthly yield of nuts from six to eight years after planting.

Leaves are plaited into kadjan roof thatching and "tattis"; these are screens soaked with water and are effective in keeping rooms cool. They are also woven into baskets and umbrellas and split to make brooms. Paper is also manufactured from leaf pulp. The trunk is hollowed out to make canoes and supplies timber for house frames.

Sap from the coconut leaves and palmyra palm leaves is fermented into toddy, a strong drink. This is made in Madras state by licence only. The juice is collected in "chattis", pots lined with lime to prevent immediate fermentation, which are suspended from the cut fronds. Tappings are taken daily and a climber can manage about fifty trees each day. With his feet tied together by a bamboo thong, the climber ascends the tree by pulling upwards with his clasped hands using his outpushed knees as levers and his feet as grips. The toddy-climbing caste of south India are the Nadars. Chatties of the sap are kept until the day following collection by which time it is about 8% alcohol. By the next day it has turned sour and if kept longer it will stink. Women boil chatties of sap to evaporate it into "jaggery", a kind of coarse sugar. This must be done immediately after collection. Distillation of the juice will produce arrack and then vinegar.

*Quoted from *Southern India* by G. Slater (Allen & Unwin, 1936).

47

The agile toddy-tapper climbs to the crown of the coconut palm. He will return later to collect the juice

When fully grown the coconut fruit, varying in colour from green to brown, will weigh 4 lb., stand 10 ins. high and have a girth of 24 ins. It is made up of four parts: an outer fibrous covering called the husk, the hard shell, a layer of white flesh and a quantity of milk. The flesh is eaten and used in curries and the milk is drunk.

To give an idea of the many uses to which the coconut is put, let us follow it from the time it is cut from the tree.

Children gather up the nuts as they fall to the base of the tree when the climber cuts them on his monthly round. They then take them to a yard where the nuts have their husks removed on a spike projecting from the ground. Strong wrists and a steady hand are needed for this work. Now the fruit is in the form that we see it in our greengrocer's window. We shall return to the husk later. The nut is then split open and the milk emptied. Men and boys squat on their heels halving the shells with one blow of a heavy knife. Women and children neatly lay out the halves in yards, open side upwards, to be sun-dried. After some days the flesh dries and shrinks and becomes detached from the shell. These empty shells are used mainly for domestic fuel and for producing charcoal. If the craftsman gets a chance he will carve them into beautiful bowls, vases and brooches. The meat is then cut into small pieces by women working deftly on large curved knives planted into the ground. After drying in the sun or in a kiln, this flesh is known as copra and is exported for the extraction of coconut oil. The average yield of copra per nut is 5 oz. with an oil content of 72%.

Oil supplies for domestic use and cooking are obtained by crushing the dried flesh in the village press. This is a large pestle and mortar worked by a bullock at the end of a boom. The oil is used for frying, lighting in lamps, hair and skin oils and for making cheap soap. What is left in the press is fed to cattle as nutritious oil-cake.

The Coir Industry   It is likely that the matting for your school cricket wicket started off as a coconut husk in a cottage in Kerala. Most of us have coconut matting somewhere in our homes. These are the end-products of the Kerala coir industry which uses the coconut husks as its raw material; 80% of the husks grown in

Much of the wealth of Kerala comes from coconuts. Here split
coconuts are drying in the sun to make copra

Kerala are used by the industry and India exports over Rs.
80 million worth of coir products each year.

Coir making is an ancient craft. In the thirteenth century Marco
Polo noticed that the Arabs sewed their boat planks with
coir yarn from India. Today, half a million workers, three-quarters
of whom are women, make a living by producing coir yarn in their
villages and selling it to the factories. Coir yarn spinning is still a

In this open yard of a coir factory women are sorting the coir brought by farmers

cottage industry because technical progress has not been able to better the traditional methods.

The husks have first to be retted. For this they are piled into large soaking pits. These are nets moored in a lagoon and weighed down with mud and stones placed on top of the husks. The gentle currents remove the tannin from the husks giving the fibre a golden-brown colour. They are left submerged for ten months. Women and children fish them out by ducking under the water. Extraction of the fibre is done, again by women, by the tedious process of beating the husks with wooden clubs. After sorting and grading the fibre is spun into yarn on a spinning wheel. It is then taken, often by the children in their small canoes, to the dealers of factories at Cochin, Alleppey or Kozhikode to be sold. From here onwards it is a factory industry.

At Alleppey and Shertallay are factories where the coir yarn is skilfully made into mats, matting, rugs and carpets on heavy

A rubber plantation in South India

looks. Colourful designs are either worked in as part of the weave or stencilled on before the mats are clipped to an even surface.

Since 1953 the coir industry has been nationalised.

FOREST AND PLANTATION PRODUCTS

The steep forested slopes of the Cardamom and Nilgiri Hills yield tropical products—spices, coffee, tea, cashew nuts, timbers and rubber. Next to coconuts, pepper is the largest peasant-grown crop in Kerala. Cinnamon, cardamoms and cashew nuts are grown in ryot plots, and also in plantations in the case of cashew nuts, but all are often collected wild from the jungle.

Of the forest timbers of south India, teak and sandalwood, a scented yellow wood, are the chief. Elephants move the logs from the timber camps deep in the jungle to loading points on the light railways. From there they are taken to ports on the coast.

Two-thirds of the cleared land in the Nilgiris is devoted to tea and coffee plantations. Around Ootacamund there are 900 tea estates. Also grown in plantations are eucalyptus trees, introduced from Australia, and cinchona trees, the bark of which is used to make quinine. The first cinchona plantation was set up by the British in 1860 and was worked by Chinese convict labour.

Rubber is the great plantation crop of the Cardamom Hills of Kerala. In that state over 100,000 acres are devoted to it. High temperatures, rainfall of 80 to 120 ins. and the shortness of the annual dry season give conditions favourable to the growth of rubber trees. The estates are situated on the lower hill slopes (at from 1,000 to 2,000 ft.) and are bounded by stone walls. Under the blanket of the closely packed trees the atmosphere is dank and humid. Coolies work at tapping, gathering the latex* from the collecting cups and spraying the trees with copper sulphide to protect them from blight. No rubber is exported because production cannot yet satisfy domestic demand. Europeans manage many of the estates but they are mainly Indian owned.

POWER AND IRRIGATION

To help to overcome the irregularity of rainfall, the larger rivers of south India that have their sources in the wet hills are controlled for irrigation and hydro-electric power. Many new schemes have been born under the Indian Government's five year plans to extend cultivation by watering new lands from regulated out-flow dams, and to supply cheap power to new and expanding industries.

The largest river is the Cauvery, flowing from the Western Ghats to its delta on the Coromandel coast. The delta has been irrigated in places since the eleventh century when the Chola kings built the 1,080 ft. long Grand Anicut. Today, the Cauvery river system produces a third of India's total hydro-electric power before it slows down on the Carnatic plain. Over 90,000 million cu. ft. of water in a lake of 60 sq. miles is impounded behind the Mettur Dam, completed in 1938. It is built across a gorge of the river, is made of cement concrete and is 5,300 ft. long and 176 ft. high. Canals issuing from Mettur irrigate 30,000 acres of land in the Cauvery delta region. Mettur, generating cheap power, supplies the cement and textile industries at Trinchinopoly and the rolling mills at Negapatam, besides supplying its own industrial centre.

Two rivers draining the Nilgiris have important electricity plants on them. With a capacity of 72,000 KW. the station at

*Latex: milky juice from the rubber tree.

53

NAZARETH COLLEGE LIBRARY

Pykara Falls (on a tributary of the river Moyar) supplies the tea plantations of the hills and the cement and textile industries at Coimbatore. The Pykara and Mettur schemes are soon to be linked. In 1956 the 204 ft. high dam of the Lower Bhavani project was completed at a total cost of Rs. 95 million. A canal network 125 miles long branches from it taking water to over 200,000 thirsty acres.

The Cardamom Hills with their high rainfall and many waterfalls are also a source of power. A 173 ft. high masonry dam impounds the Periyar Reservoir and over 1,000 acres of forest land skirting the lake have been declared a game sanctuary. Shooting is forbidden in this reserve where herds of elephant fifteen or twenty strong may be seen. By a mile-long tunnel through the hills, water is taken to parts of Madras that lie in the rain-shadow. Rs. 72 million have been provided in the second five year plan for the development of power at Periyar.

Power from the plant at Pallivasal supplies the industries at Alwaye, Cochin and Ernakulam. Besides producing chemicals and fertilisers, Alwaye is an aluminium smelting centre and now processes the atomic sands of the Kerala beaches at its Rare Earths factory. Pallivasal also drives the pumps that drain the flooded fields of the backwaters.

Tanks in Madras From earliest times tanks have irrigated the rice-plots of the Carnatic. A tank is merely a pond of water held up by a dam built across a river. Heavy rains fill the tank which stores the water for use in the dry period. Many river courses of Madras are simply a series of tanks, each feeding upon the overflow of those above it. Ditches and channels take the water from the tank to the fields. Rarely is a tank able to store water from one year to the next. High evaporation and seepage rob it of much of its efficiency.

The Kabalai of South India A mathematician from south India called Kabalai invented the bullock water-lift of the same name. Only slightly less efficient than a motor-pump, the kabalai is self-filling and self-emptying. One man and a bullock are needed to operate it whereas the north India version needs two men, one to fill the bucket and one to empty it. The kabalai consists of a large leather bucket with an open tube attached to the bottom. The ropes and pulleys are so adjusted that as the full bucket is

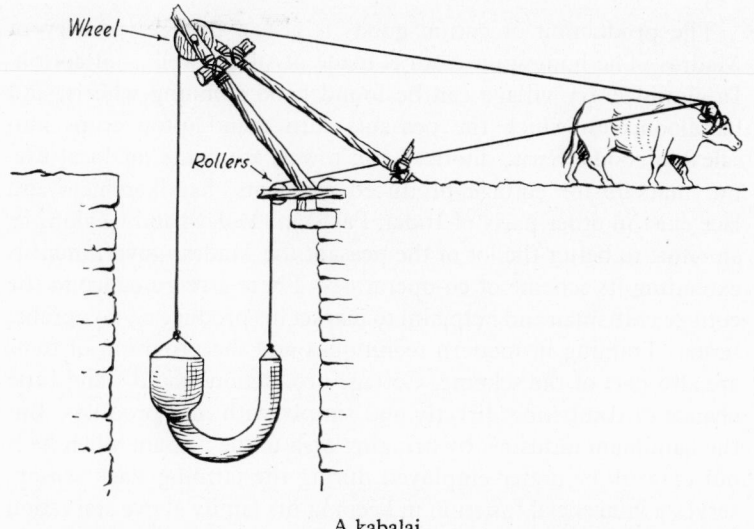

A kabalai

raised by the bullock, the end of the tube is level with the top of the bucket until it reaches the lip of the well. The tube is then automatically pulled over the lip into the irrigation channel while the bucket is pulled higher towards the top pulley. The water then rushes from the tube and bucket into the ditch and away to the fields. When lowering and filling the same principle works in reverse.

COTTON AND HANDICRAFTS

Next in importance to agriculture in Madras is the cotton industry. On the black soils of south central Madras the cotton plant is tended by the peasant cultivators and the cotton is spun into yarn and woven into cloth in their homes.

There are centres of the factory industry at Coimbatore, Madras, Tirunelveli and Tuticorin. The Buckingham and Carnatic Mills of Madras city were established in the late nineteenth century. Today, cotton is the largest single industry in the city. Local supplies of cotton and power from the Pykara Falls plant in the Nilgiris have led to a considerable expansion of the industry at Coimbatore. The mill at Madurai is one of the largest in India.

The production of cotton goods is also a cottage industry in Madras. The homespun cloth is made of silk as well as of cotton. In almost every village can be found hand spinning wheels, and handlooms on which the peasants turn their cotton crops into saleable goods. Saris, dhoties* and towels are made for local use, but markets for cottage produced garments, handkerchiefs and lace exist in other parts of India, Pakistan, Malaya and Ceylon. In an effort to better the lot of the peasant the Madras government is extending its scheme of co-operatives. These give guidance to the cottage craftsman and help him to market his produce on favourable terms. Training in modern techniques and the provision of tools are also part of the scheme. Cottage production would stand little chance of competing directly and simply with mill products. But the handloom industry, by bringing cash to the peasant when he is out of work or under-employed during the farming slack season, serves a vital social function in keeping his family above starvation level. Wisely, the state government has recognised this and is doing much to help the industry.

No part of India is more famous for its handicraft products than the south. Kerala, with its herds of elephants, is noted for its ivory carving. Figures, cigarette cases and holders all display patience and skill. Metal mirrors from the village of Aranmula, brocaded fabrics from Kottar, silver inlay work and pottery are all exquisite products of traditional craftsmanship.

Madras, too, has noted handicraft centres. Silky mats and articles made of palmyra leaves from the Tirunelveli district, cotton carpets from Bhavani, brassware from Kumbakonam and ceramics are but a few of the articles produced by cottage craftsmen in the state.

*SARI: the long outer garment worn by Hindu women. DHOTI: a loincloth.

APPENDIX 1

Annual Expenditure of an Agricultural Labourer

The family consists of the man, his wife and two male children.
(Tirunelveli district, south India.)

Item	% of Annual Income
Millets and Paddi	40
Drink	10
Oils (coconut, gingelly, etc.)	3
Salt	1
Chillies (dried)	1
Fish	6
House Repairs	2
Cloth	8
Implements	3
Washermen and Barbers . . .	2
Ceremonies	12
Religious Festivals	10
Luxuries (e.g. travelling)	2
	100 %

Adapted from *Some South Indian Villages* by G. Slater.

APPENDIX 2

Some Castes of South India

Caste	Region	Occupation
Ambalavasis	W. coast	Temple service
Cherumas	W. coast	Agricultural labourers
Chettis	Madras	Merchants
Idayans	Madras	Shepherds
Kapus	Madras	Landowners
Mannans	S. India	Washermen
Panikkans	Kerala	Barbers
Vettis	S. India	Lowest caste of village and servants who care for the burning ground for the dead

c

The Kammaralas caste is the great artisan caste of south India. It is divided into five:

Tattans	. . .	Goldsmiths
Kannans	. . .	Weavers
Tachans	. . .	Carpenters
Kal-Tachans	. .	Stone masons
Kollans	. . .	Blacksmiths

II

CENTRAL INDIA

PHYSICAL

LIKE an inverted triangle, the tableland or plateau of peninsular India stretches from about 26°N. to its southern peak in the Nilgiri Hills. It is a region of great diversity, including the group of northern mountains, the Deccan Lava Trap and the high plateau of Mysore. The central block has a tilt downwards from west to east.

On the west the edge of the region is clearly marked by the high, and often precipitous, Western Ghats (average height 3,500 ft.); to the east the lower Eastern Ghats (average height 2,000 ft.) form the limit of the plateau. Separating the block from the Indo-Gangetic plains in the north are high plateaux and the heavily forested Aravalli, Miakal and Vindhya mountain ranges, with heights varying from 1,500 to 4,000 ft. These ranges are among the oldest mountains in the world. This peninsular block is composed in the main of very old and hard crystalline rocks, particularly granites and gneisses,* and the lavas of the Deccan Trap in the north-west region.

The surface of the plateau is not even. The mountain ranges to the north, and the deep troughs between them, are heavily forested and inhabited by backward tribes. Rivers have dissected the plateau into a series of shallow valleys and intervening ridges. Weathering of the granite rocks has produced reddish-brown soils and left behind granite-domed residual hills that litter the country-side. These are much like the tors of south-west England. One

---

*GNEISS: a rock which is formed in layers, such as quartz or mica.

such hill, Nandi Hill near Bangalore, reaches a height of 4,851 ft. above sea-level. On its summit is a temple and a large dak bungalow (travellers' rest house) near which is a sheer drop of 1,000 ft. over which Tipu Sultan is said to have thrown prisoners of war.

The landscape of the Mysore plateau might be quoted to give an idea of one type of countryside in a region of varying countrysides. Great pinnacled ant-hills, some more than 8 ft. high, baked hard by the sun, are common sights. Dried up water-courses, called "nullahs", cut deep into the ground. Apart from cultivated areas around the many tanks, there is little vegetation besides cactus, used as hedges to the fields, thorn bushes and plantations of casuarina trees.* These trees are useful to the villagers as they can be split easily with a hand knife into building timber. Many of the dry, dusty roads are lined with fig trees often inhabited by monkeys and tree rats. And throughout the area can be found the barren, reddish hills made up of granite boulders.

The Deccan lava region is one of widespread cultivation and close settlement. Lava weathers into a fertile, easily worked soil and the region is a great cotton producer, with millets as a close second food-crop. The lava, the depth of which varies between 2,000 and 5,000 ft., escaped through fissures, or cracks in the earth's crust to spread rapidly over a vast area.

This region experiences the main seasons common to the rest of India; the hot season from March to June with temperatures in the nineties, the rains from June to October, and the cold season from October to February. Because the monsoon rains have to pass over the Western Ghats, the plateau is in a rain-shadow. Annual averages vary with individual situations, but are mostly within the 20 to 40 in. range. Even this amount is irregular, and dry years fail to fill the tanks on the river-courses and famine follows. One very arid area is the Thar Desert. The variety of climate begets a variety of natural vegetation coverings. On the wetter Western Ghat slopes is dense, moist forest, but in areas with less rainfall dry deciduous forest, low thorn bushes and savanna grassland exist.

The large and important rivers, with the exception of the Tapti and Narbada, flow eastwards with the tilt of the plateau. The coastal streams flowing into the Indian Ocean from the Western

*CASUARINA: Tree with leafless branches like huge horse-tails.

60

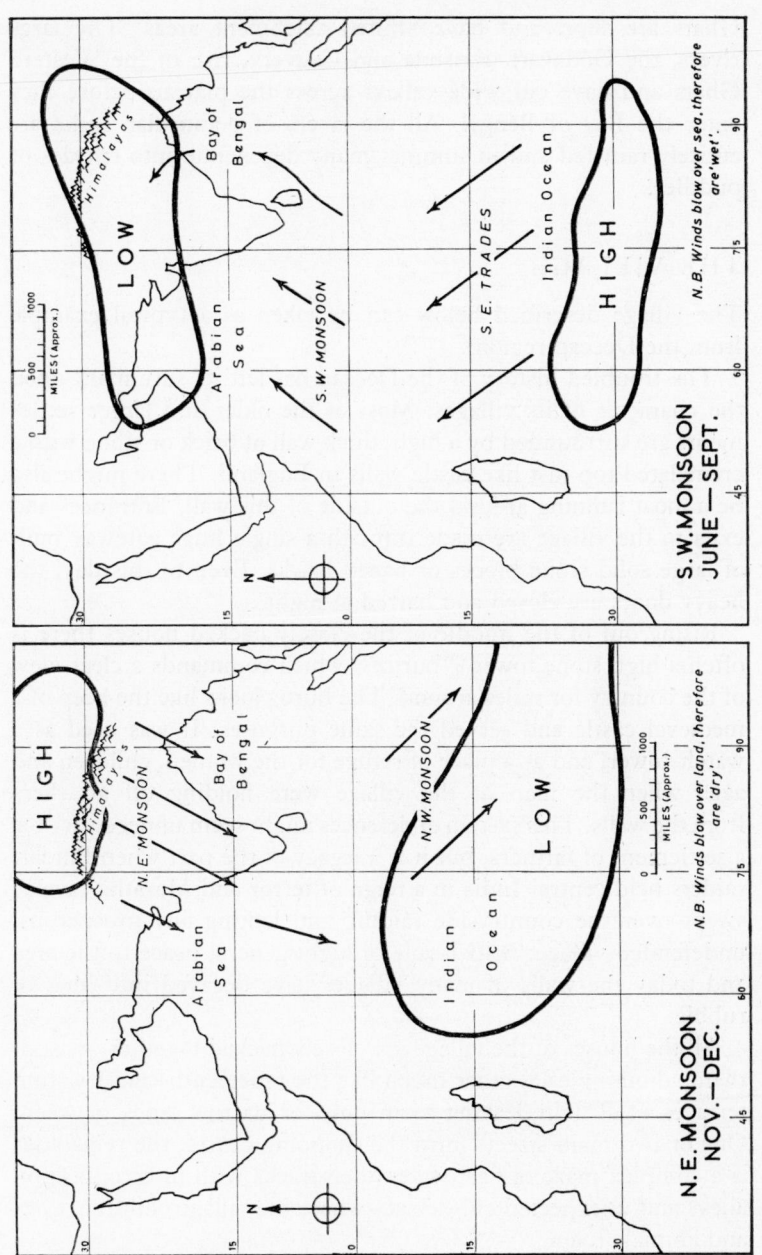

N.B. Winds blow over sea, therefore are 'wet'.

S.W. MONSOON
JUNE — SEPT.

N.B. Winds blow over land, therefore are 'dry'.

N.E. MONSOON
NOV.—DEC.

Ghats are short and have limited catchment areas. The large rivers, the Godavari, Krishna and Cauvery, rise in the Western Ghats and have cut wide valleys across the plateau before they enter the Bay of Bengal. All the rivers of peninsular India are entirely rain-fed and in summer many degenerate into trickles or puddles.

THE VILLAGE

The village described below can be taken as a typical example from the Deccan region.

The troubled history of the Deccan has left its sure mark upon the character of its villages. Most of the older and larger settlements are surrounded by a high, thick wall of brick or stone with a crenellated top just like castle walls in England. There might also be a moat running around the outside of this wall. Entrances and exits to the village are made through a single huge gateway built of large solid stone blocks or baked bricks. Even to this day, the heavy doors are closed and barred at night.

Rising out of the middle of the closely packed houses there is often a high stone tower ("buruz") which commands a clear view of the country for miles around. The buruz looks like the keep of a medieval castle and served the same purposes. It was used as a watch-tower, and as a place of refuge for the women, children and aged when the men of the village were holding off attackers from the walls. This system of defences might seem unnecessary for a settlement of farmers, but it is a legacy of the past when Pindari raiders held central India in a reign of terror and Maratha cavalry swept over the countryside raiding and looting any prosperous, undefended village. British rule brought general peace to the area and today the walls of many villages have decayed into lines of rubble.

All the houses of the village are closely packed together, most of them adjoining each other much like the nineteenth-century slum terraces of Britain, leaving room only for narrow lanes between. One or two main streets form the shopping centre; the remainder is a complex maze of narrow, earthen tracks with interconnecting alleys and unexpected cul-de-sacs where the village children, dogs and animals roam.

Deccan landscape, with a typical hill fortress

The houses of the village are all made from local materials—stone, burnt bricks and mud—which keep the interior of the house cool in the hot Deccan summers. The "wadas" of the landowners, mostly Brahmins, and of the village chief are the largest houses in the village. They occupy the most pleasant sites and are set in large compounds. Many of the older houses of the richer families look like small forts with their high, solid walls of stone and masonry or bricks. The few windows, when there are any at all, face the street and are very high up the bare walls for fear of burglars. In a large house such as this there will be many rooms, including perhaps accounting offices, a family temple and a treasure room.

The very poor, low caste, out-caste and tribal people live in separate "cheries" on the outskirts of the village or beyond its walls. Their houses are small, dark and flimsy, with thatched roofs and woven-reed walls plastered with mud or cow-dung.

Between these two extremes of the social scale come the majority of the villagers—the great mass of the tenant-farmers renting their land from the "wada" owners, and the castes of the carpenters, metal-smiths, barbers, cobblers, etc. The tenant-farmer's house has mud or burnt brick walls and a flat roof with a little parapet and clay drainage pipes. The roof is made of layers

The village of Hangala Pura in the Deccan (Mysore State). See section on Village Life in India, pp. 139

of branches and sugar-cane leaves resting on wood beams and fully covered with a 6 in. layer of mud to make it proof against rain. If the farmer is prosperous the roof will be made of tiles. In front of the house is a small open porch, a platform raised above street-level. Here crops are dried in the sun and here also the family sleep on warm summer nights. The front door leads into a main room, part of which is at a higher level. The lower section is used as a cattle pen; the higher section is the family's living quarters, both by day and by night. In one corner of the room the stocks of grain are stored either in gunny bags or earthen pots. At the back of this main room the kitchen is set apart. The walls of the farmer's house are covered with paintings of Hindu gods, and with red and white stripes to scare away the spirit that brings cholera.

Few of the houses will face south, firstly because this exposes them to the direct rays of the sun; and secondly, because Yama, the god of death, lives in the south.

The interior of a rich man's house in Hangala Pura

The village receives visitors from time to time. In the rainy season the shepherds of the waste ground and the hills, will come and pitch their tents of cotton or wool outside the village. They make compounds from thorn bushes to protect their goats and sheep from the panthers and wolves. During their stay, the shepherds earn a little by working as casual field labourers for the farmers.

The main street of the village is the centre of its life as here are found the shops, refreshment stalls, offices, the larger temples and the once-weekly bazaar. The school, too, certainly the most modern of all the buildings, will also be near the centre of the

In Hangala Pura the threshold grain is stored in holes, about
fifteen feet deep, dug in the main street

village. Outside the village walls lie the cultivated fields and beyond
them the grazing waste, hills and bush. The Deccan is an area of
dry crops and not much rice production. The main crops are
millets, cotton (a great cash crop), and oil-plants like the peanut.
Some smaller plots are irrigated from the brick-lined village well
to produce sugar-cane and vegetables.

FARMING IN CENTRAL INDIA

Most people will tell you that Indians eat rice as their staple grain
item of diet; but this is only partly true for rice needs plentiful

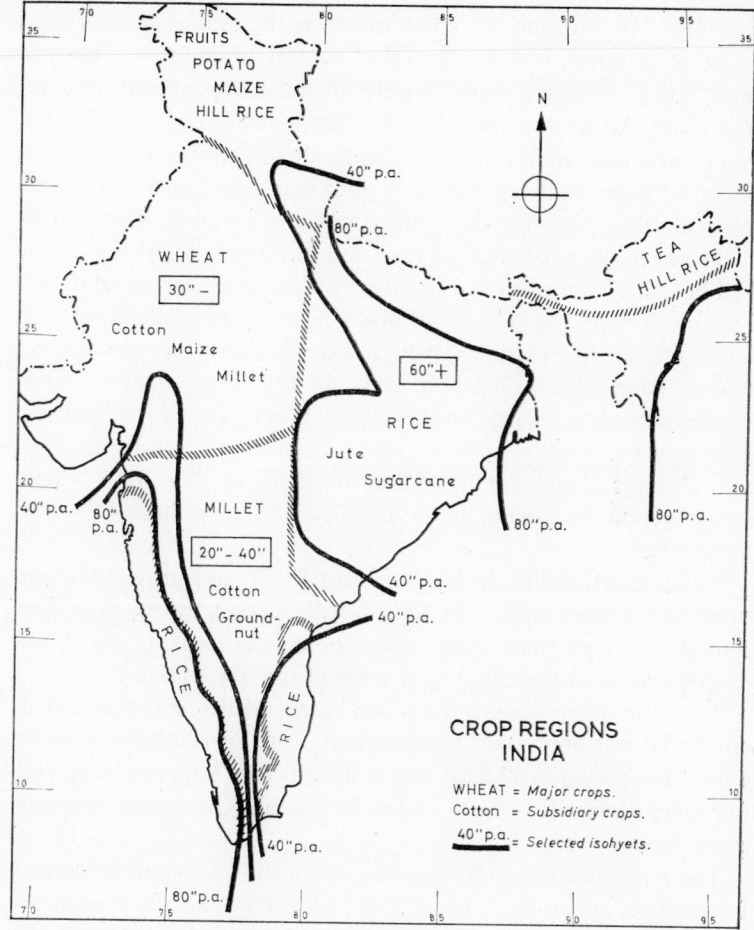

CROP REGIONS INDIA

WHEAT = *Major crops.*
Cotton = *Subsidiary crops.*
40" p.a. = *Selected isohyets.*

rainfall and there are areas of India that do not get sufficient. The Deccan is one of these. The climate of central India is hot and dry (20 to 40 ins. a year) so the peasant farmers must grow crops that will survive under these conditions and cannot grow rice except on the wetter fringes of both ghats and the river valleys of the lower east.

The three major crops of central India will be examined: the food-grain, millet; the cash crop, cotton; and the oil-seed crop, groundnuts.

Millet In England we know millet as the grass-like seed that is fed to canaries, but the farmer of central India grows "jowar" and "bajra" (the two main varieties of millet) to a height of 8 ft. and more. Millet was probably the first grain to be cultivated by prehistoric man and is today grown in all Indian states, especially on arid fringes. It is regarded as a poor man's food as it is a coarse grain and less palatable than milled rice, but its great value is that it thrives in hot, dry areas of poor soil unsuitable for rice.

The cultivation of Jowar, or Great Millet, is concentrated in the Deccan proper. One variety of jowar has a grain head round and hard and red like a cricket ball. Jowar takes only four months to mature from sowing to harvesting, and the farmer rotates it with cotton on the black soils of the Deccan. It may be grown as a "kharif" (monsoon) season crop, being sown in May just before the first rain showers come over the Western Ghats, or as a "rabi" (dry) season crop, then being sown after the last rains have fallen in September.

Bajra, Pearl Millet, is hardier than jowar and grows in even drier and poorer soils. In fact it will survive the most severe droughts but will not yield where rainfall exceeds 35 ins. It is mainly grown in Rajasthan and areas of the Thar Desert.

The other main millet, "Ragi" or Finger Millet, is concentrated on the laterite (red and clayey) granite soils of southern Mysore where it is grown as a kharif and irrigated crop. Ragi can be stored for more than fifty years under favourable conditions without going bad.

There is much misunderstanding about the food value of millet. Its yield per acre is less than that of paddi (jowar 400 lb. compared with 860 lb. of paddi), and therefore it is less suitable for a heavily populated country; but its stalks and leaves give good fodder for the farmer's cattle. The actual food value has been proved to be higher than that of milled rice. An experiment was conducted on the relative goodness of diets of certain selected areas of India. Rats were fed on the foods and it was found that those given millet were heavier (Deccan diet weight, 225 grammes) than those fed on milled rice (Bengali diet weight, 185 grammes). The Marathas, a millet-eating people, are one of the most energetic of India's regional communities.

Cotton picking

Cotton The Greek writer Herodotus, says in his *Histories*: "India has wild trees that bear fleeces as their fruit and of these the Indians make their clothes". He was, of course, describing the cotton plant that grows in the tropical regions of India. Cotton in India is centred on the sticky black soils of the Deccan lava country where climatic conditions meet the requirements of the plant; minimum temperatures rarely fall below 70°F. and rainfall rarely exceeds 35 ins. a year.

If the farmer grows millet as his main food crop, he grows cotton to sell to the mills of the industrial towns for cash. Because he has only a small plot of land, he mixes his crops in order to produce as much as he can in one season; he will sow cotton between the tall growing millet rows. Deccan cottons are short stapled ($\frac{3}{8}$ in. to $\frac{5}{8}$ in.) and are called "oomras". India cannot meet her home demand for cotton and much has to be imported; to help the small peasant farmer, whose lack of capital prevents him from improving the yield and quality of the cotton crop himself, the Bombay State Government is financing a scheme by which seeds of improved varieties are given to him. Thus India hopes to reduce her imports.

The Deccan harvest is picked in April; the farmer, his wife and children go into the fields and pluck the bolls by hand. There is no mechanisation and few farmers can afford to hire labour. The cotton is baled by the farmer and he loads it on to his bullock cart and takes it to the nearest cotton market town. Perhaps he takes it to Gadag where the agents of the Bombay mills will give him a fair price for his crop. To avoid cheating by middlemen at these collecting centres, the Bombay Government appoints inspectors who supervise dealings. Having sold his cotton, the farmer buys cloth for a new sari for his wife, a small toy for each of his children and a wad of betel* for himself. But he has made other things besides a small bag of rupees out of his cotton crop. After taking the lint from the boll, he feeds the soft shell of the seed to his cattle; he puts the seeds into a bullock-driven oil-press and crushes out the oil which his wife uses for cooking; the oil-cake that is left in the press is again used as cattle feed.

These thousands of peasant cash-croppers of the Deccan lava country make Bombay state the greatest cotton producer in the Indian Union. It has half the total cotton acreage and half the total output of India.

Groundnuts While we in Britain use mostly animal fats for frying and cooking, the people of the Indian sub-continent use only vegetable oils. On all farms of the sub-continent are grown

---

*BETEL OR ARECA NUTS: The ingredients of betel are pan leaves, areca (or betel) nuts, lime and various flavourings. It is a favourite "chew" with many people in the tropics. Fresh leaves of the betel pepper ("pan" leaves) are smeared with lime and cutch, which has a spicy flavour, cloves may also be added. Pieces of areca nut are added and the whole bolus placed in the mouth and chewed with great relish. It is a mild stimulant. It causes the spittle to appear blood-red and much spitting is part of the fun of chewing it.

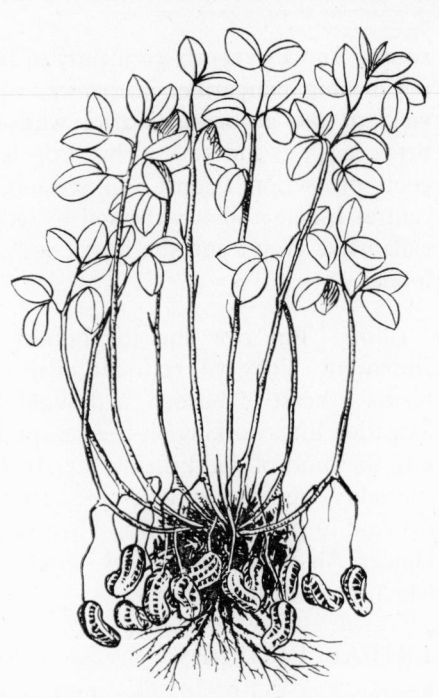

A groundnut plant

whatever oil-seeds are best suited to the local conditions of soil and climate. In the extreme south coconut oil is used, but there are also sesamum, linseed, rape oil and mustard seed.

Groundnuts, or peanuts, were introduced into India in the sixteenth century by the Portuguese. Today India is the world's greatest producer with 32 % of the world's total output. Groundnut cultivation is concentrated in peninsular India, mainly in the states of Madras, Bombay and Hyderabad. The plant will grow dry, but for heavy yields needs irrigation. Rainfall of 30 to 40 ins. per annum is the optimum, but the plant will thrive with as little as 20 ins. or as much as 50 ins. It occupies the ground for five months, but, because it is a low plant, the farmer often combines it with taller crops like cotton and jowar. Newly developed varieties take only a hundred days to mature so the farmer can get two crops each year.

Peasant farmers grow groundnuts chiefly as a source of cooking oil or as a food, but many sell their nuts to the large exporting

71

houses. India's exports go mainly to Europe where the oil is used for making margarine, medicines, varnishes and soap. The oil yield of the groundnut varies with the different types, but is between 43 % and 54 %. This crop has other advantages: it is a good protection against soil erosion, a very potent danger in central India; it allows the soil to recover after supporting more exhaustive crops; and the leaves and stalks can be used as cattle fodder.

Cattle The cow and the bullock are pervading features of Indian life. They will be found in all villages, and have many jobs to do: a beast of burden, a draught animal, threshing, working irrigation lifts, working oil-presses, puddling building clay, trampling the mud of paddi fields, etc. In Mysore cattle breeding is a speciality, and the varieties produced by that state are in great demand in peninsular India. Their fame goes back to the days of Haidar Ali who bred a very tough and hardy type of bullock which he used in warfare.

TRIBAL PEOPLES

Scattered in the forests and difficult mountains of central India are ancient and primitive tribal groups whose remote homes have isolated them from the advance of civilisation. These people, like the Juangs who still wear skirts made from leaves, live today much as they have for centuries past. All tribes are very superstitious and worship gods; the gods of the Korku tribe are painted stakes driven into the ground. They also believe in unseen demons who live in the dark forests and bring illness, disease and poor crops to the village. The forest people have many natural enemies, elephants, tigers and wild pig amongst them, but the greatest enemy of all the tribes is the anopheles mosquito, the bringer of malaria which takes heavy toll in the monsoon season.

Every tribe has its own magician, or wizard, but those of the Baiga tribe are regarded by all the neighbouring tribes as being the greatest professional magicians in the world. The Baigas are a poor, semi-nomadic people who live in the dense forests of the Maikal range to the east of the Satpura Mountains. They scratch a few scanty crops from burned jungle clearings with hoes or axes, but are forbidden to use the plough, since they believe it will tear

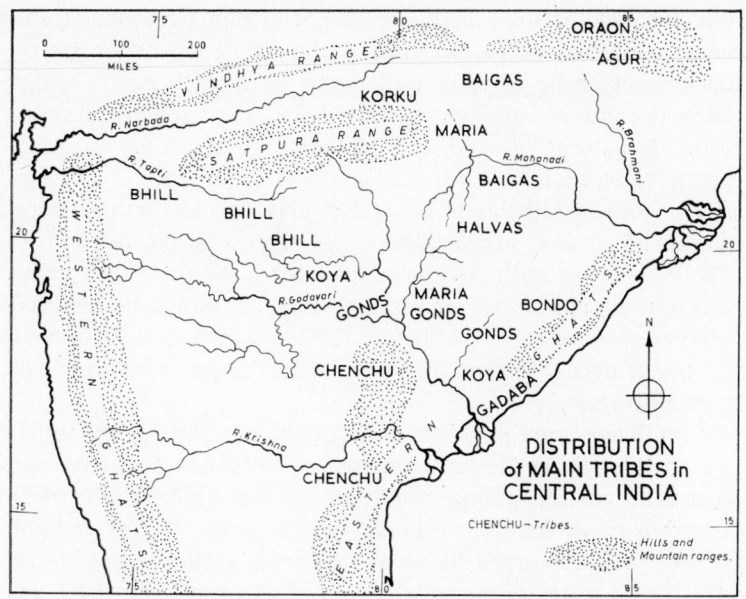

DISTRIBUTION
of MAIN TRIBES in
CENTRAL INDIA

CHENCHU—Tribes.

Hills and
Mountain ranges.

the skin of their Mother Earth. They also collect berries and fruit
from the forest and trap fish in the streams; they think fish-food
gives keener eyesight. Baigas are skilful hunters with spear and
bow and arrow; the latter they tip with a vegetable poison which
is potent enough to kill tigers. The bow, made from a length of
sturdy bamboo, is decorated with strips of silk each representing
an animal killed and stained with its blood. All the forest peoples
eat their food from large leaves instead of plates.

The Baigas, however, make their living mainly as "gunias",
magicians serving neighbouring tribes. Other tribes pay well for
the Baiga to officiate at ceremonies and effect cures for illness.
Armed with a straw stick and a winnowing fan and his magic, the
gunia has numberless duties; he will bless crops to fertility, ward
off diseases, pacify ghosts and turn demons from the village, give
protection from snake-bite, bring or stop rainfall, help the course
of love. His cures vary greatly, but the gunia always enters a
trance to effect them. He can make love potions from crushed
crane's bones, butter and dust from the girl's footprints; he can
transfer sickness from a person to a lizard by drawing the lizard

73

over the sick person's body; he can stop rain by catching and burying the first drops. So great is the reputation of the gunias that they are believed to be on friendly terms with tigers. Nanga Baiga, the ancient father of the Baiga tribe, was given the power to close the mouths of wild animals by God, according to Baiga legend. Now, when a tiger makes itself a great nuisance in a village, a Baiga gunia is called in to help. He will drive a nail into a nearby tree and this nail is supposed to fix the tiger's mouth shut so that it will starve to death. In the jungles there are trees with many nails in them and below are scratches that are said to be the claw marks of starving tigers. Although the Baigas are thought to have this power over the tiger, they believe that if they wash they will be eaten by one.

If the Baigas are the powerful magicians of tribal central India, then the Gonds are the great warriors. The Gonds conquered the other tribes and set up large kingdoms and today they are the most numerous of all the tribes. Their weapon is the "tangi", a light axe with a long, curved blade which comes vertically out of the shaft. Gond warriors are capable of killing tigers with the tangi in single combat. Women of Gond tribes decorate their legs with tattooed designs; large forest thorns are used in place of needles and wood soot for dyes.

One of the sub-tribes of the Gond people, the Kond, used to offer human sacrifices to their gods. The victims were not members of the tribe, but captives or strangers kidnapped for the ceremony. Today the place of the human victim has been taken by young goats. Another branch of the Gonds, the Marias, are great bison hunters. The horns of the bison are made into large head-dresses that are worn at ceremonies. In the Kond wedding dance the dancers charge each other and beat large drums that hang around their necks. The drum is regarded as sacred by all tribes in central India and bad luck comes if it is broken. The face of the drum should be made from the hide of an animal that has been killed by a tiger for this will make it roar like a tiger. Drums are called by many graphic names such as "the thing that growls at the least touch" and "the elephant's stomach in which there buzzes a fly".

In the Satpura Mountains live the Korkus. The name of this tribe comes from two words, "koru", meaning man, and "ku", meaning many; hence the name Korku means "many men". They make

Gonds dancing

their homes in the thick forests where teak and bamboo grow, and it is from these valuable timbers that the Korku make their living. In the rainy season, when all roads and tracks leading out from the forest are impassable bogs, the Korkus cut and trim the logs ready for carting. They fell the large trees with only a light axe which they use with skill and speed. In the dry summer the Korku transport the logs to the timber depots. The carts travel in convoys for protection against tigers. The animals and men rest in the heat of the day and move during the cooler nights.

Korku villages are like all tribal settlements; they are small clusters of flimsy huts built of woven bamboo or teak walls with thatch roofing. The walls are heavily plastered with mud, and each house has two or three rooms to accommodate the large family. Built on to the huts are cattle sheds where the animals shelter at night, reasonably safe from attacks by tigers and panthers.

Korkus grow wheat as their staple grain food. Teams of oxen pull the wooden plough under the guidance of the man, whilst the woman follows behind dropping seeds into the furrow through a bamboo pipe attached to the plough. Raids by wild pig and deer from the forest diminish all the carefully tended crops, and a continual watch has to be kept over the growing plants to ward off

75

hungry birds. Wild honey is gathered freely from forest hives and the Korku seem impervious to the stings of the large jungle bees. A fruit which the Korku call "mohwa" also provides food. During the months of March and April this small white fruit falls from the tree at night and is collected the next morning. It is sun-dried and stored in large jars and kept as a reserve for when other foods run short. A strong drink is also made from mohwa. Korkus use flint and steel for making fires, and they call them "chuck muck"!

All the people of the forest live very near to nature. The jungles around their homes abound with wild animals, some of which they fear greatly. Korkus have little fear of the tiger or the panther, but go in dread of the ill-tempered bear who comes to share the mohwa fruit harvest. The Korkus have many tales about the animals that roam the forest: for instance, there is the bird, so they say, which is so nervous that it sleeps on its back with its legs in the air in case the sky falls on it.

Customs of the other tribes of central India vary greatly. The Bondos, who live in the Orissa Hills, have reversed fashion. The women shave their heads while the men allow their hair to grow very long and spend hours combing and training it. Women of the Bondo tribes are also forbidden to wear anything more than a plain loincloth. Bondo legends give the reason for this; a goddess was bathing in a pool when some Bondo women passed by and laughed at her; the goddess, in her anger, threw a loincloth at the giggling women and cursed them into wearing the single cloth from that time onwards. Bondo women make up for their bare heads and plain clothing by wearing dozens of strings of beads around their necks and many bracelets on their arms.

Bondo men are vain, indolent and drunken. They have a very easy life, simply hunting or drinking whilst the women do all the household tasks, fishing and other work. The men are drunk for most of the day and the first thing they grab for in the morning is the jar of strong palm spirit that stands near their beds. Permanent semi-intoxication makes them very aggressive and the Bondos have been described as the most murderous of all Indian tribes. In 1952 an expedition was attacked as it approached a Bondo village and two porters were wounded by the arrows.

"Mudar", a plant which is held sacred by the Bondos, supplies the fibre for the tribe. Tribal taboos declare that it may be cut in February only, after which it is scraped, dried, beaten between stones and then spun into yarn. Human spittle is applied to make the tough yarn pliable. The yarn is dyed yellow, red and black with dyes from jungle plants and woven into cloth on a primitive handloom.

Living near the Bondos are the Gadabas, but unlike Bondo women the female Gadabas dress in many sorts of finery. They wear red and white striped cloth which, so legend tells, copies the tiger-skins they wore in more primitive times. They also form bustles of cloth, tie their hair into a ringed knot at the back, and wear heavy silver bracelets on their arms and big rings through their ears.

Perhaps the least primitive of all tribes in the Orissa Hills are the Saoras. Their houses are built in compounds fenced by high walls of stone and their large herds of cattle roam within these. The Saoras cultivate rice on terraces that are fed with water by complex irrigation devices. They make yarn from a shrub, but tribal laws forbid weaving, which is done by neighbouring peoples.

The Saoras are one of the few tribes of central India that produce artistic works. Painting is entirely an expression of their religious beliefs. Walls of huts are covered with designs that keep disease away, make crops plentiful and pay homage to gods, spirits and ancestors. The walls are painted red, so the artist draws his designs with a white paint made from rice flour. Often there is a professional artist in the village; he will sleep near the wall upon which he is to work and the gods will send him a dream showing what he has to paint. Figuring often in the paintings are gods and their pets (tigers and monkeys especially), the porcupine who is the priest of the spirit world, and automobiles, trains and aeroplanes—even Saora gods ride about in these. Usually these murals are put on to the darkest wall of the hut so that the prying eyes of humans shall not offend the ghosts.

BAIGA GAMES

Young Baigas delight in imitating their parents. They hold bazaars at which they haggle fiercely over the prices of rare goods brought

These children in Hangala Pura are having a gymnastics
lesson. Their teacher earns about 25/– a week

from "foreign parts"—sticks, stones or forest leaves. They build
small reed huts in which the girl cooks rice and lentils (mud and
sand?), whilst her "husband" hunts with miniature bow and
arrows that his father made for him. Proudly he marches home
with his fowls and ham-strung wild pig (leafy branches and round
stone?) to feed his expectant, hungry family.

Kanda-kel is a strange Baiga sport. A line of boys sit with their
legs outstretched, and twigs representing roots are wedged between
their toes. One boy and one girl are given this "crop" to
grow and their first job is to plant it by banging the heads of the
boys on the ground. Other children play the part of ants and their
act is to pinch the plants—the line of boys. They play their part
well for jungle children know how ants bite. Enter the villains of
the game—one robber and one policeman. They steal the crop by

The fort at Jodhpur stands impressive and impregnable on a rock
outcrop above the city

plucking the twigs from the grubby toes, and escape into the nearby
bush. The game ends with all the remaining children chasing the
miscreants. Such is Kanda-kel: I cannot see the point of it, can
you? But then, we do not live in the Indian jungles.

THE THAR DESERT

The large state of Rajasthan is divided into two natural regions
by the Aravalli mountain range; to the west of this is the arid,
little settled and sparsely populated region known as the Thar
Desert (or, strictly speaking, the eastern and larger section of that
desert, for much lies in Pakistan); to the east is an area with a more
favourable climate, better agriculture and many large towns.

Rajasthan is the home of the Rajputs, a noble race whose
history is a glorious one of wars and battles for a dying cause. They
were heavily defeated by the invading Muslim forces of Muhammad
of Gur in 1192, after which they retired to their fortresses built
high on the ridges of the desert margins. Jodhpur, for example, is
built amongst sandstone hills; its centre is a large fort and around
the city is a 6-mile wall with seven huge gates: a very formidable
city to attack. The code of life of the Rajput warriors might be
compared with that of the Knights of the Round Table.

79

But it is the western section of Rajasthan that is of interest. The Thar is almost complete desert with scanty, dry scrub, stretches of bare rock and great sand-dunes rearing before the winds. Some of these dunes reach nearly 500 ft. in height. Only 10 ins. of rainfall comes annually to the Thar, and temperatures range from 60°F. in winter to 100°F. in summer. This vast expanse of sand is 100,000 sq. miles in area. Very little cultivation is possible here. Farming of dry crops like bajra is done in wetter valleys but most farmers are herdsmen who care for flocks of sheep and goats. One important product is salt from Pachbhadra Lake, a huge marsh. It is thought that the salt has been carried by winds from the tidal marshes of the Rann of Kutch. A railway serves the salt workings.

Main towns in the Thar, Jodhpur and Bikaner, are, like all desert cities, caravan-route centres for trade across the desert. Whilst railways have come to the Thar, these cities are still trade centres and the camel is still the most common form of transport.

SOME ANIMALS

In the forests and on the open savanna parklands of central India live a great variety of wild animals. Here, nature has made her usual balance of meat-eaters (e.g. tiger), who prey upon the fast grass-eaters (e.g. gazelle). There is ample opportunity for hunting with both camera and rifle, but "shikars" (hunting expeditions) and "kills" are closely controlled by the state governments. Before animals can be shot, and some cannot under any circumstances, a permit must be obtained from the Divisional Forest Officer. Much of India's animal-life has been ravaged in the past by trophy hunters, and governments are now protecting their fauna by law.

The Asiatic Lion   Living in the Gir Forest in the Bombay Ghats are the few remaining Asiatic lions, which enjoy complete protection from hunters. No one may shoot these proud beasts which were once found in great numbers in central India, but have been brought to the verge of extinction by shooting. Visitors are encouraged to observe the lions and a guest house run by the Government stands in the centre of the forest. The best time to see the animals is from March to May when the grass is at its shortest. The only difference between this lion and the African species is that it has a less luxuriant mane.

An Asiatic Lion

The Sloth Bear   This animal, a rather scruffy bear, lives in caves or amongst the boulders of rocky hillocks in the jungle. It eats wild fruit, grubs, berries, honey, flowers and insects. Despite its name, the sloth bear is a bad-tempered, aggressive beast, especially if a female has cubs, and is liable to attack on sight. When it is surprised, which happens often for its eyesight and sense of smell are poor, it is made very angry. Many of the jungle people fear it more than they fear the tiger.

The Cheetah   This is another animal that is almost extinct. The few that remain live in the rocky hills of central India preying upon gazelle and deer. Though not a leopard, it is often called the Hunting Leopard because it may be trained to hunt animals, and becomes almost as docile as a pet dog. The rajas and princes of India kept hunting cheetahs for sport just as the kings of England kept trained falcons. The cheetah's skill in hunting depends upon its stealth and phenomenal speed; it is reputed to be the fastest animal alive and can easily outpace the fleetest gazelle. Over clear and regular ground this long-legged cat can travel more than 90 miles an hour for short distances.

The Indian Wild Dog   This is a true dog which hunts by day in large and savage packs. Like its village cousin, it is a scavenger. The wild dog has a rich red coat and a very bushy tail like an English fox. Packs of these dogs can terrorise a whole village when their natural prey is scarce; and, like the many wolves and hyaenas that roam central India, they have been known to carry off children from houses.

The Mouse Deer   This strange little fellow (about 10 ins. high and 6 lb. in weight) is a deer, but moves with the starting, scurrying run of a mouse. It has no horns. It is very common in the Deccan, but the hunter and the traveller will rarely see it.

The Barking Deer   This deer, a small one, has a very peculiar characteristic. As it wanders about the thick jungle in which it lives, it makes a soft "clicking" noise with its tongue. When it is alarmed and frightened, it runs and makes this noise very rapidly and barks just like a dog.

The Mysore Kheda   Some of the finest specimens of the Indian elephant live in the Karapur forests 35 miles from Mysore city. These fine animals are wanted the world over for zoos and circuses, and especially in India for festival parades and temple service. But the elephant will not breed in captivity so it must be captured and trained.

Periodically, hunts or "khedas" are organised. Whilst the elephants are feeding in the forest they are surrounded by a human circle of 2,000 beaters who, at a signal, blow blasts on trumpets, shout at the tops of their voices and beat drums. The alarmed elephants panic and stampede, but they are cleverly driven by the beaters towards a large stockade of tall, heavy tree-trunks built in the jungle nearby. The leader is driven in first, and when the faithful herd follows, the heavy gate is closed. The stockade then becomes a mass of trumpeting, bellowing, trampling and rearing "jumbos". They are allowed to kick their heels for a while and later are roped and led out of the stockade to begin their training under their "mahout".

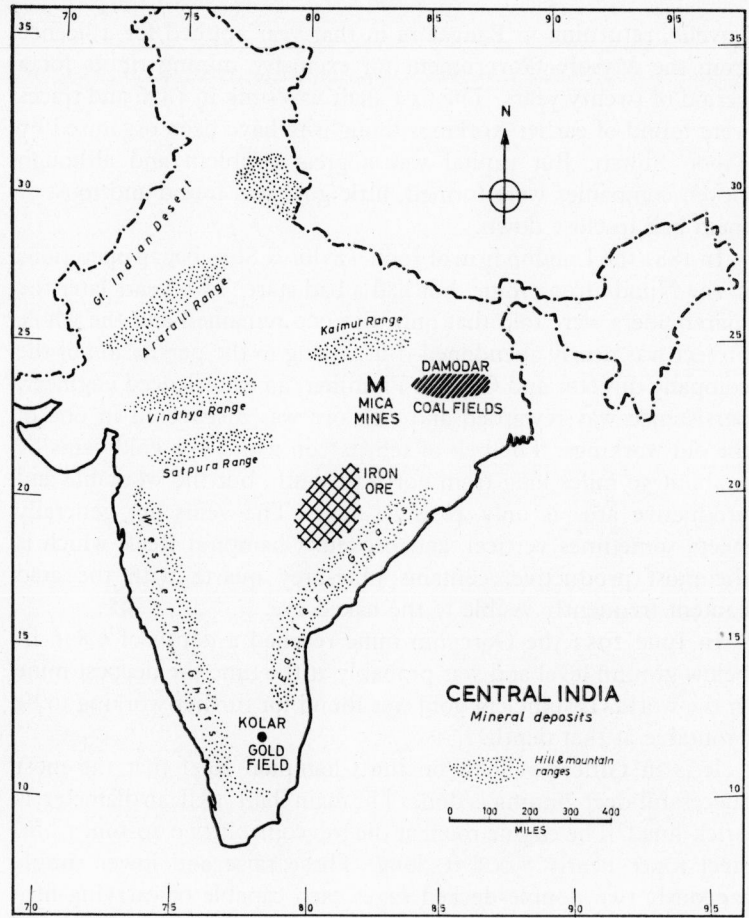

Map labels:
N

Gt. Indian Desert
Aravalli Range
Kaimur Range
Vindhya Range
MICA MINES — M
DAMODAR COAL FIELDS
Satpura Range
IRON ORE
Western Ghats
Eastern Ghats
KOLAR GOLD FIELD

CENTRAL INDIA
Mineral deposits

Hill & mountain ranges

0   100   200   300   400
MILES

GOLD-FIELDS OF THE DECCAN

The most important mineral product of the Deccan is gold, nearly all of which comes from the Kolar gold-fields in Mysore state, 44 miles east of Bangalore. The modern history of the mining goes back to 1802 when Lt. John Warren examined and reported on the area while working on a survey. Although prospecting took place during the next seventy years, it was not until 1873 that things really began to happen. An Irish soldier, Michael

83

Lavelle, returning to Bangalore in that year applied for a licence from the Mysore Government for exclusive mining rights for a period of twenty years. The first shaft was sunk in 1876 and traces were found of earlier workings thought to have been organised by Tipoo Sultan. But capital was a great problem and although eleven companies were formed, little gold was found and most of them had to close down.

In 1881 the London firm of John Taylor & Sons began operations in the Nundydroog mine, but had a bad start. Two years later the shareholders were told that only £13,000 remained and the whole project was nearly abandoned. But, owing to the persuasion of the company director and Captain Plummer, an experienced engineer, persistence was rewarded and rich ore was discovered in one of the old workings. The belt of schists* on which the gold veins lie is about 50 miles long from north to south, but the workable and productive area is only $4\frac{1}{2}$ miles long. The veins are generally steep, sometimes vertical, and broken. Champion Reef, which is the most productive, contains blue-grey quartz with the gold content frequently visible to the naked eye.

In June 1953 the Ooregum mine reached a depth of 9,876 ft. below ground level and was probably at the time the deepest mine in the world. Insufficient gold was found for further working to be profitable at that depth.

It is in Gifford's Shaft on the Champion Reef that the most successful deep mining is done. The main shaft, 18 ft. in diameter, is brick-lined. The engine room at the top controls two 20-ton, $1\frac{7}{8}$ in. steel ropes nearly 7,000 ft. long. These raise and lower simultaneously two double-decked cages each capable of carrying fifty men or 5 tons of ore.

As temperature falls with altitude so it increases with vertical depth, about 1°F. for every 110 ft. down into the earth. The actual rock temperature at 9,000 ft. is 140°F. Pressure also increases with depth. To overcome these naturally unfavourable conditions air-conditioning plants have been installed on the surface and underground. These cool and reduce the humidity of the down-cast air, pumping as much as 200,000 cu. ft. of fresh air through the mine every minute.

*SCHIST: a rock made up of layers of different minerals that split into irregular sheets.

There are 600 miles of roadways and tunnels underground, the main ones being broad and well-lit. Total tunnelling costs are about £8 for every foot advanced into the rock.

The mining method is called "open-stopping". The ore is drilled to receive a charge of high explosive which reduces it to small enough pieces to be transported to the surface. Here, after sorting out much of the waste rock, the ore is crushed into a fine product called "slime". During the crushing operation the ore is passed over coarse blankets which catch gold particles and other minerals. This produces, after further treatment, about 75 % of the gold content of the ore. The slime goes into the cyanide works where another 20 % is recovered. In the final smelting, gold bars are produced which contain 925 parts per 1,000 of fine gold and 70 parts per 1,000 of fine silver. These bars are sent to the Bombay mint where they are refined again and sold, with silver, in the Indian market. Each ton of ore brought to the surface contains about $2\frac{3}{4}$ oz. of gold.

Some 130,000 people are employed in the mining community, including just under 200 Europeans. They live in a well-planned town with its own dairy, hospitals, schools, welfare clinics, and sports and social clubs.

Years ago the workers lived in colonies of "tattie" houses built of timber, baked mud and grass-screen walls. Today modern prefabricated houses are laid out in neat rows, each group with its own shops, laundries and cattle sheds. The rent for these houses varies between 8 annas and one rupee (1s. 6d.) per month. This may seem very low, but it must be remembered that the general cost of living is also low. The average wage for a shift worker is Rs. 75 to 100 (£5 to £7 10s.) per month.

All newly engaged mine workers attend courses in accident prevention and selected men receive special instruction in mine rescue work. Others can attend night school for courses in reading, writing and arithmetic, with promotion to the technical school to learn more about the theory and practice of mining. Great skill is needed in any mine and it takes time and money to train the workmen. However, because of the inherent craftmanship of the southern Indian, and the experience many gained in the Indian Army during the 1939–45 war, suitable labour has become less of a problem than it was in earlier years, and the gold-field has helped to make Mysore state one of the most progressive in India.

MINERALS AND IRON AND STEEL

Iron ore, manganese, chromite, bauxite, zinc and other minor minerals are won from the ancient rocks of peninsular India. Gold mining at Kolar in Mysore has been described; now mica mining and the big industrial centre at Jamshedpur, with its surrounding supplies of ore and coal, will be covered (see map showing mineral deposits, p. 83).

Mica Mining in Chotanagpur Mica is used in making electrical equipment, one of the world's most modern industries, but the winning of mica from the deposits of Chotanagpur is a very primitive business in great contrast with the industries which it supplies. The mica is dug by hand from tunnels driven into the hillsides. No machinery is used and the labour is supplied by poor cultivators from the locality. They work for just over half the year, and when the monsoon is due they return to their fields. In the mining season the workers live in camps in the jungle, but they are paid very low wages. Mica mining deserves the name "sweated labour". The men do the mining and carrying whilst their wives and children split and process the mineral. The women can split the mica into sheets of one-thousandth of an inch in thickness.

About 30,000 miners are engaged in extracting mica in Chotanagpur, and more than three times this labour force is engaged in splitting and dressing the mineral. From this primitively organised industry, 75 % of the world's mica comes.

Iron and Steel at Jamshedpur There are many industrial centres in peninsular India: the aircraft industry at Bangalore (meaning "town of boiled beans"), the cement factory at Kymore (Madhya Pradesh), the large cotton mills at Indore, the iron and steel works at Rourkela, Burnpur and Bhadravati, to name only a few. But none is more important than Jamshedpur in the north-east corner of the peninsula. Here, set in the paddi-covered valleys of the Kharkai and Subarnarekha rivers, are works which produce

86

A view inside the factory of Indian Telephone Industries Ltd., at Bangalore. The assembly of the telephone is carried out on a moving conveyor belt. At the end of the belt a complete telephone appears every three minutes of working time

about half of the total Indian iron and steel output. They specialise in pig iron, railway and bridge parts, agricultural tools and ploughs and armoured vehicles for the Indian Army. The hills around are covered with jungle that contrasts sharply with the huge modern blast-furnaces and rolling mills of the industrial plant.

To the north of Jamshedpur is the Damodar valley with its string of coal-mines. Here the coal, including good coking coals, is found in regular seams from 15 to 30 ft. thick. Labour, drawn mainly from the Santal tribes of the hills, is cheap, but productivity is low for there is little machinery and the workers are at the mines for two-thirds of the year only. Until 1939, women were employed in digging the coal underground. Despite the low output per man, the Damodar coalfields are the greatest producers in India and vast reserves have been proven.

The giant Bokaro Thermal Power Station in the Damodar valley. Bokaro uses the coal from the Damodar coal fields to produce electric power

To the south of Jamshedpur are the vast deposits of iron ore of the Singhbum region. India's estimated deposits of ore are amongst the highest in the world. Another advantage which Jamshedpur enjoys is easy rail communications with her largest market, Calcutta. Much of the produce of Jamshedpur goes to the ship-building yards of that city.

Jamshedpur itself is the favourite and most successful child of the great Tata enterprises. Tata is the largest name in Indian industry, controlling interests as varied as soap making and aeroplane assembling. In 1908 Jamshedji Tata mooted the Jamshedpur scheme and work was begun in 1911. The First World War gave a stimulus to the project for India's supplies of iron and steel were cut off then, and she had to rely upon her own domestic output. Jamshedpur is something of a model town. Tatas have provided sports grounds, housing of a very high quality, medical centres and most amenities found in large towns. About 20,000 people are employed in Jamshedpur town itself; most of the unskilled labour is supplied by the Santal tribes of the hills, but technicians and skilled labour are drawn from all over India.

III

WESTERN INDIA

PHYSICAL

FROM the heights of the Nilgiri Hills in the south to the Gulf of Cambay in the north, the Western Ghats run parallel to the Bombay-Goa coast like an unbroken giant's wall. Between these great land-cliffs and the Arabian Sea, there is a narrow coastal plain which is the heart of our region. The climate of western India and of the odd Kutch-Kathiawar area is considered below.

The Western Ghats are very high (average elevation 3,000 ft.) and steep on the slopes that face the coast. There are no wide or important gaps through the Western Ghats as there are through the Eastern, but two considerable breaks in the heights behind Bombay carry railways to Poona and the south-east, and to Nasik and the north-east. Down to Goa the ghats are formed of horizontal lava strata which have been weathered into step-like formations. Cutting into the scarp slopes are narrow ravines and canyons that have been carved by the short, swift streams running down from the high watershed to the Arabian Sea. These streams are of little use for river-traffic, but many are harnessed for hydro-electric-power schemes. Here and there one sees magnificent waterfalls cascading hundreds of feet. The most impressive of these are the Jog Falls of the Sharavati river on the Mysore-Bombay boundary. They form four separate waterfalls and the one known as Raja crashes vertically down 850 ft. The Mahatma Gandhi Power Station at mist-enshrouded Jog supplies electricity to a large area.

It is thought that the Western Ghats are ancient sea-cliffs which have been raised to a high level by massive earth-movements. The evidence quoted for this theory is the raised beaches, complete

89

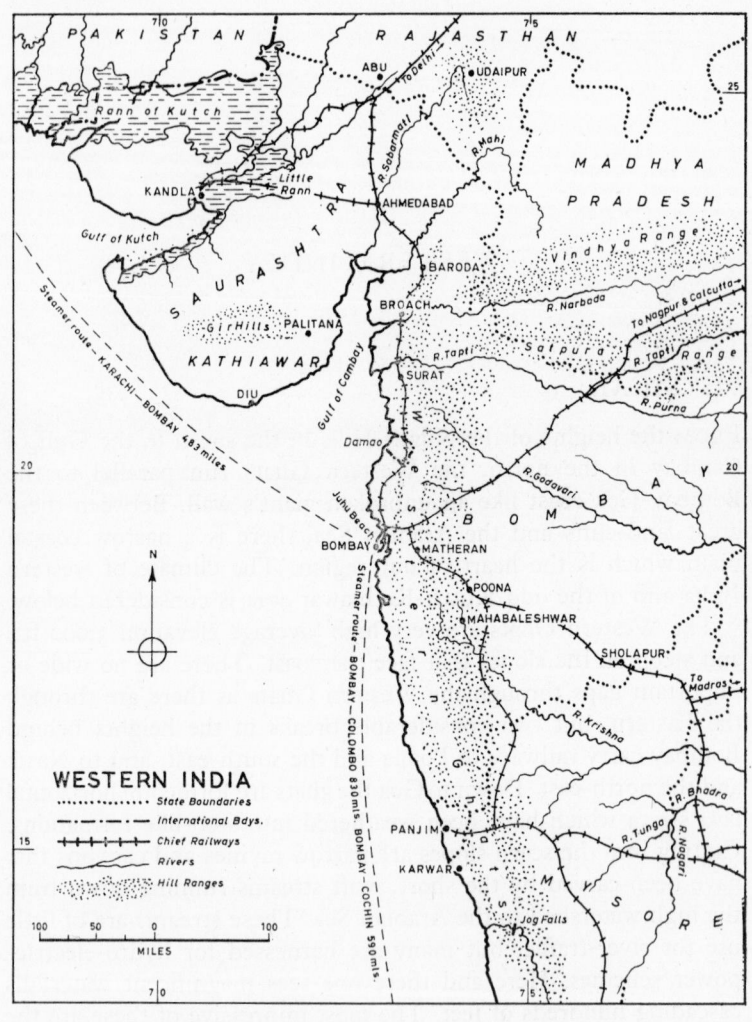

with sea-shells and pebbles, that are found high up the ghats and far away from the present shore. The ghats are covered with dense tropical evergreen jungle which thrives on the high temperatures and plentiful annual rainfall. There is little farming here except primitive shifting cultivation by tribal and backward groups.

The Western Ghats. The seated figure on the right-hand side of the picture gives an idea of the scale

Some spices and cashew nuts are produced on small plantations in the southern section of the area. The forest, however, supplies valuable timbers, especially teak, ebony, sandalwood and bamboo, and the logs are floated down the streams to coastal towns like Karwar.

The strip of lowland which forms the coastal plain proper varies in width, but averages 30 to 40 miles along most of its length. In places it is quite hilly where low spurs from the ghats jut out or harder rocks stand up amid the alluvium, but for the most part it is flat alluvial land. The soils of the coastal plain are fertile and the rainfall is plentiful and regular, so it is heavily populated and rice occupies most of the cultivated land. On the poorer laterite (friable red clay) soils of the lower ghat slopes, millet is grown. Most of the farming is subsistence farming, i.e. food production for local consumption and not for trading or export, but the area around the metropolis of Bombay supplies the city's Crawford Market with rice, vegetables, poultry, meat and fruit—especially the mango, for which Bombay is famous. This fruit has a tough golden skin covering a fleshy and juicy interior. It is shaped something

Fishermen tending their net

like a small squashed marrow and tastes like a hybrid between an apple and a very juicy orange.

Immediately adjoining the sea are sand-banks and magnificent sandy beaches lined with coconut palms that sway gracefully in the breeze. In places, however, there are unattractive and smelly mangrove swamps. Small fishing villages pepper the whole length of the coast, and those near Bombay send their catches to the city after they have been dried. The tropical beaches near Bombay have become holiday resorts; Juhu Beach, reached by rail and road, provides excellent bathing and offers chalets for rental during the season, which lasts from the end of one monsoon to the beginning of the next.

THE SOUTH-WEST MONSOON

The breaking of the South-West Monsoon on the west coast of India is as spectacular as the towering wall of ghats behind Bombay city. As our plane neared Bombay on its route to Singapore, black,

A fisherman casting his hand-net from the shore. Although it looks simple, splaying the net takes considerable skill

fast-moving clouds followed below us coming in from the Indian Ocean. This was in September and for another month they would race eastwards until the monsoon faded in October. These clouds first hit the western shore in June; officially, the monsoon "breaks" in Bombay on 5th June and reaches Bengal by the 15th of the month. "Break" is an accurate description of what happens at the start of the rains.

From the end of the Cold Season (November-February) onwards, temperatures over India rise rapidly. Bombay reaches 91°F. by May and Nagpur (central India) 109°F. in the same month. Towards the end of May a few short showers herald the approach of the coming monsoon; these are called "mango showers" in peninsular India. Inland, on the Deccan plateau, the pre-monsoon weather disturbances take the form of violent dust storms that reduce visibility to a few yards. As the time of the rains approaches,

The monsoon clouds, heavy and dark with moisture, bring life-giving rain to India

the weather gets hotter and hotter and more oppressive so people sleep in the open on roof-tops or even in the Bombay streets.

On or about 5th June a complete and sudden change takes place in the weather. At one hour the sky above Bombay is blue, cloudless and shimmering in the heat; at the next a violent wind rushes in from the sea carrying with it black, towering clouds heavy with moisture. The temperature falls sharply and suddenly the heavens open and rain pours from the overcast sky. In the city the monsoon drains fill to overflowing within minutes. The streets are awash (this helps to clean them) and neglected roofs leak. In the country the tropical forest is drenched, kadjan roofs fail to stop the rain from pouring into huts, and mud walls are washed away. If the monsoon has been delayed, the farmer, anxious about his paddi, will rush out into the downpour with relief for he knows that the monsoon is vital to his crops. The monsoon has come, and from June to October rain will fall almost every day in torrents. While the rains are essential for the farmer's paddi crops, they may be disastrous in other ways; the sudden heavy downpour might wash his paddi away, and in drier areas of the interior it might wash his

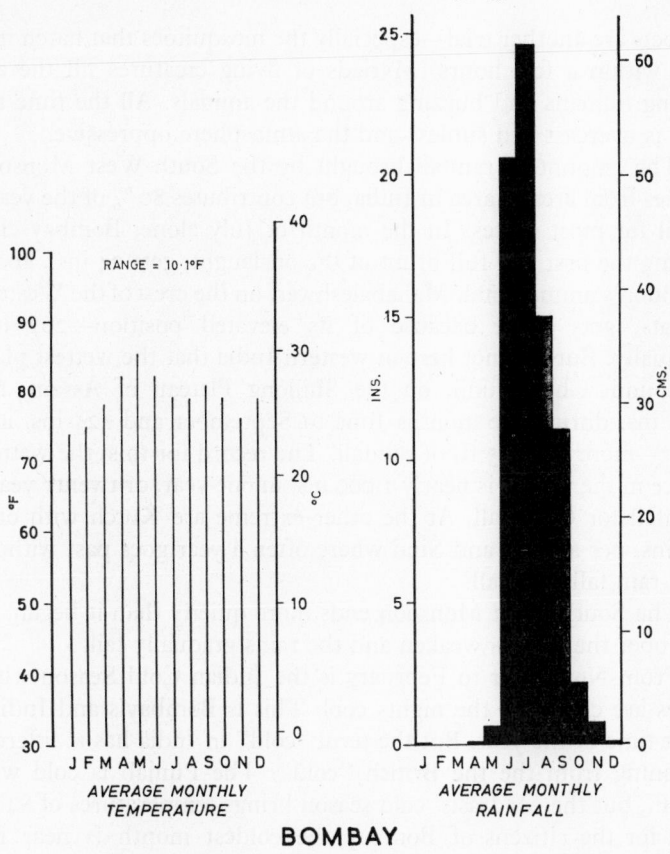

RANGE = 10·1°F

AVERAGE MONTHLY
TEMPERATURE

AVERAGE MONTHLY
RAINFALL

BOMBAY

soil away too. Rivulets form everywhere, brown or red with the topsoil they carry.

In the city, life is just as uncomfortable; clothes are difficult to dry and they have to be hung over fires, often with cow-dung for fuel which gives them a peculiar odour called "dhobi-smell"; cuts and scrapes refuse to dry up and heal in the excessively damp atmosphere; books, shoes and all leather goods quickly develop fungus and mildew; the salt on the lunch table is wet and congealed and the sugar almost water. The European sweats continuously and has to increase his intake of salt to keep up his health; clothes quickly become soggy with perspiration. The insects are another trial—especially the mosquitoes that hatch into life within a few hours. Myriads of flying creatures fill the air, biting humans and buzzing around the animals. All the time the sky is overcast and sunless and the atmosphere oppressive.

The amount of rainfall brought by the South-West Monsoon varies from area to area in India, but contributes 80 % of the year's total for most places. In the month of July alone, Bombay city, facing the first and full brunt of the onslaught, gets 24 ins., about London's annual total. Mahabaleshwar, on the crest of the Western Ghats, gets more because of its elevated position—261 ins. annually. But it is not here in western India that the wettest place is found. Cherrapunji, on the Shillong Plateau of Assam, has 320 ins. during the months June to September and 425 ins. in a year—more than 35 ft. of rainfall! The record for this, the wettest place in the world, is nearly 1,000 ins. in one year, or twenty years' rainfall for Cornwall. At the other extreme are Kutch with only 12 ins. per annum and Sind where often a year goes past without any rain falling at all.

The South-West Monsoon ends more quietly than it began. In October the storms weaken and the rains gradually fail.

From November to February is the Indian Cold Season when skies are clear and the nights cool. This is Bombay's and India's best time of the year. But the term "cold" in India has a different meaning from the the British "cold". The Punjab is cold with 55°F., but the Madrasis' cold season brings temperatures of 84°F. and for the citizens of Bombay the coldest month is near the 80's also. In other words, our hottest summer has the same temperature as winter in Bombay.

In March temperatures rise as the sun creeps over the Equator. The land becomes hotter and hotter; the parched soil bakes into hard-pan and people flag in the great heat. By May temperatures have reached their maximum—91°F. at Bombay, over 100°F. in the Deccan and Punjab and nearly 120°F. in Kutch. (A reading of 126°F., the highest temperature recorded in the sub-continent, was taken in Jacobabad, now in West Pakistan.) This, the Hot Season (March to May), is the time when schools take their long holidays and officials and the wealthy can move to the hill stations of the Western Ghats. Matheran and Khandala are particularly popular and are only a couple of hours' journey by train from Bombay.

Repairing damage done by the monsoon

A number of devices have been used for keeping rooms cool in India. The poor weave grass screens ("tatties") which are drenched with water; the water is kept in porous pots which allow evaporation and thus keep the water cool. Punkhas are an ancient method of keeping a room breezy; the punkha is a curtain which is pulled to and fro by a servant to set up cooling breezes in a room. Modern appliances include large electric fans hung from the ceiling, and the air-conditioner. The latter is a large electric air-cooling machine fitted into the wall; it sucks in warm air from outside, cools it and ejects it into the room.

Such is the seasonal round of India. The dominant feature is the South-West Monsoon; the name "monsoon" comes from the Arabic "mausin", meaning season. The monsoon can be cruel or kind. If it fails or is weak, famine can threaten the villager; if it is too strong he may lose home and property by floods.

The Mechanism of the Monsoon As you can see from the map, the South-West Monsoon is simply a movement of air from a high-pressure zone below the Equator to a low-pressure zone in the region of northern India. Air, like water, will always try to even

97

out and find its own level. Think of a low-pressure area as a dip in the surface of a pool of water, and a high-pressure area as a bump on the surface. The water will shift until the surface is perfectly even and level. Air behaves something like this. Therefore, all winds are caused by areas of varying barometric pressure. The change in the direction of the monsoon winds when they cross the Equator is caused by the deflection of the spinning earth.

Here is another way of looking at the monsoon. In March and May the air over India becomes very hot. This hot air rises and cooler air rushes in to take its place. The monsoon winds pass over great oceans and accumulate water-vapour. When they reach the west coast of India they are forced to rise over the high wall of the ghats. In rising, the air cools, the water-vapour condenses and falls as rain.

BOMBAY CITY

Voyagers to India by sea get their first sight of the country as they enter Bombay harbour and face the welcome of the Gateway of India, a tall and impressive triumphal arch standing on the water-front. Bombay city is built on an island of seven lava peaks that nestles below the Western Ghats. It is joined to the mainland (Salsette) by road and rail along the Sion and Mahim Causeways.

Bombay is the most important commercial city in the Indian Union and is the seat of the Government of Maharashtra state. Like other great industrial cities of the world, it has its gracious districts and its slums. Malabar Hill and Marine Drive are cool, comfortable and spacious residential areas for the more prosperous Bombayites, but in the northern suburbs where the great cotton mills are, there is bad overcrowding of the Hindu labourers and their large families.

Bombay has its race-course, galleries and museums; there is the zoo in Victoria Gardens where children may ride camels, and Brabourne Stadium where "Test" matches are played between the Indian National Cricket team and British or Australian touring sides.

You can drink the water from Bombay's taps without fear of poisoning (a rare thing in the East), but on alcohol the Government

The Victoria Railway Terminus, Bombay

has imposed prohibition and only visitors may buy it—and then by special permit on a quota.

Bombay's streets are always busy. Early in the morning the office workers stream out of the electric trains that bring them to the city from the dormitory suburbs just as they do at Charing Cross. To get from place to place you may take a tram (driven by electricity from power stations in the ghats) or go by taxi. You will easily recognise the taxis for they are black with yellow roofs. You pay by the meter—if there is no meter then the driver should have a card showing the standard rates—but take care if you are a stranger in the city for a journey of 500 yds. might be made into 4 miles by devious and roundabout routes.

The poorer people of the city walk barefoot or in flimsy sandals on the hot pavements. They may often be seen carrying large bundles of laundry or baskets of fruit on their heads. On special occasions they will hire a cycle-rickshaw, or trisha, to carry them through narrow streets where automobiles cannot go. Buses run on certain routes and people crowd into them until there is almost no room for the conductor.

The commercial centre of Bombay city is the "Fort" area. This has grown up around the ruins of the original Portuguese fort. Bombay has the Indian Mint and the Reserve Bank of India (India's equivalent of the Bank of England) in its territory and care. The huge railway station, Victoria Terminus, is here too, and from it you may take trains to all parts of India. The "Fort" is very cosmopolitan and might easily be in any of the great cities of the world. English is widely spoken and English dress and habits linger. This is the area of the luxury Taj Mahal Hotel, the great banks, the trading houses, insurance buildings—and money.

But leave the Westernised part of Bombay and take a trisha to the poorer northern areas of Dadar and Patel. First you enter Mazagaon. This district of "Indian Bombay" is just behind the docks and here live small craftsmen: cobblers repairing sandals on the street corner; silversmiths turning their tools delicately round the metal; fruit, nut and betel vendors; tea makers, their stalls offering curry puffs and very sweet cakes; the Muslim cloth dealers. Here are the bazaars where prices are fixed not by the value of the article, but by the skill in haggling of customer or seller.

Further north are the industrial areas of Dadar and Patel distinguished by the high chimneys of the cotton mills. Around the mills are the "chawls", the tenements of the Bombay wage-labour force. Bombay's mills employ 200,000 workers and most of them are squeezed near their work in the Dadar and Patel areas. "Squeezed" is the correct word for overcrowding is chronic. A quarter of a million people here live at the rate of nine to a room; 80,000 at the rate of ten to nineteen per room; and 15,000 at the rate of twenty or more per room. Such are the chawls. Many of Bombay's poor prefer to sleep in the streets. Any night you may see them snoring under the stars with a step for their pillow and a pavement for their bed. Much is being done to drain off the excess population of Dadar and Patel into new colonies and estates in open parts of the island. When the whistle sounds at the end of the day the mills disgorge their workers who emerge covered with cotton lint, white fluff on brown skins. And what do they earn for their work? The annual earnings of a Bombay mill worker are

Like well-regimented soldiers on parade: thousands of spindles in the spinning department in a Bombay cotton mill

Rs. 1,400 at the most, or about £105 per year. This wage is very low, but so are the cost and standard of living in Bombay compared with British industrial towns.

The busiest section of Bombay is the 5-mile strip of docks fringing the eastern shore of Bombay Island—the leeward side away from the driving South-West Monsoon winds. There are 75 sq. miles of deep water harbour. Large liners call and depart daily, cargo boats are tied to jetties and berths, loading cotton goods and grain for export and unloading machinery from abroad. Oil tankers pump their cargo to the storage tanks at Sewri. Wandering among the big boats anchored in Bombay harbour are the "baghlas", local boats of old Arab design of about 400 tons with high poops and cateen rigs, that carry goods north and south along the coast, but often as far as Aden. Cottons bound for tropical Africa are loaded by the coolies. One of Bombay's major exports in the last century was opium.

These country craft are at anchor in the small port of Mahim, north of Bombay. Such sailing boats carry much of the coastal trade of western India

There are other industries in Bombay city and more in her developing suburbs. India's most productive film studios are in the northern suburbs (India's film industry is reputed to be the largest in the world). Engineering industries, born of the mills' need for textile machinery, are on the island, and in Salsette there are leather industries, the Kurla match factory and Abernath chemical works.

But Bombay is primarily a sea-port. The Portuguese recognised its favoured position in the early sixteenth century when they founded the city and gave it the name of Bom Bahia—Fair Bay. It came into British hands as part of the dowry of Catherine of Braganza, daughter of the Portuguese king, when she married Charles II. This was in 1662, but Charles thought it more of a

Indian Coolie women

liability than an asset and he let Bombay to the East India Company for an annual rent and a loan of £50,000. Its early days were troubled. The Marathas from the mainland threatened its existence until their defeat in 1818. The tidal flats around the island were malarial and a local saying has caught the spirit of that time—"Two monsoons are a man's life". But the city survived and when supplies of cotton from the southern states of America were blocked by the American Civil War, Bombay experienced a boom which established the character and greatness of the city. At first Bombay had exported raw cotton, but now she began to make it into cloth. In 1854 there was one cotton mill; thirty years later there were fifty employing 30,000 workers, and today there are 200 employing 200,000. The advantages that Bombay enjoyed were not entirely geographical; she is on the edge of India's cotton belt and is a great port facing Europe, but her cotton industry grew more because of the banking and credit facilities that existed at an early date.

Greater Bombay's 2 million people are a very mixed population. With the growth of her cotton mills over the years people from many parts of central India came looking for jobs. They came to overcrowded quarters and for little pay.

Today, Sikhs drive taxis, and they are very fine and skilful mechanical engineers. Women from Goa take jobs as maids in the luxury hotels and men from Goa join the crews of the Bombay shipping lines' vessels. Men from the "Koli" tribe of west India came to labour in the city and work in the mills. From their tribal name the English word "coolie" is derived. There are also the Marathas who worship the god "Khandoba ("khanda" means sword) and wear slippers with turned-up toes. Muslims run shops and the Gujeratis own many of the cotton mills. These and many other communities make Bombay the most colourful of India's major cities.

PORTUGAL IN INDIA

In the sixteenth century Portugal dreamed of an Indian empire, but was not strong enough to build it in the face of competition. Three small territories on the west coast—Goa, Damao and the island of Diu—like the crumbling cathedrals, convents and forts that they hold, are lingering memories of Portugal's grandeur in the East.

Diu is a hot, rocky little island 8 miles long off the barren coast of Kathiawar. Though almost nothing grew, or grows there, the Portuguese considered it of major strategic importance in their scheme for trade and conquest in the sixteenth century. They obtained permission in 1535 to erect a fortress there, which they built on the eastern tip of the island. This fortress was attacked in 1538 by the Turks and again in 1546 by Gujerati forces from the mainland, but it held firm. Over the years the defences were improved and expanded; the giant moat below the precipitous walls was hewn out of the solid ground-rock so that at high tide the sea fills it and completely severs the fort from the rest of the island. The massive walls of the islet-citadel at Diu still stand today and there are even cannon facing the sea as if to defend the ghosts of the past garrisons.

The territory of Goa, 12,000 sq. miles in all, consists of Tissuary Island and an arc of the mainland. Its people farm the land for rice and grow coconuts. Mormugao, at the end of a peninsula on the mainland, is a considerable and well-equipped port dealing with $\frac{1}{2}$ million tons of shipping annually and exporting coconuts, salt and fish. It also exported 6 million tons of iron ore.

But the glory of Goa lies in the past. On the island of Tissuary is the ruined city of Old Goa, the Lisbon of the East. Here only the great whitewashed cathedrals are kept alive by priests; while the laterite churches, convents and forts are overgrown with jungle.

Goa was a Moorish city when Albuquerque, founder of the Portuguese empire in the East, captured it in 1510. For 200 years it thrived; the city grew to 6 miles in circumference, its population to 200,000 (75% of whom were Christians); churches, convents and cathedrals were built and the Portuguese intermarried with the Indians. The shipping roads of the Mandavi river were crowded with trading ships and the docks busy. But decline set in, malaria from the muddy river spread pestilence and the capital moved 7 miles away to Panjim, or New Goa, in 1759.

The palace of Albuquerque in Old Goa is now decayed and so are many of the churches, but the glorious cathedral, Casa Professa Bom Jesus where the body of St. Francis Xavier rests, is still standing. St. Francis came to Goa in the sixteenth century and from there went to Ceylon and Japan. In his lifetime he made 200,000 converts to Catholicism before he died while returning to Goa to organise a mission to China in 1552. At intervals the body is exhumed to be displayed to the faithful. It is in a wonderful state of preservation and pilgrims come to kiss the foot of St. Francis. It is said that on one occasion, however, a pilgrim was overcome with bliss and she bit off and ate one of the saint's toes. The last exhumation was in December 1952 when not only Christians, but Hindus and Muslims also, came to the Bom Jesus shrine.

THE NEW PORT AT KANDLA

India today is a land of striking contrasts; old India, the India of 1861, is still there in the poor villages, the sweated labour of the "bidi" (cheap cigarette) workshops, the rickshaws and the destitute; but the new India is a land of power industries, higher wages, mechanisation and progress. Throughout the nation flourishing projects are bringing more secure and congenial employment, improved housing, better education and economic improvement.

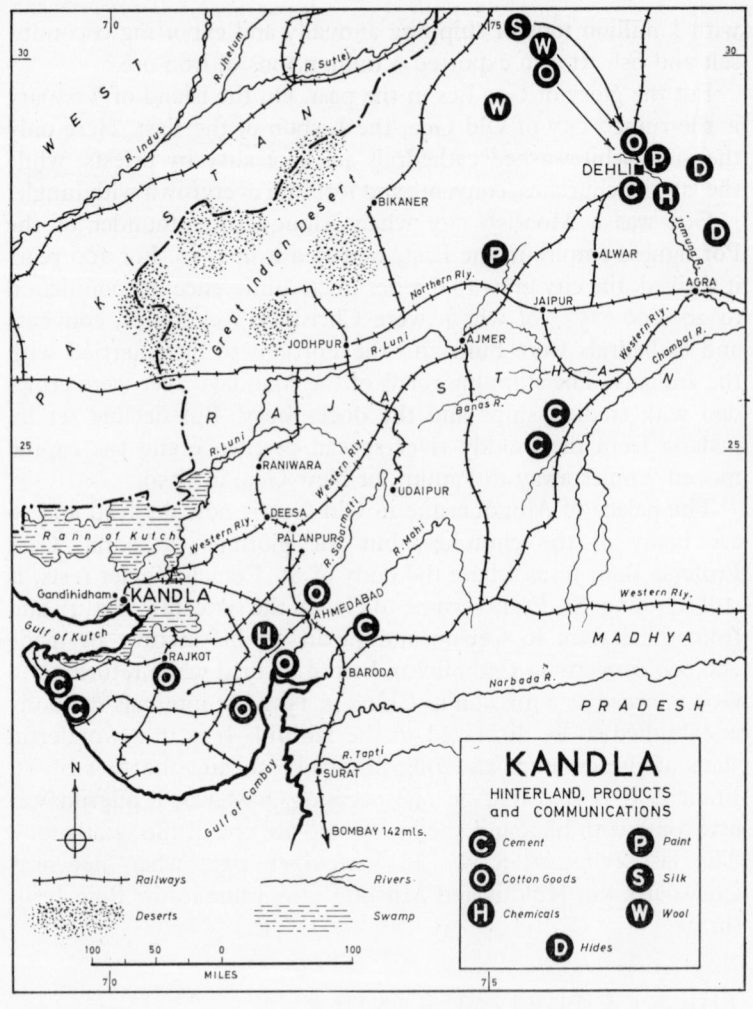

KANDLA
HINTERLAND, PRODUCTS
and COMMUNICATIONS

C Cement   P Paint
O Cotton Goods   S Silk
H Chemicals   W Wool
D Hides

One such symbol of India's modern spirit is the new port of Kandla in Kutch.

By 1946 the need was felt for another port in north-west India to relieve the growing pressure on Bombay. Partition and the loss of Karachi to the new state of Pakistan aggravated this need and left the vast hinterland of the north-west (principally Delhi,

Kandla port. A view of the cargo jetty

Rajasthan, Punjab, Kashmir, western Uttar Pradesh, Gujerat and Kutch) with no outlet for its goods apart from far-off Bombay.

In the eastern section of the Gulf of Kutch there existed a small, local port called Kandla which was built in 1933 to serve the little developed Kutch region. Study parties, sent by the Indian Government, reported that the harbour was good and the site suitable for development. The work of expanding Kandla began in 1949; on 10th January 1952 Premier Nehru laid the foundation stone of the new port, and five years later the large cargo berths were officially opened. Today Kandla is a major Indian port with prospects of handling more than 1½ million tons of goods annually.

The once remote and quiet creek at Kandla has been flanked with jetties, berths for cargo-ships, warehouses, offices and port buildings; there is open space for stacking goods to a million sq. ft.; there are trained pilots, the channels are dredged regularly and are marked by lighted and radar equipped buoys; business facilities are at hand including banks and insurance agents. All dockside equipment is modern and mechanised; there are twenty-one mobile electric cranes that serve the berths from the jetties; railways join the docksides to the warehouses and sheds; there are auto-trucks and mechanised lifts for moving cargo and huge grabs for handling coal and ore. The harbour is sheltered and easily navigable by ocean-going vessels. The oil-tanker jetty can cater for ships up to 600 ft. in length with 29 ft. draught, and pipe-lines run direct from the berths to the oil installations. New and powerful tugs and lighters lie offshore ready to come into service when needed. These facilities already exist and the Government plans to add more berths in the future. All this stands where once were reed huts in a wilderness of sand and marsh.

The exports now handled at Kandla include cement, food grains, cotton, hides, salt, sulphur, glass, crushed bones and bauxite; but when the giant Bhakra Dam* opens up more farming land in the Punjab and Rajasthan, Kandla will have to deal with vastly increased traffic. Kandla is a cheaper port for the area than Bombay; for example, handling, transporting and warehousing costs for imports of machinery to Delhi are cheaper by Rs. 8 per ton through Kandla than through Bombay, and exports of Udaipur zinc are cheaper by Rs. 10 per ton.

Forty thousand workers and technicians have been brought to Kandla and housed near the port in a modern, spacious town called Gandhidham, named after Gandhi who gave his blessing to the scheme. Gandhidham is still growing for it expects eventually to accommodate 150,000 people, the total labour force at work when all is completed. To plan a modern, attractive and well-serviced model town, the Indian Government brought planning experts from the United States. Housing for the families is excellent and suited to individual needs. The town is divided into community units each with its own amenities. There are cinemas, clubs, libraries, a maternity ward, post offices, shops, gardens and playing fields, schools and banks.

Light industries have been attracted to the town. Established ones are saw mills, automobile workshops and cement works and soon others will be building on their reserved plots, including food

---

*The Bhakra Dam is being built across the river Sutlej, in a Himalayan gorge just before the river enters the plains.

processing, steel works, furniture making and manufacturing of agricultural implements. To attract these light industries to Gandhidham the Government allows sites to be rented, bought for cash or on favourable hire-purchase terms.

There were a number of problems facing the planners of the port and town. Communications with Kandla's hinterland were poor and inadequate for serving a major port; now it is linked by rail with Delhi, Ajmer and Jodhpur and a new broad-gauge line and a highway are being constructed to link the port with Ahmedabad.

The water supply also presented a difficulty for this is arid country (about 12 ins. of rain annually). Deep drilling has discovered and tapped underground reservoirs, one of which gives 35,000 gallons per hour. Power, too, is supplied to the port and town by a new thermal-electricity station.

KUTCH AND KATHIAWAR

These two areas in the north-west of the region are worlds apart from the lush, green Bombay-Goa coast.

Kathiawar is the large square peninsula between the Gulfs of Cambay and Kutch. It is composed mainly of lavas associated with the Deccan flows and has a central core of highland covered with dry forest (the Gir Forest). Being off the track of the South-West Monsoon, Kathiawar is an arid land averaging 15 ins. of rainfall on the lowlands and 30 ins. on the central hills annually. But even this is precarious, and agriculture (wheat and millet) is confined to the more fertile valleys where irrigation water is drawn from wells.

Kathiawar was almost severed from the Indian mainland at one time. Stretching from the head of the Gulf of Kutch to the head of the Gulf of Cambay is the old tidal channel, now silted up. There are marshes (Little Rann) and a string of lakes where this channel once ran. While this part of the land has been "raised" by silting, other parts have fallen below sea-level into the Gulf of Cambay. Here there are sunken forests, and ancient tree-stumps with their roots still clinging in the soil appear 15 ft. below low tide and 30 ft. below high tide.

Kutch is even more desolate and dreary than Kathiawar. The southern highland is barren and rocky, and during the monsoon the Rann of Kutch is a vast area of tidal flats—a wilderness which looks like a lost world of science fiction. It is a useless, bare, hot and almost uninhabited country. The people that do live there cultivate a little wheat and cotton in more favoured and irrigated valleys, but the low rainfall (about 12 ins. annually) makes agriculture very difficult. More important are the large numbers of animals raised by the Kutch herdsmen who live in small, isolated hamlets and keep their stock in large paddocks nearby. Goats figure largely on the list, but the Kutch region is more renowned for its horses and camels. The latter are used as pack animals by the traders who take their caravans over the few tracks that cross this barren, almost desert land.

During the retreat of the monsoon (November to March) the Rann is a dry, hot land covered by salt-scum pans, ". . . there is nothing beyond a few bleached skeletons of cattle, salt dried fish, or remains of insects brought down by the floods . . ."* Not quite lifeless, however, for herds of wild asses roam the flats and large flocks of long-legged flamingoes wade in the marshes.

The Rann was once an inlet of the Arabian Sea, a large northern extension of the present Gulf of Kutch. This was in historical times, and prosperous ports lined the old coast. Remains of these ghost-towns can be found today littering the barren fringes of the marshes. Silt brought down and deposited by the rivers filled the inlet and created the marshy flats. In 1819 an earthquake shook Kutch and 2,000 square miles in the western section dropped 15 ft. and became a sea. Sindree Fort fell beneath the waters until only a single one of its turrets stood above the flood. To compensate for this sinking, a great wedge of land was raised several feet above the level of the surrounding plains. This ridge was given an apt name by the local people who were naturally overawed by the sudden change in the shape of their countryside. They called it "Allah Bund", meaning "built by God".

INDIAN RAILWAYS

Rome gave England her first fine, straight roads; when England gave up India she left her a complete network of railways (about 34,000 track-miles).

*WYNNE: *Memoir of Geological Survey of India*, Vol. IX (1872).

Before the coming of railways, travel in India was precarious and not lightly undertaken. Boats glided up and down the great navigable rivers and carts rolled along the dusty, bare roads, but travel by these means was both uncomfortable and slow. The "dak" mail carts, Indian equivalents of Wells Fargo, were introduced in 1831. In the hot season canopies were rigged over the carts and boats of the rich to protect them from the scorching sun; in the wet season, too, they were erected to keep off the rain, but anyone travelling then was bound to be soaked. The poorer people, on the rare occasions when they made a journey, such as a pilgrimage, had none of these facilities.

But there were more than inconveniences, there were real dangers. Wild beasts were often encountered, especially by the foot-traveller, and the man-eating tiger was the most feared of all because he was not afraid of man. Human beasts also prowled about the country—robbers, gangs of bandits and the dreaded "thugs". Robbers are to be met all over the world, but in India they lay in wait right up to the city walls where the local ruler might be in league with them. But more terrifying than bandits were the "thugs"; these were professional murderers who, as part of their worship of Kali, the goddess of death, strangled for the religious glory of killing and then looted their victim's belongings. Their weapon was a single strip of cloth and their practices were too horrible to describe, but before they massacred their prey they held a short service to Kali. To gain protection from these "thugs", traders and merchants travelled the roads in large groups, but the "thugs" were cunning. The unsuspecting travellers sometimes found that the very friends they had made at the last town and who also pretended to seek company for protection, were the "thugs" they feared. Thanks to the valiant and daring efforts of a Cornishman, Sleeman, the thugs were destroyed.

Slowness, too, made journeys wearying. In 1856 it took six weeks to travel up the Ganges by boat from Calcutta to Banaras, and the hire of the vessel alone cost not less than Rs. 100—a price far beyond the reach of the ordinary peasant. At the turn of the century the same journey took fifteen hours by rail and cost Rs. 26 for first-class accommodation.

Since it was the British who built the railways it was to be expected that the routes should spread over the sub-continent from those centres which the British held to be most important—Bombay, Calcutta and Madras. It was from these coastal centres, the first places in India to have railways, that the great iron web spread over India. The story of how tracks reached all corners of the empire is too long to tell here. Only some of the highlights will be looked at.

On 16th April 1853 the first "iron-horse", the *Lord Falkland*, a 2–4–0 tender engine, rumbled heavily over a track on Indian soil—only twenty-eight years after the world's first locomotive made its historic journey in England. *Lord Falkland*, bound for Thana some twenty miles away, pulled out of Bombay to the loud cheering of a great crowd and an almost royal salute of a twenty-one gun salvo. Two days later Sir Jamsetjee Jeejeebhoy, an Indian who was a director of the Great Indian Peninsula Railway Company and a father of India's railways, booked the whole train for his family to make the journey to Thana. This Bombay-Thana line, the first track of railway to operate in India, was followed a year later by a rival at Calcutta. The first passenger train ran from Howrah to Hooghly on 15th August 1854, and only a few of the 3,000 people who sent for tickets for the journey were able to get seats on the train. The south was not far behind and on 1st July 1856 the Madras Railway Company opened its first line.

But these facts do not give the best picture of the development of India's railways. Few countries faced more or greater difficulties in the laying of railway tracks. That was in the second half of the last century long before bulldozers, giant earth-moving machines and mobile cranes were invented. Most of the transporting, cutting, embanking, moving and laying was done by armies of labourers using picks to dig and baskets to carry earth. And what work these labourers did! They cut deep notches in giant mountain spurs, built high viaducts over gorges, embanked miles of track over dips, and tunnelled for miles more until a gently sloping track was laid over the broken, high and steep Western Ghats.

In the mountains behind Bombay there were marshes, jungles, loose, shifting soils on the alluvium and the danger of flooding. But let us have a closer look at the problems that faced the engineers who were ordered to lay tracks over the Western Ghats from Bombay to central India in the 1850's and 1860's. The object was to link Bombay through the Bore Ghats to Poona and the south,

An aircraft factory in Bangalore

and through the Thal Ghats and thence to Delhi and Calcutta. In 1870 the great ports of Bombay and Calcutta were at last linked by rail, but only after the ghats had been overcome.

One must remember that the workmen were laying a metal path over mountains and through jungles that had not been disturbed since time began. There were only horse tracks and rugged roads climbing the ghats, and it was over these that all the sleepers, rails, girders, bricks and other materials were transported by bullock carts, mules and often human carriers. There were dangers lurking in the thick jungle. The *Illustrated London News* of the period shows a picture of an engineer and his Indian helpers fleeing from a family of tigers which had squatted on the rails. Wild animals and snakes were often encountered by the pioneers. The weather in the hills also made working unpleasant even for the Indians; in the rainy season work often stopped completely and in the dry season it was difficult to get water. Malaria struck with regularity and epidemics of disease broke out in the large labouring camps; in the working season cholera took a heavy toll amongst the 30,000 workers in the ghats. Other hazards, landslides and rock-falls, added to the difficulties of working. But they were

113

eventually overcome, and the engineers planned and executed the viaducts, tunnels, cuttings and bridges that carried the steel road over the rugged Western Ghats.

Now, one hundred years after the "battle of the Ghats" was won, Indian Railways are improving the lines by widening tunnels, strengthening viaducts and laying new tracks—but they are working on the firm basis laid a century ago.

Bombay, again, was the first to electrify part of its line in 1925. Later, the rail over the ghats to Poona and Igatpuri was electrified to speed up traffic over the mountains. The steam locos, working up gradients approaching 1 in 37, found difficulty in coping with the increasing traffic. The electrified trains now carry passengers faster (the *Deccan Queen* makes Poona from Bombay in three hours) and do not have to take on booster engines or break the trains into manageable units as they had to with steam power.

Today Indian Railways (they are nationalised) boast one of the finest and most efficient networks in the world. Dining coaches, air-conditioning (introduced in 1936), sleeping berths, pleasant and helpful officials (even translators who help the illiterate passengers to read signs and time tables), make travelling in India less of a trial than it was just over a century ago. But still the old India plays its part—a large proportion of passengers using the railways in a year are pilgrims making their way to Hindu holy places and festivals.

JAINS AND PARSEES

Western India is the home of two religious minorities rarely found elsewhere in India except as small communities in large cities like Calcutta. The Parsees are concentrated in Bombay city and the Jains are more widely scattered in Bombay state, the Kathiawar peninsula and Rajasthan.

Jains claim great antiquity for their religion. For a Jain all life, even that of the lowliest of insects and the simplest of creatures, is sacred and must not be taken. So as not to violate their creed they wear white scarves over their mouths to avoid swallowing any flying insect by accident. It is said that a Jain will not light a candle for fear that he will kill a moth in the flame. This habit of

Parsees leaving a Bombay Fire Temple

covering their mouths led the Greek Megasthenes to write that there were people in India without mouths.

Jains are divided into two sects; the Digambaras consider clothes unholy so they go naked and their name means, appropriately, "sky-clad". The Svetambaras wear white cloth only and their name means "white clad".

Jains are notorious as successful and ruthless financiers and moneylenders who may be found plying their trade in most of the great commercial cities of India. Much of their wealth is devoted to enriching the magnificent and ornate temples of the religious order and supporting the monks and priests that live therein.

Like all religious orders, Jainism has its sacred places of pilgrimage. The most revered is Mount Abu in the Aravalli Hills where there are white marble temples carved in a very delicate, almost filigree fashion. An interesting place of Jain pilgrimage is the hill of Shatrunjaya near Palitana in the Kathiawar peninsula. Pilgrims have to toil up the flight of hundreds of paved steps in

Jain temples at Palitana, Kathiawar

the hillside to reach the top of the 1,000 ft. mount, a journey which takes an hour and a half. For the rich and aged there are porters who carry a "dolis" (chair) slung on their backs. On the summit of the hill there are no fewer than 863 separate temples in the magnificent Jain style of architecture. The temple of Sri Adisvara houses a fabulous collection of priceless jewels. There were originally two peaks at Shatrunjaya, but the intervening valley has been almost filled in at the order and cost of a rich Jain merchant.

All Jains try to make the sacred journey to Shatrunjaya at least once in their lifetime and for the rich man the climax of his pilgrimage is to have a temple built in his name and at his expense. This accounts for the large number of temples already standing.

At Sravanabelgola in Mysore state the Jains hold a great festival once every fifteen years with the ceremony of bathing the statue of a Jain saint. But the image is 57 ft. high, so a scaffold is built over the massive statue and thousands of Jain monks stand upon this to shower the saint with offerings. Very expensive items go into the anointing-pots that are emptied over the holy statue, including flowers made from gold and silver, gold coins, gems and precious stones, honey and milk.

Near the Hanging Gardens on Malabar Hill in Bombay city are the "Towers of Silence", the burial ground of the Parsees. When one of their number dies his body is taken to the cemetery by the "carriers of the dead", the funeral attendants. The bier upon which the corpse is carried is strewn with beautiful blooms. Only the carriers are allowed to enter the cemetery, even the relatives of the deceased must wait outside the gates. The carriers lay the body in a cubicle and as they retire they clap their hands. At this signal great black vultures swoop down from their homes in the tall towers and within half an hour have cleaned the corpse of all its flesh. The carriers then take the skeleton and drop it into a deep well. This strange form of burial is an expression of Parsee beliefs. They are taught that the earth and fire are too holy to be contaminated by a corpse so they neither bury their dead as we do nor burn them as do the Hindus.

Parsees are not of Indian origin. They came to the country from the town of Pars in Persia in A.D. 717 to escape religious persecution at the hands of the Muslims. They settled in western India and today almost half of the 100,000 Parsees live in Bombay city.

Parsees are followers of Zoroaster who preached in his code of life the sacredness of good deeds, words and thoughts. They are mistakenly thought to be fire-worshippers because the fire Zoroaster brought from Heaven is kept burning in all their temples.

Parsees have adopted many aspects of the Western way of life from the British. They, like the Jains, are a virile community who have contributed much to India's economic life. Parsee shipwrights and money established the large Bombay shipbuilding industry in the eighteenth century. They have put much capital into Bombay's trading houses and have organised commerce in that city. Dadabhai Naoroji, a leading Parsee, played a central part in the early nationalist movement of India. The Tatas are Parsees and nothing could speak more for Parsee talent than this. Tatas took the lead in hydro-electric development with the first Indian station in 1915, they own a great variety of large and successful enterprises and have contributed more to Indian industrialisation than any organisation outside the Government. (See p. 88).

IV

EASTERN INDIA

PHYSICAL

EASTERN India is the wide, irregular coastal plain lying between the Eastern Ghats and the Bay of Bengal in the states of Orissa and Andhra Pradesh. Compared with the western littoral, i.e. the land lying along the coast, the east plain is very wide and at places, for example the lower valley of the Godavari river, penetrates through the river valleys far into the interior of the peninsula. The drop from the plateau is also less spectacular, for the Eastern Ghats are lower and frequently dissected by large rivers. In addition to the plain, there are large deltas where the rivers crossing the peninsula have deposited alluvium as they leave the ghats and slow down to enter the Bay of Bengal.

Rainfall decreases from north to south. Cuttack has 60 ins. a year while Madras (just out of our region) has 10 ins. less. This is because the South-West Monsoon sweeps up the Bay of Bengal in a wide arc and hits the northern coast direct, but the areas to the south lie on the fringes of the rain-bearing winds. This fact is important because in the northern part of this region rice is entirely rain-fed, but in the south must be irrigated. Temperatures are high (Cuttack has a May maximum of 101°F. and a December minimum of 81°F.), but bracing sea-breezes in winter turn many of the towns into popular resorts.

For the most part, the immediate coast consists of sandy beaches backed by dunes, often reaching 50 ft. At Puri the shore seas are very shallow for a mile and at Masulipatam, which was once a thriving port, ocean-going ships have to anchor 5 miles

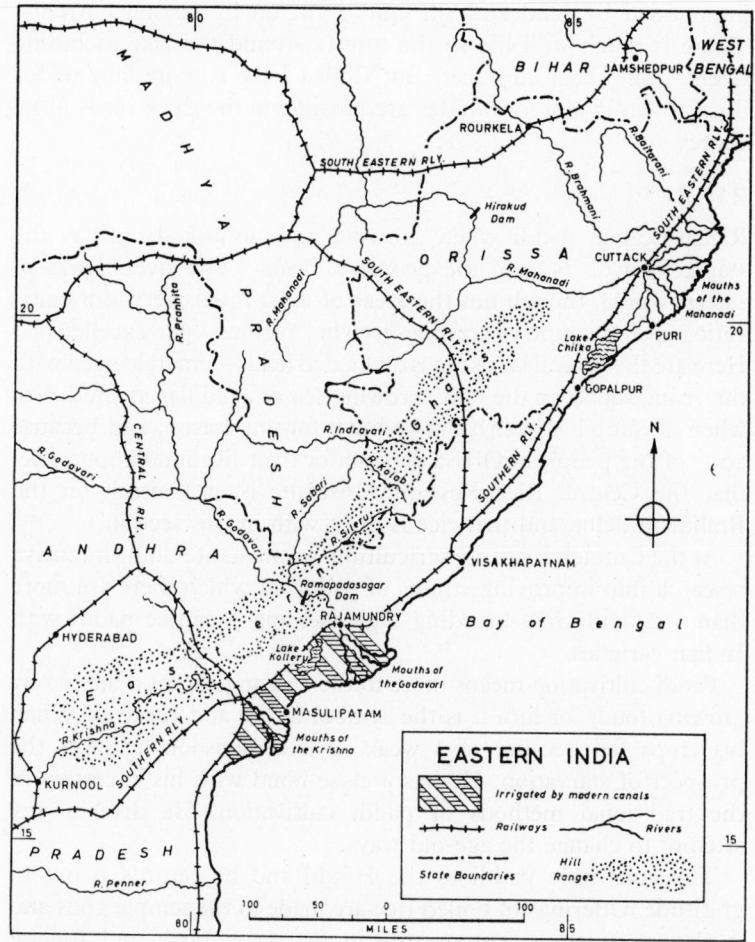

offshore because of the shallows. The sea edges of the great deltas are fringed with dense mangrove swamps.

Directly behind this coastal belt lies a wide strip of rich agricultural land cropped with paddi, coconuts, mangoes and vegetable gardens. On the western edge of the region the land rises up to the ghats.

One interesting formation is Chilka Lake. This is a large sheet of salt water (45 miles long and 10 miles wide) which has been impounded by sand and silt spits built up by coastal currents. There is much wild life in the forests around the lake including tigers, bears, boar and deer. But Chilka Lake is more famous for duck shooting and ideal hides are possible in the thick reeds of its shores.

RICE

Rice is called paddi when growing and unhusked, and is the staple food of 75 % of the people of India. The river deltas of eastern India, though not the areas of most intensive paddi cultivation in the country, are rice-growing regions "par excellence". Here are the typical landscapes of flooded fields—emerald geen with the rising shoots in the rainy growing season, and baked mud flats when the crop has been harvested. It is for this reason, and because 80 % of the people of Orissa depend for their livelihood upon rice, that the Central Rice Research Institute is at Cuttack on the Brahmani delta, and that rice is dealt with in this section.

At the Cuttack Institute agricultural scientists are doing intensive research into improving strains of paddi (of which there are more than 400) and cross-breeding high yielding Japanese paddi with Indian varieties.

Paddi cultivation means more to the Indian peasant than merely growing food; for him it is the symbol of life and survival. When his crops fail because of a weak or late monsoon he faces the prospect of starvation. He has a close bond with his ancestors in the traditional methods of paddi cultivation. He dislikes any attempt to change the age-old ways.

The gods gave paddi to the Hindu and he returns it out of gratitude. Offerings of boiled rice are made to the temple gods and it also plays an important role in marriage, birth and funeral ceremonies. Every stage of rice culture, from sowing the seeds to threshing the harvest, has to be started by some ritual or custom which seeks favour from the gods. So utterly dependent is the Indian peasant upon rice that during the Great Famine of 1942, when thousands died because the rice supply failed, people starved to death in the streets of Calcutta after refusing other foods that were available in plenty.

Rice is eaten mainly with hot curries of fish and vegetables, but still the grain forms almost 90 % of the poor man's diet. By way of

Before he is able to plant his paddi, the farmer must prepare his fields by puddling the flooded soil with a heavy wooden board pulled by his ox-team

contrast, millet flour is used for making chapatties (pancakes) in the Deccan, but this forms a far smaller proportion of the diet than rice does in, say, Bengal. Rice is well suited for cultivation in a heavily populated country for it gives a large yield of grain per acre. But the Indian peasant, reluctant to abandon his traditional inefficient and laborious methods, gets an average yield of only 860 lb. from an acre compared with the Japanese 2,500 lb.

Farming practices vary from area to area; three crops are taken each year from the fertile muds of the rain-soaked Ganges delta; other areas can barely raise one without the aid of irrigation. In places where labour is short, the seeds are sown broadcast over the fields direct, but the practice of transplanting seedlings raised in carefully tended nurseries is becoming more popular. This method involves more back-breaking labour, but the reward is in much higher yields.

Rice is a crop entirely dominated by the monsoon. Where 80 ins. of rain falls annually, it can be grown without irrigation (thus in the Balasore region of Orissa, 95 % of the paddi is unirrigated).

After the fields have been made ready comes the back-breaking work of planting the paddi shoots in rows. Each shoot has to be planted individually

But as rainfall diminishes, so irrigation becomes more essential; tanks are used in Mysore, canals in the Cauvery delta of Madras, and wells in the Deccan. Paddi also prefers heavy, clayey soils and the areas of greatest paddi cultivation are the large deltas of India (e. g. in Bengal).

Paddi cultivation gives the Indian peasant a very irregular life-tempo. When he is tending the crop by seeding, ploughing or weeding, he is overworked; when the crop has been gathered in he is indolent.

Cropping Paddi Times of sowing vary throughout India, but most of her paddi is a winter crop; it is sown or transplanted in June and harvested about November. Thus it occupies the ground when the South-West Monsoon is bringing heavy flood-rains. But before the paddi is actually put into the ground much work has to be done in the fields.

First, the bunds, or raised embankments around the fields, have to be prepared. Paddi needs to be in flooded fields during its period of growth so the best soils are water-retaining clays. The bunds have to be secure to keep the water in the fields. The water comes from the monsoon rains or irrigation channels.

Threshing and winnowing corn

Next, the fields have to be "puddled" and ploughed by the buffaloes. Their hooves churn and mix the mud and the vegetable matter that is used as manure. About a week before transplanting, cartloads of cow dung are tipped and spread in the fields.

The seedlings are then pulled carefully from their nursery beds, tied in bundles and taken to the main fields for transplanting. Each shoot is individually planted, about 6 ins. to 9 ins. from its neighbour, by the women. This is very hard work and the women sing paddi songs to keep their thoughts from their aching backs.

Now the paddi crop is in the fields, but there is no time for rest. The giant flocks of birds have to be kept from the emerald shoots, weeds have to be pulled and the threshing floors prepared.

By about November, the paddi crop is ripe for the harvest. Men and women go to the fields with their sickles in a happy mood— if the monsoon has not failed and the crop is a good one.

The cut paddi is taken to the threshing floors where it is laid on the hard-baked earth. A team of bullocks is driven around a central stake and the trampling of their hooves separates the grain from the husks. Where there are no bullocks, men and women trample the grain. When it has been fully threshed, it has to be winnowed. The paddi is lifted up in cane winnowing scoops and thrown into the air. Often the man who is doing the winnowing stands upon a high bamboo platform to throw the paddi. The heavier rice grain falls in a heap at the foot of the platform, but the lighter chaff is blown further away before it falls. Thus the rice and the husks are separated into two piles by the natural force of the wind.

His harvest is in and it is a good one. The farmer does not forget the gods who have given him his food for the coming year. The grain is stored in large jars in his house, but a little is kept aside to be offered as a thanksgiving at the temple.

THE DELTAS

The great deltas with their silt and fertility renewed each year are the heart of the eastern coastal plain. In the north is the combined Brahmani-Mahanadi-Baitarani delta which measures 125 miles at the coast and spreads for 50 miles inland. The coastal margins are of little use except as a source of wood-fuel for they are covered with swamps and jungle. But behind this strip is the older, more stable and fertile alluvium. This is intensely farmed with paddi, oil-seeds, vegetables and jute. The latter is becoming increasingly important as India expands her acreage to supply the jute-mills of Calcutta that have had their established source in East Bengal cut off by Partition.

This is an essentially agricultural region for only 4% of the people live in towns and there is little opportunity for industry at present. The hydro-electric-power and flood-control project being developed in a gorge on the upper Mahanadi river may attract industry in the future. Until this happens, the only products are handicraft goods from places like Puri which specialises in textiles, soapstone carvings, silver work and vases. There are also the small units which process local farm products: the mills for husking and polishing rice and those for crushing oil-seeds.

The delta of the Godavari in the rainy season is much like Bengal for it floods to some depth and the only spots above water are roads, village and house sites, field bunds and embankments. Another natural hazard to life is the tropical cyclones that visit the area; in 1864 a cyclone was responsible for the deaths of more than 30,000 people. Like the more northerly delta, the Godavari is a rice region (it is one of the few areas of India that produce a yearly surplus), but here there is often a need for irrigation. Other crops are tobacco and sugar-cane, which has to be protected by bamboo thickets against the strong winds.

There is slightly more industry in the Godavari delta than farther north, but again all the units are small. There are seventy-seven rice mills in East Godavari with a total labour force of 1,800 workers. At Rajahmundry there is a paper mill with a yearly output of 3,000 tons. It draws its raw material—paddi straw and bamboo —from local farms, as do all Indian paper mills for there are no supplies of soft woods in the tropics.

THE CAR FESTIVAL AT PURI

The most striking features of the cultural landscape of India are her thousands of Hindu temples. They are found in the most humble of villages, in the centres of modern commercial towns and in remote, abandoned cities where the decaying ruins speak of a glorious past. Some, like the shrines in Elephanta Cave, have been hewn from solid rock. Others had universities and observatories attached to them. All the temples are carved in minute detail with figures of gods and goddesses, monkeys, cobras, cows and elephants, so that the very stones appear to writhe with life.

The temple is the centre of the Hindu's life. Some towns, like Puri in Orissa state, depend completely upon the temple for their existence and their citizens make a fair living from pilgrims. In addition to the national all-Hindu festivals, each temple has its own festival in honour of its patron god or goddess. These celebrations are too numerous for all to be mentioned, but any book which sets out to describe the life of the people of India would be incomplete if no reference were made to them. So far we have not come upon one of these Hindu festivals, but now that we are in Orissa state we can see one of the most famous and spectacular— the "Rath Yatra" or Car Festival at Puri.

The temple at Puri is a famous place of pilgrimage. Built in the thirteenth century, its centre is a large rounded tower capped by Vishnu's giant wheel. Being whitewashed it is called by the

Konrak Temple at Bhubhaneshwar, Orissa State. It was built in the seventh century

Puri people "The White Tower". It has the usual four chambers found in Hindu temples: the Hall of Offerings, the Pillared Hall for the dancing girls, the Hall of Audience and the inner sanctuary containing the sacred images. No one not a Hindu may enter any part of the temple or the surrounding courtyards, but worshippers of that religion throng there daily in their hundreds.

Although the Jagannath (Juggernaut) Festival is a local one, the city is crowded with almost $\frac{1}{4}$ million pilgrims at the time of the Car Parade in the Hindu month of Ashadha, corresponding with our June or July. From every corner of India people come—men from Kerala, women from Calcutta, families from Madras, and sadhus (holy men) come from their caves and huts in the hills. The climax of "Rath Yatra" is when the sacred images of the god Jagannath (a form of the god Krishna) in whose honour the festival is held, his brother Balabhadra and his sister Subhadra, are put on

126

Jagannath car ready for
the Festival

to huge "cars" (chariots) and taken from the temple to Gundicha
Bari two miles away, where they stay for a week. This commemorates Krishna's journey from Gokul to Mathura. Jagannath's
car is almost 50 ft. high and 35 ft. square at the base, and its sixteen
wheels are 7 ft. in diameter. The thousands of teeming, pushing
and rejoicing pilgrims follow the cars on their journey through the
gaily decorated streets. Some push the cars from behind; others
fight and struggle for the honour of getting their hand on the long
ropes by which their fellow pilgrims pull the cars on their way.
The journey of two miles can take as long as two days if there has
been rain and the wheels sink deep into the sands. It was thought
that fanatical worshippers sometimes committed religious suicide
during the procession in order to gain great blessedness. Hindu
penitents do mutilate themselves at festivals with spikes, hooks and
knives, and when someone was crushed under the great wheels of
the cars at Puri it might have seemed intentional. But the probable
truth is that these unfortunates were pushed under the wheels by
the vast scrum behind them.

The holy images are large; Balabhadra's is 6 ft. high and painted black; Subhadra's is 4 ft. and painted yellow, and the great white Jagannath is 5 ft. They are carved in wood and clad in colourful dresses. The males have arms coming from their ears and Subhadra has no arms or legs. Being of wood the images need to be renewed from time to time, but the interval depends upon signs from the heavens. It might be twelve or twenty-five years, but after a long period certain ceremonies have to be observed in the carving of new statues. The wood must be of the "neem" tree; there should be no nests in the tree chosen, no shadow from another tree should have been cast on it, snakes should have been living beneath it and there should be markings of a wheel and a conch-shell under its bark. After the new images have been shaped, a Brahmin, blindfolded and gloved, takes an article from the old image of Jagannath and puts it in the new one. The Brahmin must not see or touch the article which is believed to be Krishna's bones.

Why are the images at Puri temple so holy? The reason is given in Hindu myth-history. Hinduism believes in a "Supreme God" who is represented in his varying forms by idol-gods; there is a trio of great gods and a number of minor gods. The Hindu trio are Brahma the Creator, Siva the Destroyer and Vishnu the Preserver. Jagannath is a form of the god Krishna who is an incarnation of Vishnu.

Legend tells us that King Indradyumna sent Brahmins to find Vishnu. One, who went to the land of the aborigines, was shown Lord Jagannath who appeared as a blue stone. Delighted, the Brahmin returned to his king with the news. But when Indradyumna came to the spot, the god had disappeared. The unhappy king prayed to the gods and heard a voice telling him that Vishnu would come to him, not in the guise of a blue stone, but as a log with certain markings on it. A log did float in with the tide and Indradyumna had it placed on the spot where the Jagannath temple now stands. The king brought carpenters and ordered them to carve from the log the image of Jagannath, but their chisels would not cut the wood. But then the miracle happened, for the great god Vishnu came to the place as a carpenter and was put in the room where the log was. After fifteen days the room was opened; the carpenter had disappeared, but there in the room were the three images of Jagannath, Balabhadra and Subhadra. This

The main street in Puri

miracle performed by Vishnu has made the images and temple at Puri one of the "Charo-Dham", the four most holy places of pilgrimage in the whole of India.

Puri is a town of some 20,000 people; it has no industry for the population makes its living by catering for the pilgrims. Puri craftsmen carve and cast images of the gods to sell outside the temple, and food vendors pitch their refreshment stalls in the streets. The festival crowd is not only made up of pilgrims; the scene is much like a market day in medieval England. Out come the sherbet sellers and the betel vendors with their trays of "pan" leaves, lime and areca nut; there too are the peanut sellers and the tea-men; the sellers of fruit—bananas and mangoes when they are in season—shout their wares; here too are the sellers of holy water, holy medallions and charms and little images of the gods; at the steps of the temple sit the sellers of rose and jasmine leaves which the faithful will scatter over the statues within. All these do a flourishing trade during the festival and a steady trade for the rest of the year.

Beggars also come to Puri for the festival—hundreds of them, to ask alms from the pilgrims. Let us have a closer look at them.

Beggars are found everywhere in India. Here at a corner of an alley leading to the Puri temple is a sadhu. He is a religious hermit

Sellers of fruit and sweetmeats in the temple
entrance

who has renounced life and work, and spends his time wandering
about, thinking, and living on the charity of others. He is almost
naked, painfully thin and filthy. Over his head he has thrown ashes;
on his face white stripes are painted; his hair is long and greasy
with dirt. In front of him is a bowl into which passing benefactors
drop rice and small coins.

Around the next corner is a blind beggar, or a cripple or a man
with no hands, collecting a lot from the passers-by. Hinduism
teaches that a man wins great merit by giving to the beggar and it
has become a tradition of Hindu life that no one will refuse to give
alms. So here they are at Puri, hundreds of beggars. Some are
genuinely poor or crippled or helpless, but others are not. Some

A 'holy man' (sadhu) outside his hut. He begs gifts of
money or rice

have made a profession of begging. The little boy, thin and dirty
with a sad expression on his face, who is pushing a metal cup at
that man, might be one of a small army of similar little boys who
have been hired from their parents to beg for a master-beggar.
They will get a part of all they collect. This one has his leg tied
behind him in order to appear limbless.

Around the next corner might be a little girl leading a fully
grown man with a head the size of a baby's. This poor, drooling
idiot is a "pin-head" who has come from northern India for the
festival. As a sign of gratitude to the gods for granting a wish, a
father might offer his next-born son as a "pin-head". He will

then encase the baby's head in a metal helmet so that as its body grows its head and brain remain the size of a child's.

Such is the colourful Jagannath Festival at the holy temple-town of Puri in Orissa. Though the ritual will vary in other Hindu festivals of India, the social scene described above remains much the same.

SHIPBUILDING AT VISAKHAPATNAM

Have you ever seen a ship launched down a slipway that had been greased with thousands of bananas? Have you ever seen a ship launched by having a coconut broken over its bows in place of the traditional bottle of champagne? Most likely your answer will be no, but this is what happens when large ocean-going vessels are sent gliding down to the water in India's largest shipyard at Visakhapatnam in Andhra Pradesh.

The yard was first constructed and opened by a private company, the Scindia Steam Navigation Company, during the Second World War. Seven years later the first ship was completed, in March 1948. But by 1952 the Scindia company found that bringing the raw materials to Visakhapatnam was too expensive and they contemplated closing the yard. Steel had to be brought by rail from the mills at Jamshedpur more than 500 miles away, and coal from an equal distance. Though labour at Visakhapatnam is cheap, the heavy transport costs outweighed this. The Indian Government, however, was not prepared to see the shipyard close, so in March 1952 it bought up the Scindia company and the yard now works under the control of the Hindustan Shipyard Company. More than twenty ships have so far been launched, and plans for the 1960–1 year envisaged five more going down the slipway.

Visakhapatnam has a deep harbour suited for berthing large ships, which is the result of large-scale dredging operations undertaken when the site for the port was being prepared for its opening in 1933.

Besides being India's largest shipyard, Visakhapatnam is also her fifth largest port. Most of its exports (1 million tons per annum) draw on the immediate hinterland and include manganese and oil-seeds. The Caltex Petroleum Company has recently built a

A view of the excellent harbour of Visakhapatnam, Andhra Pradesh

refinery plant here which has berth room for two modern tankers at a time.* Thus, from a rather unhappy start, Visakhapatnam is developing into a port of major value with the direct aid of the Indian Government.

DALEISERA: ORISSA'S TRIBAL COLONY

The governments of the Indian states do not regard their tribal peoples as freaks fit only for the attention of anthropologists. Most of them are helping in a number of ways to raise the standard of living and improve the health of their backward communities. Orissa, for instance, is a state with many tribes living in its hills (see "Central India", section on tribes), and by degrees it is helping sections of these tribes to improve their lot. But this is not an easy

*Apart from its ocean-going trade, Visakhapatnam also serves coastal traffic, as it lies half-way between Madras and Calcutta.

A Chenchu aboriginal,
The Chenchu are one
of the wild tribes of
Hyderabad

task for many of the tribal peoples themselves do not readily accept the new ways: new homes, schools and a confined village life. One such colony, Daleisera, has been established near Bonaigarh in Orissa state.

Ninety families of the Bhuiya tribe were brought down from the western hills to found their own village on a chosen site. The Bhuiyas were unused to building brick and tile houses, and sinking brick-lined wells and cutting field-irrigation channels, so the state authorities employed wage-labour to do the work. The Bhuiyas did what came naturally to them—they cleared and burned the trees and undergrowth. But old ways die hard and some of the Bhuiyas preferred to erect and live in their traditional grass-thatch huts.

Clashing farming methods also presented the authorities with a problem. In their hills the Bhuiyas practised shifting cultivation. They burned the jungle, scratched the soil and then scattered seeds of rice and vegetables; when the land became exhausted, they moved on to another patch. In the Daleisera colony they took their first crops and then tried to clear more of the surrounding forest for new land. The Government Forester, the resident official in charge of the colony's land, would not allow this. The Bhuiyas could not understand why until lecturers and demonstrators

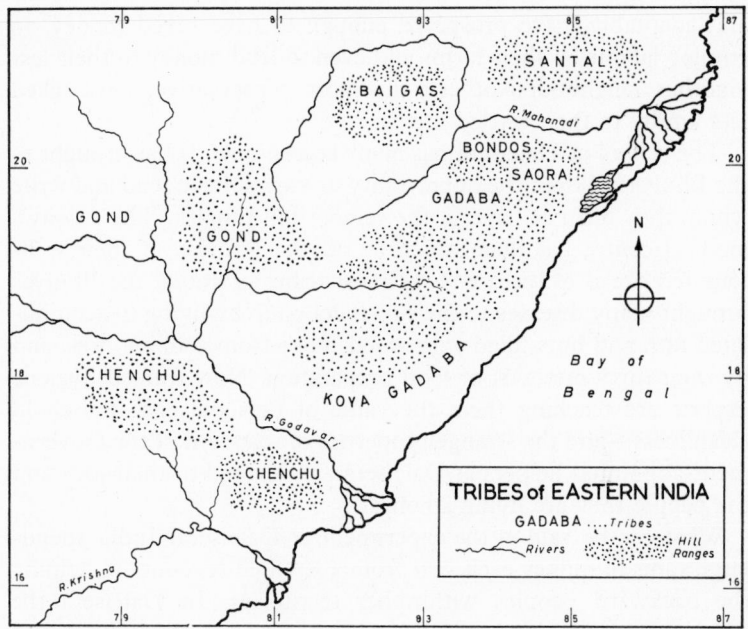

TRIBES of EASTERN INDIA
GADABA ....Tribes
Rivers
Hill Ranges

taught them how to farm irrigated paddi lands and use them year after year in a settled community. Now most, if not all, of the Bhuiya families have better crops and more food than they reaped from their inefficient cultivation in the hills.

The Orissa Government was very generous to the Bhuiyas of the settlement. Under the guidance of the "amin", or revenue surveyor, each family was given five acres of wet (irrigated) land and three acres of dry hill land as their share. These plots the people cleared for themselves. Each family was also given tools for farming, including a spade and a pick, and a pair of buffaloes— the utility animals of Indian farming. They were now richer than they had ever been for in the hills one pair of buffaloes was shared between five families. Now the Bhuiyas grow crops of cucumber, maize and mustard which they sell in the markets of nearby villages; in return they buy extra rice, vegetables, salt, cooking oils and cheap mirrors, combs, brushes and trinkets. The Bhuiyas have taken variously to their new life. Some, perhaps the young

135

and adaptable, have prospered enough to have saved money, to employ labour on their farms and even to lend money to their less vigorous neighbours; others, the more conservative, have taken less kindly to their settled life.

The school at Daleisera has many keen pupils. It has brought to the Bhuiya children the opportunity to learn how to read and write which they did not have in the remote hill jungles. The colony's medical centre has done much to rid the Bhuiyas of their well-founded dread of disease. Like most tribes of India, the Bhuiyas brought many diseases to their own doorstep by living in accumulated filth and huts filled with woodsmoke from cooking fires, and by their dirty methods of food preparation. Now trained hygiene experts are teaching them the value of personal and household cleanliness—and the strange properties of soap! All of the Government-appointed helpers at Daleisera are devoted to their jobs and the people they are living amongst.

What can be said of the experiment at Daleisera? India spends large sums of money each year from a strained revenue on helping the backward peoples within her territories. In Daleisera the Bhuiyas are healthier, more prosperous and having more and better foods than when they were in the jungle. This success alone proves the value of such Government schemes, but where success is slow in coming, the fault is in the ingrained conservatism of many of the tribal peoples. In time, this too will diappear along with the general poverty of India.

ANDAMAN AND NICOBAR ISLANDS

Far off the east coast of Madras, in fact nearer Burma than India, are two groups of islands that are directly administered by the Indian Government. The northern group, the Andaman, has 204 separate islands, but this is dominated by three large islands, the North, Middle and South Andamans. These are separated by shallow, narrow channels and mangrove swamps which indicates that they were once joined. The land sank and the deeper valleys were flooded. The southerly group, the Nicobars, has nineteen islands (seven uninhabited) of which the Great Nicobar (133 sq. miles in area) is the largest and most southerly, being only 90 miles from Sumatra. All the islands are remnants of a partly submerged mountain chain, the northern ranges of which form the uplands of Burma, and the southern ranges the hills of Sumatra.

The Nicobars In the middle of the last century these islands were the base of a band of Malayan pirates. A renegade from the British Royal Navy was their leader and chief. When storms raged in the Bay of Bengal, ships often made for the Nicobars looking for shelter, water and provisions. The pirates fell upon these ships, plundered the cargo and murdered the crews to a man. In 1869 the British occupied the islands to protect the trade routes.

Today, these scantily populated islands are important for their trade with Malaya and Burma. Most of the traders are Chinese with contacts in Penang who deal in goods demanded by the Chinese communities in Malaya. Edible nests are collected from the forest for making Chinese soup, trepang (sea-slugs) are fished from the shores and exported, and rattan canes are cut and dressed to supply the cane-workers of Malaya and Singapore. Coconuts grow everywhere in the Nicobars and are the chief export. To some extent they form a currency, and purchases may be made with them in place of money. It was estimated that the people of the Nicobars owned 29 million coconuts in 1915. A prosperous Nicobar family will use 300 nuts in a day; two-thirds of these will be used as pig-feed. The main imports are rice (there is little grown on the islands), Burmese knives ("dahs"), cloth and tobacco.

The Andamans Most of these islands are heavily forested. They have a long-standing connection with crime in India: after the Great Mutiny, convicts, murderers and undesirables were transported there from the mainland to the Port Blair penal settlement. Eventually these men under life sentence were freed and permitted to build homes and work for the Government. Many had their wives with them and others married on the islands. A more recent development is the settling of displaced persons there; in 1948 a large number of families went there from East Bengal.

The aborigines of the Andamans, of whom there are few left today, have a reputation for ferocity and murder. Like the natives of the Nicobars, they would kill shipwrecked and sheltering mariners, and they are still very suspicious of strangers—an attitude due, perhaps, to the unwelcome attentions of Malay slave-traders in earlier centuries.

In the jungles of Little Andaman, the most southerly of the Andaman Islands, lives one of the last remnants of the tribes of the islands—the Onge. The Onge are pygmies, the men standing only 4 ft. 9 ins. high and the women less; they have black skins and thick, curly hair. In the past they killed and possibly ate the sailors calling on their shores.

The Onge are a very primitive people; they do not know how to make fire; they do not cultivate crops; they cook in and eat from cans cast up on the shores and from large shells (for instance, the large nautilus shells are used for drinking cups). They still wander about almost naked: the men wear a scanty loincloth held by a belt of bark fibre which also serves to carry their knives; the women wear skirts of leaves. But, like all primitive peoples, they take great trouble over personal decoration and adornment. Both men and women wear bracelets and necklaces of coloured sea-shells. The women of the tribes decorate themselves and their men-folk by tracing designs with their fingers in red and white clay paste on the body and head. This paste is also used as a cure for aches, being painted on the sore spot.

Each tribe, consisting of about a dozen families, has well-defined hunting and fishing grounds. The main village has only one hut, a large structure of twigs and leaves, in which the tribe lives a communal life. Certain sections of the large hut are apportioned to the families. When they are out hunting, the Onge build temporary lean-tos from large leaves resting upon branches. One peculiar custom of the Onge is their method of greeting friends and visitors. The host squats on the ground and the visitor sits on his lap and hugs him!

The Onge eat almost anything they can pick, kill or collect. From the sea they get large turtles and fish. These creatures are speared or shot with arrows from large dug-out canoes with outrigger attachments. Wild pigs and birds are shot in the jungle and honey is collected in sections of the giant bamboo. It is interesting to note that the metal for arrow-heads comes from past shipwrecks.

VILLAGE LIFE IN INDIA

Hangala Pura, meaning Little Hangala, 60 miles south of Mysore, has 500 inhabitants of the lingayat caste. The village possesses 1,000 acres of good land for growing cereal and cotton and for raising cattle. It has 300 cows, 80 pairs of oxen, 120 sheep and 50 buffaloes. There are no pigs, goats or poultry. The lingayats are vegetarians.

The 'dhobis', village launderers, wash clothes in the nearby river and lay them out in the sun to dry

Every morning at 6 o'clock the village women fetch water for the day's needs. For the rest of the day they will be doing housework, preparing meals and milking cows

Like all village industries in India, milling grain into flour is done by hand. This miller uses a method which has not changed at all over the centuries

In England we take soap for granted, but this little village girl has to make her own. She is pressing oil from vegetable seeds. This oil will be boiled and then set into blocks to harden. Increasing supplies of cheap soap is a major aim of the Indian Government in its drive to make villagers more hygiene-conscious.

Literacy in India is increasing slowly. Here a little boy is doing his homework whilst his mother prepares food. Of the 500 people of Hangala Pura, 200 could read and write, 20 had secondary education and 5 girls were attending secondary school

The fight against disease is a constant one in tropical countries. Here a milk inspector checks the quality and purity of milk

The village tailor

V

THE GANGES PLAIN

PHYSICAL AND COUNTRYSIDE

IN THE Himalayas, about 13,000 ft. above sea-level, there is a glacier called Gangotri, and from a small ice-cave nearby a little stream emerges to carry away the melt water. Sixteen hundred miles and many tributaries later, this trickle enters the Bay of Bengal as the mighty and holy Ganges after having watered its flat and fertile plain. The boundaries of the region are as follows: in the north the edge of the Siwalik Hills, in the south the irregular edge of the central mountains, in the west the elevated watershed of the Punjab, called the "doab", and in the east the sea-face of West Bengal.

The Ganges Plain is geologically and physically the most simple, but the most staggering of all the regions of the sub-continent. Where the plain now is there was once, far back in geological history, a trough or depression about 1,300 ft. deep. Geologists have different theories about this trough, but some think it was formed by the upheaval which raised the mighty Himalayas. Whatever its origin, this vast trench lay between the high Himalayas and the old block of peninsular India. Then the rivers rising in the mountains to the north of the trough rapidly wore away the obstacles in their course and carried down layers of silt, sands and gravels until the trench was filled. It might seem beyond belief that a depression of this size could be filled by river action, but it has been estimated by experts that the river Ganges carries one million tons of silt into the Bay of Bengal daily, and this is in addition to material laid down on the plain. These clays and sands

146

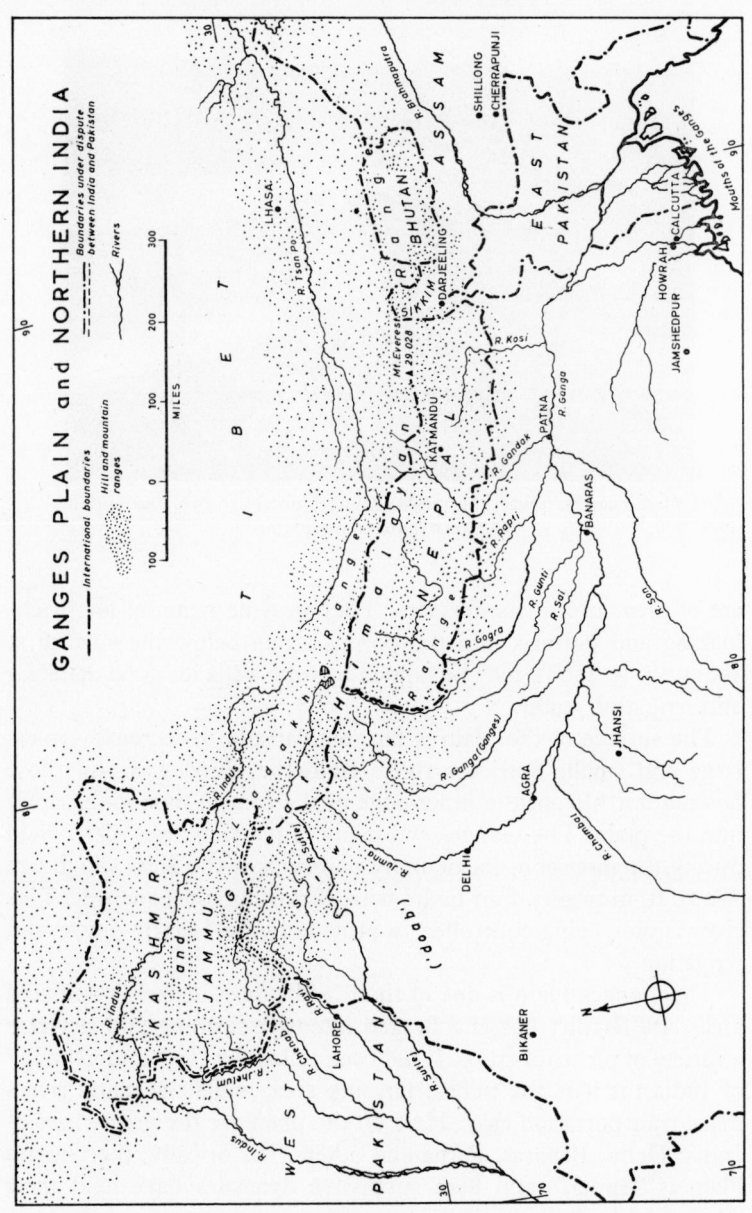

GANGES PLAIN and NORTHERN INDIA

International boundaries
Boundaries under dispute
between India and Pakistan
Hill and mountain
ranges
Rivers

MILES

100   0   100   200   300

Here near Hardwar, the mighty Ganges breaks from its mountain
course on to the plains

are of great use to the farmers. They provide material for brick-making and pottery, and the porous strata below the surface at about 200 to 400 ft. may be tapped by tube wells for good drinking and irrigation water.

The surface of the plain is flat, regular and dissected by rivers large and small. Both the rivers from the Himalayas and those flowing north from the inner edge of the central mountains drain into the plain. The Ganges and many of its tributaries often flood during the monsoon. Particularly notorious is the Kosi which can rise 30 ft. in twenty-four hours with disastrous consequences. This river is now being controlled to provide hydro-electric power and irrigation.

The Ganges Plain is one of the world's most densely populated areas. Its fertility has encouraged intensive farming and it yields a variety of plentiful crops. It has been called the "soft under-belly" of India for it is the richest farming area, while the many rivers make transportation easy. Here on the plain are the great cities of India: Delhi, Banaras, Patna and others. Historically, the Ganges Plain is "India," and here successive dynasties have held their courts and built their capitals.

148

The plain is fully settled and there are no forests hiding primitive tribes as in other parts of India. Emperors did hunt elephants, tigers and lions on the banks of the Ganges as late as the sixteenth century, but the natural covering of forest has made way for farming land and thousands of villages and mud-brick homesteads.

West Bengal is the dead delta of the Ganges. It is flat and cut by old river-courses and flooded dips. The landscape of this area is very similar to that of East Bengal.

AGRICULTURE

Farming occupies 90% of the people living in the fertile Ganges valley so we must concern ourselves with agriculture in this chapter. The great plain is a vast patchwork of small farms tilled by the peasants with plough and hoe. As their techniques differ little from those of other regions already described in this book, here we will study the crops.

Farming depends upon many factors, but none more important than rainfall and it is this which gives rise to different crops in the Ganges valley. The plain may be divided into three regions on the basis of rainfall and crops—the Upper, Middle and Lower (or Ganges Delta) sections of the valley. What causes the variation in rainfall?

As the South-West Monsoon winds sweep up the Bay of Bengal they are diverted westwards up the Ganges valley because the great wall of the Himalayas prevents them from crossing into Tibet. As they drive up the valley, the winds weaken and drop their rain. By the time they reach the Punjab they are almost exhausted and dry. Therefore, rainfall decreases as one moves up the Ganges valley and the Punjab is much drier than Bengal. In the dry season the upper reaches of the plain are dusty, brown and dry, but the Ganges delta remains green with vegetation all the year round.

We will briefly survey the crops grown in the three areas and then consider in detail some of the more interesting, if not the most important, crops.

UPPER GANGES PLAIN

By the time the South-West Monsoon reaches this region there is little rainfall left and the average total for a year is about 40 ins. This

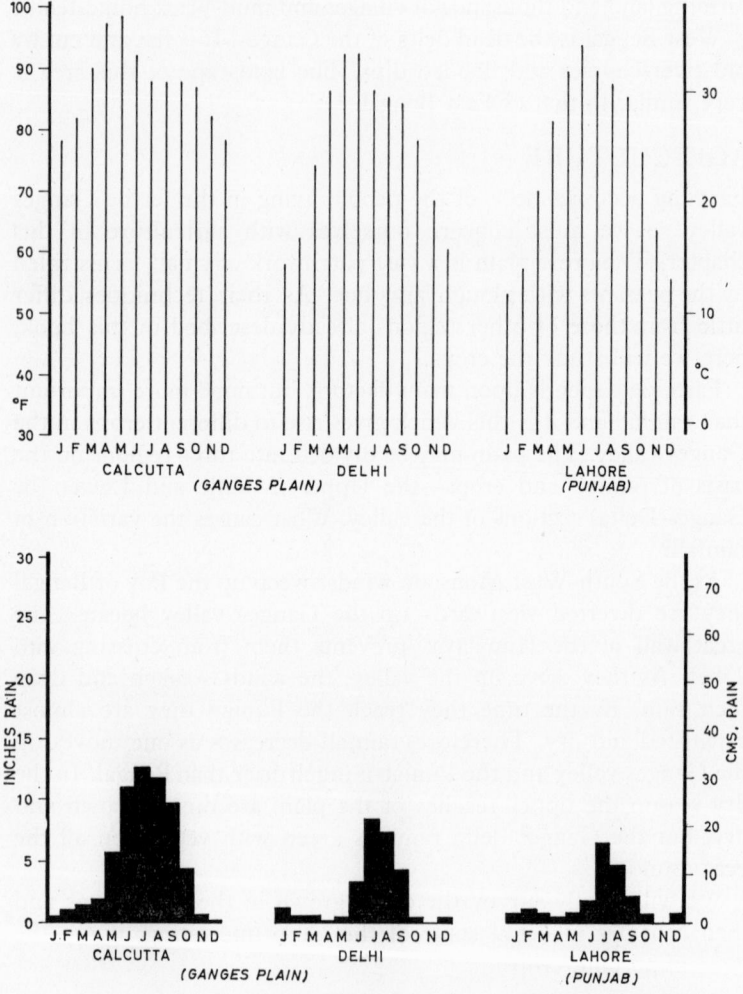

Temperature and rainfall graphs for Calcutta, Delhi and Lahore

A proud farmer displaying a new wheat variety which gives a better yield per acre

means that irrigation is necessary and about half the crops are irrigated with water from the network of canals that interlaces the country between the rivers. Wheat, barley and rice are the main irrigated crops and millet the main dry crop. Rice here is of little importance for the climate is both too dry and cool for its growth. Wheat is the staple grain food of the Punjabi and is eaten in the form of chapatties.

Wheat This grain requires conditions opposite to those on which rice thrives. The lower temperatures and moderate rainfall of the Punjab allow the peasant to sow this "rabi" crop in October, after the monsoon, and harvest it by sickle in March. While wheat is grown by the peasant mainly as a food crop, 45% of India's total harvest is sold as a cash crop chiefly in small markets and bazaars or to dealers in the cities.

MIDDLE GANGES PLAIN

Here rainfall is more plentiful, varying within the region from 40 ins. in the western margins to 60 ins. in the eastern margins; rice,

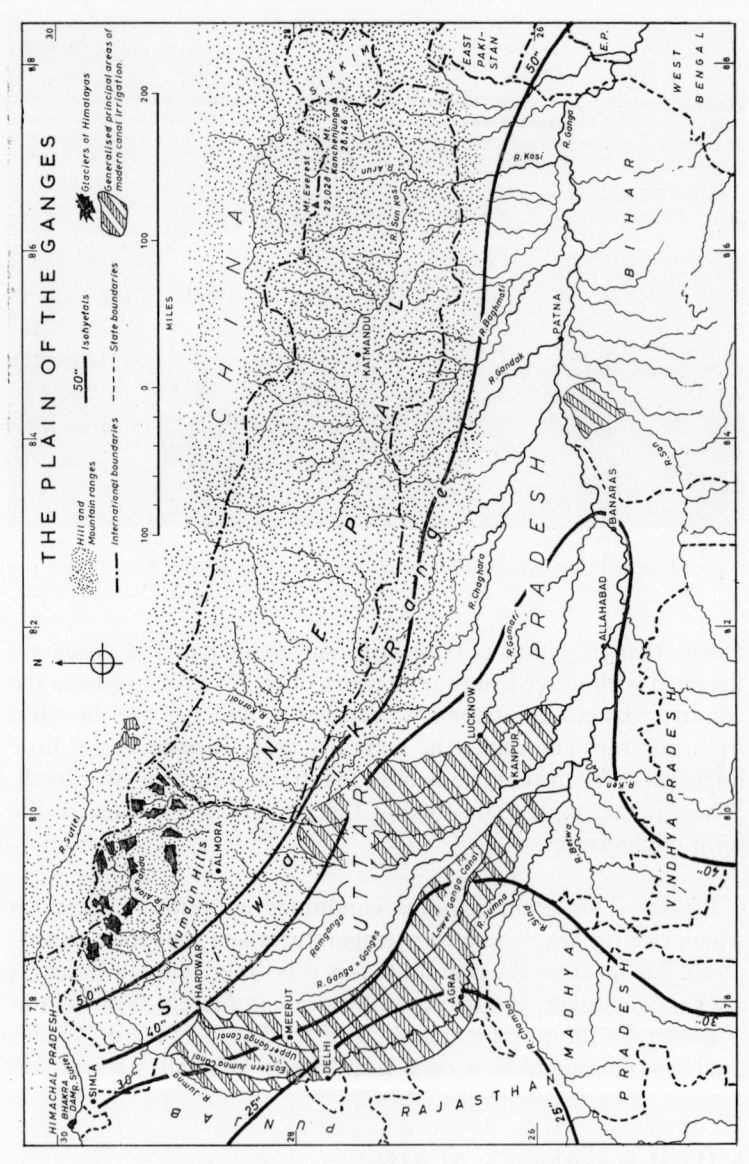

THE PLAIN OF THE GANGES

International boundaries
State boundaries
Hills and Mountain ranges
50" Isohyetals
Glaciers of Himalayas
Generalised principal areas of modern canal irrigation.

MILES
100   0   100   200

therefore, occupies a larger area than in the Upper Plain, but wheat is still important, with maize and millet close competitors. An interesting crop grown widely both in the middle and upper Ganges Plain is sugar-cane.

Sugar-Cane On their return from the Indian campaign, Alexander's soldiers told the Greek people that they had seen honey "not made by bees" in India. In fact, what they had seen was the brown "gur", or coarse sugar, made by peasants from their sugar-cane crops. India is the original home of sugar-cane, a tropical plant, and it is cultivated in most states of the Union, but Uttar Pradesh produces 50% of the national sugar total. Notice that the Ganges Plain, the centre of sugar-cane cultivation, lies outside the tropics, yet sugar can be produced because the climatic conditions in the Ganges valley are ideal for cane growing. Rainfall ranges from 30 ins. to 40 ins. per annum, there are few frosts and temperatures are uniformly high in summer.

Sugar-cane is a peasant cash crop. The farmer grows it either to turn into "gur" for his own use or for sale in the village bazaar; or if his farm is near one of the great sugar factories of Kanpur, Lucknow or Allahabad, he will cut his cane and sell it to the factory which will make it into white sugar. The latter is a luxury in India only afforded by the rich.

Sugar-cane needs much attention from the farmer. Before he can plant the cane he must take his bullock team and plough over the land four or five times to get a good tilth. When the warm season is due he then plants his cane for it needs high temperatures in its early growing period (April). "Setts", cuttings from selected cane, are planted in rows in the fields at the rate of about 12,000 per acre. In the early stages, the farmer must manure and irrigate the crop through the channels between the lines of cane and hoe all the weeds away by hand. In ten or twelve months the cane is high and ripe for cutting. The farmer and his helpers, usually his family, go into the fields with sickles and cut the tall cane stalks.

"Gur" making is done on the farm by the farmer himself. His methods are centuries old. The cane is first stripped of all leaves with a knife, and then it is crushed in a mill. Village mills are worked by a team of buffaloes tethered to a beam from the crusher.

153

F

Crushing the juice out of sugar-cane. More often
cattle are used to provide the power

As the buffaloes circle the mill so the beam turns the crushing
cylinders in the mill. One man drives the animals while the other
feeds the cane stalks into the crusher. The juice is collected into
large containers and then boiled in a bath. Boiling brings a crust of
crystalline syrup to the surface of the juice and this is scraped off
and moulded into loaves of "gur". Some of the loaves the farmer
keeps for his own family use, but the surplus he takes to the local
bazaar to sell.

About half of India's cane crop is made into "gur" in this way,
whilst one-third is made into factory white sugar. The yield per
acre of Indian cane is the lowest in the world, but the Indian
Institute of Sugar-cane Research at Lucknow is producing better
varieties in an effort to increase this yield.

Hessian and jute goods from the raw material to the finished product

GANGES DELTA (WEST BENGAL)

This again is monotonous, flat country—an expanse of alluvium brought down by the Ganges. It is cut by old river channels and much land is swamp (the local name for a swamp is "bhil"). West Bengal is the dead delta of the Ganges and is a green land covered by palms, bamboo and fruit trees very similar to the active delta region in Pakistan's East Bengal. The houses and villages are built upon raised land and the peasant drains the "bhils" to grow his rice, jute, mesta and vegetables and fruit. With rainfall well over 60 ins. the delta is intensively cropped, with rice predominating as the food grain, and jute for the mills of Calcutta.

Mesta whose original home is the Sudan, is a fibre similar to jute but coarser and is used as a substitute for jute in the mills of Calcutta. Since Partition cut off Calcutta's supplies of jute from East Bengal, more and more mesta has been grown in West Bengal. The acreage under mesta has increased twentyfold. It is too coarse

155

for making the finer materials, but the mills produce good ropes, sacking and canvases from it. Bengal paper-mills also use mesta for making wrapping paper.

Mesta is more hardy than jute and can grow on less fertile and even stony soils. The stages of cultivation, preparation and manufacture are similar to those of jute (see section on Pakistan), but its higher yield makes it increasingly popular with the West Bengali peasants as a cash crop. The advantages for the farmer, who is tending to grow more and more mesta, are many; it needs less attention than jute; it can survive the natural hazards of drought and flooding better than jute so there is less chance of a crop failure; it can grow on poor soils thus leaving the better alluviums for rice or jute, which fetches a higher price.

Cattle Every farmer needs a pair of buffaloes or bullocks to do the farm work of pulling ploughs and carts, and a cow for breeding. In the Ganges Plain with its million of cultivators this need has produced a huge cattle problem. India has one-third of the world's cattle population, but they are thin and weak and in the main unhealthy. In this region there is almost one cow or bullock to one acre of sown land. But the demand for food by the millions of people means that the land is too precious to use as grazing meadows or for growing fodder crops, and the cows are forced to be scavengers on waste land, road-sides or stubble fields. Although the cow is sacred to Hindus and they must never kill it, it is very badly treated; it is underfed, overworked and beaten. Bullocks fare better than the cow. They are given straw from paddi and wheat crops for they are working animals, but the cow must find its own food as best it can. India is, therefore, overpopulated with cattle. Almost five-eighths of the vast cattle population are rendered useless by disease and malnutrition.

The hot climate of India means that dairying as we know it in Britain is of little importance for milk quickly turns sour in the heat, but the treatment of cattle skins is a major industry in the Ganges Plain. Because of the religious taboo, the cattle are not slaughtered, but the death rate amongst them is so high that there is little need to kill them. Hides are taken only from cattle that have died from natural causes—the fact that 20 million cow hides and 5 million buffalo hides are produced every year in India

A boy on a buffalo

testifies to the terrible state of health of the cattle population. The skinning and preparation processes are in the hands of Muslims and the leather-working Hindu caste called "Charmar". Other Hindus will have nothing to do with this unholy work, as their religion calls it.

IRRIGATION

With its light rainfall coming from a weakening monsoon, the upper section of the Ganges valley has many schemes that ensure sufficient water for the farmer's crops. Both canal and tube-well irrigation feed water to the fields of wheat, sugar-cane and rice. The network of canals is very complex, but we will look at two schemes, one old and the other new.

The Ganges Canal In 1837 Proby Thomas Cautley, the Superintendent-General of Canals in British India, was traversing the jungles of the upper reaches of the Ganges river surveying the land and looking for the best route along which to build a canal. In that year the monsoon failed completely, the crops were ruined and a dreadful famine came to the land. This catastrophe awakened the authorities to the need for irrigation.

Cautley drew up a scheme, but many factors stood in its way; swift monsoon rivers cut across the route planned; the country was rolling and hilly which made canal construction difficult; the river gradient was very steep. Hostility between the British and Sikhs also made the work dangerous and the Hindu Brahmins resented the engineering interference with their holy river. But in 1839 Cautley began the canal, still in the face of much opposition. Today the Ganges Canal irrigates 1,700,000 acres and from the eight power-stations on its banks electricity is fed to villages, their small industries and the pumps that raise water from the thousands of tube-wells.

The Ganges Canal was completed in 1854 and water for irrigation flowed from it in the following year. The total cost of the canal was low (£1.4 million) mainly due to the availability of unlimited and cheap labour. The labourers, mostly from the professional digging tribe of the Oades Gipsies, were paid the high wage of 3d. per day. They dug the great trench of the canal with hoes and picks and carried the waste soil and rock away in baskets. When Cautley gave them wheelbarrows to transport the rock and soil, they put them on their heads as they were used to carrying their wicker baskets there.

There are 103 bridges and an aqueduct (3 miles long) on the Ganges Canal and Cautley found difficulty in getting bricks for their construction. In the masonry sections of the canal alone, 300 million bricks were laid and many million more were crushed to powder for mortar. These bricks were made on the spot from local clays, but the problem was in their baking. A special type of kiln was copied from that of Sind which could use the quick-burning local woods without ruining the bricks. More than 100 sq. miles of jungle were cut for fuel, and every day 2,000 bullock carts were carrying bricks from the kilns to the bricklayers working at the canal cutting. Mortar was reinforced with some unusual ingredients: lentils, certain jungle fruits, the country sugar and jute.

Many extensions have been added since 1854, but today the farmers of the upper reaches of the Ganges valley still water their crops from the canal which was built by the persistence, faith and vision of Proby Thomas Cautley.

The massive dam at Bhakra (Punjab) when it was near completion in February 1962

The Bhakra-Nangal Project Work began on this scheme in 1946 and the main work was finished by the end of 1962. Near the small village of Bhakra on the Sutlej river, about 225 miles north of Delhi, a dam 740 ft. high and 1,700 ft. long has been built to straddle a gorge before the river flows out on to the plains. The project is designed to irrigate $3\frac{1}{2}$ million acres in Indian Punjab and Rajasthan. From the flanks of the 50-mile-long reservoir 650 miles of main channels and 2,000 miles of distributary channels spread over the wide area like a giant spider's web. All these channels have been excavated by hand by thousands of labourers, women as well as men, drawn from low-caste and tribal groups. With their simple tools, picks and hoes, they have dug out the soil and waited for the dynamite-gangs to blow their charges, then carried away the waste in small wicker baskets balanced on their heads.

Before the foundations of the Bhakra Dam could be laid, 10 million cu. yds. of rock and earth had to be blasted and carried away by the labourers. In their place, 5 million cu. yds. of concrete,

This camel-driven Persian wheel is raising water from a main canal into feeder channels leading to the fields. Why do you think the camel is blindfold?

fed to the layers by a conveyor-belt from the mixing centre, were laid down. Upon this the wall of the dam was built. The most modern construction techniques employing a minimum of unskilled labour were used in the building of this dam. This is in contrast to the use of much unskilled labour in the digging of the canals.

Power-houses are being built on the Bhakra Dam, and on the Nangal Dam 8 miles down-stream to draw electricity from the turbines fed by the head of water in the reservoirs. These will give electricity to villages and industries of the region.

Wells Permiable layers of gravels and sands under the surface of the Ganges Plain hold vast reserves of water which are being tapped by the many tube-wells of the upper Ganges valley. The water is raised by pumps powered either by oil or electricity from the development schemes. The farmer lifts the water from the distributing channels on to his land by ancient methods. For instance, "Persian wheels" are common. These are vertical wheels turned by a bullock or camel with the aid of a beam. The animal turns the beam which turns the wheel. As the wheel revolves the pots below the water in the channel fill, are raised to the crest of the wheel and tip the water into the field channel.

It is fitting that Delhi, the city of "seven cities" and a thousand monuments, should be the capital of the young Indian republic. The "city", standing upon a bridging point on the sacred river Jumna, presents a summary in masonry of late Indian history, and here are the tombs of eleven prominent emperors while the rest of India has only four altogether.

Here the fine, spacious and modern buildings of New Delhi, those like Parliament House and Broadcasting House (the home of All-India Radio) contrast with the colourful and crowded quarters of the Old City (Shahjahanabad) in the north. Old Delhi, with its narrow bazaars and small craftmen's workshops, was built by Emperor Shah Jahan in the seventeenth century, and is still surrounded by its massive walls and defended on the riverside by the Red Fort, so named because it is built of red sandstone.

In fact, Delhi is not one but eight cities, and an area of 70 sq. miles around the present capital is littered with decayed walls and buildings of past capitals like Tughluqabad, the "Delhi" of the fourteenth century Tughluq dynasty. From its establishment as a Muslim capital in about A.D. 1200 until the British built New Delhi between 1920 and 1930, a series of magnificent cities have risen, flourished and fallen as new emperors ordered new capitals to be built. The general movement of the capitals was northwards to higher ground where it was cooler.

The first city at "Delhi", Indarpat, flourished at the beginning of the Christian era. In 1192 the invading armies of the Muslims defeated the forces of the Hindu Confederacy at the second battle of Taraori. The Muslims swept across the desert country to the Hindu capital of Ajmer in Rajasthan, sacked and looted it and left it. Ajmer was too far into the desert for the Muslims to adopt it as their capital and the choice of the new rulers of north India fell upon the second capital of the Hindus, the city at "Delhi". In 1206 "Delhi" became the capital of an independent Muslim empire in India under Qutb-ud-din, the first Slave Emperor (he was once the slave of Muhammed Ghori). The new capital grew up around the old fortress of the defeated Hindu Rajputs.

Why did the Muslims choose a secondary Hindu town as the site for their capital? The answer to this question is given by

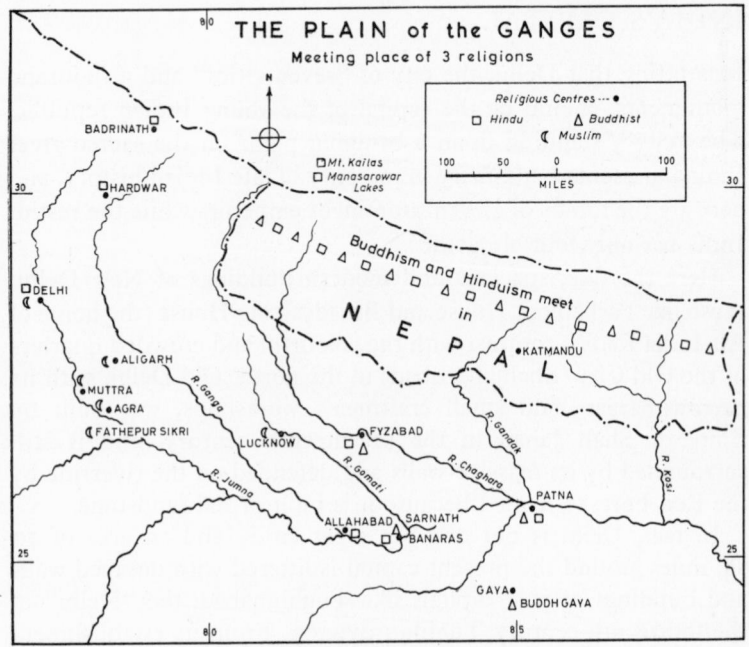

THE PLAIN of the GANGES

Meeting place of 3 religions

geography and strategy. It must be remembered that the Muslims were intruders in India, aliens in a foreign country with the prospect of rebellion by their defeated subjects always facing them. Besides, until they had been established in India for some time, the Muslims depended upon their homeland for supplies of troops and administrators. Therefore they did not want their capital to be too remote and disconnected from their former home. "Delhi" was just half-way between Bengal and the eastern borders of Persia and Turkestan. Thus, here they were near home and in a position to control the fertile plains of their new conquest.

"Delhi", too, is the cross-roads of northern India: from the south, between the Thar Desert and the central mountains; from the east, up the Ganges river and valley; and from the west, up the Indus plain. From "Delhi", astride the saddle between the Indus and Ganges valleys, they could rule, control and extract taxes from the fertile river valleys. Once established in its strategic position, "Delhi" remained the capital of northern India with few interruptions.

New buildings in a government housing scheme

In the fourteenth century Muhammed Tughluq tired of the capital and decided to establish a new one, Daulatabad, in the Deccan. He forced the people of "Delhi" to move with him—many of them died on the long and arduous journey—and "Delhi" was deserted. However, Muhammed soon realised that he had made a mistake and returned with his court and people.

In 1399 Timur the Lame invaded India and sacked "Delhi". With the establishment of the Mogul Empire, Akbar moved to a new capital at Agra (in 1556), but a century later (in 1650) Shah Jahan made "Delhi" a capital once more when he built the last of the "Indian" Delhis, Shahjahanabad. As the Moguls lost their grip on their empire other eyes of greed were shining from the West. In 1739 the people of Shahjahanabad foolishly murdered some of the troops of the army of Nadir Shah, the new invader from Persia. Filled with rage, Nadir massacred the population and looted the city. For 200 years "Delhi" was of no importance until the British moved their Indian capital there from Calcutta. The end of "Delhi's" eclipse came when a great "durbar" was held there in 1911. At this durbar King-Emperor George V made a speech in which, without any warning to the Indian people, he declared Delhi the new capital of the Empire. India was delighted.

Delhi, under British rule, had three districts: the Old City (Shahjahanabad) where the mass of the people lived, the Civil Lines where the British administrators and rich Indians had their

163

large bungalows, and the Cantonment or barracks area occupied by the military.

With the declaration of Delhi as the new capital, the British Government initiated the building of the new garden-city of New Delhi. Work began in 1920 and finished in 1930. Today, New Delhi has an administrative area, but in the Old City the people live and work at various small industries such as cotton milling and making articles of ivory and gold for tourists. The goldsmiths' centre is Chandni Chowk, "Silver Street", in the Old City. Today modern factories and estates are growing up around the town.

CALCUTTA

In 1692 Job Charnock, a servant of the East India Company, chose a swampy site on the east bank of the Hooghly river to build a trading station. At the time there were three small villages among the marshes, today the city of Calcutta stands on the drained site. Calcutta has grown and spread over and around the banks of the river, with the industrial centre of Howrah on the west bank and jute mills skirting the river up to the town of Hooghly, 25 miles to the north.

Calcutta is new as Indian cities go. There are no ancient ruins, no famous old temples, and no traditions except the remnants of British supremacy. Calcutta was the capital of British India from 1773 to 1912, but every summer the brassy heat drove the Government away from Bengal to Simla in the Himalayan foothills, a journey of more than 1,000 miles.

Greater Calcutta, including Howrah, is the most industrialised of Indian cities. She has the world's greatest concentration of jute mills and the world's most miserable industrial slums. But Calcutta is also a port, and a home for almost 3 million people.

The Port Calcutta is one of the largest ports in the East. The concentration of dockside berths and jetties is in the Kidderpore area, and through the port nearly half of India's total sea-borne trade passes—$3\frac{1}{2}$ million tons of imports and $4\frac{1}{2}$ million tons of exports a year. Calcutta has as its hinterland the vast and productive Ganges Plain from which she draws jute, hides, coal and

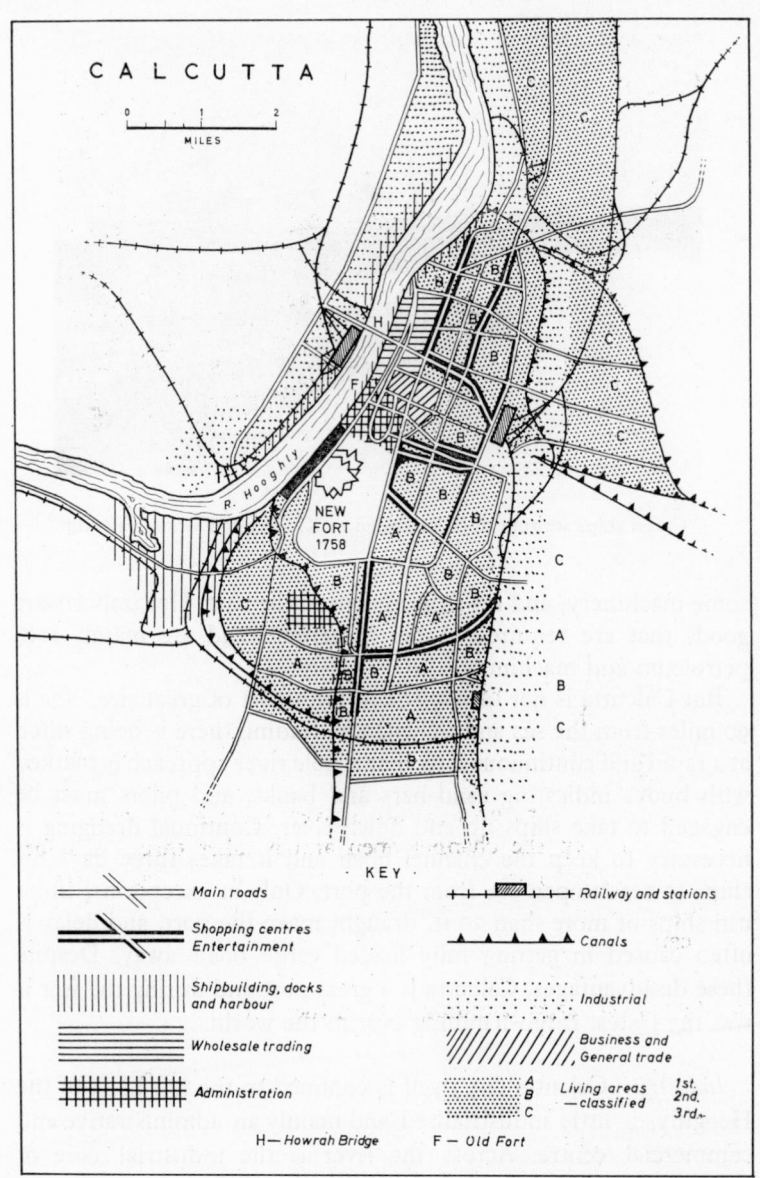

CALCUTTA

0   1   2
MILES

NEW
FORT
1758

R. Hooghly

C

C

C

C

C

C

A

B

C

B

B

B

B

B

A

B

A

B

A

A

C

B

A

A

B

B

B

A

H

F

KEY

═══ Main roads

━━━ Shopping centres
     Entertainment

▓▓▓ Shipbuilding, docks
     and harbour

≡≡≡ Wholesale trading

▓▓▓ Administration

╂╂╂▨╂╂ Railway and stations

▲▲▲ Canals

∷∷∷ Industrial

⁄⁄⁄⁄ Business and
     General trade

A
B   Living areas   1st.
C   —classified   2nd.
                      3rd.

H — Howrah Bridge   F — Old Fort

Cargo ships waiting to be unloaded at Kidderpur Docks, Calcutta

some machinery, and tea from Assam in the east. Her imports are goods that are required in her hinterland and are mainly salt, petroleum and machinery.

But Calcutta is not ideally suited for a port of great size. She is 90 miles from the sea and the channel leading there is being silted at a rapid and continuous rate. The whole river approach is marked with buoys indicating sand-bars and banks, and pilots must be engaged to take ships up and down river. Continual dredging is necessary to keep the channel open and it takes three days for ships to reach open sea from the port. Only at exceptional times can ships of more than 30 ft. draught make the port, and delay is often caused in getting fully loaded cargo boats away. Despite these disadvantages, Calcutta is a great port and during the war it was the fastest cargo-handling port in the world.

Industry Calcutta city itself is confined to the left bank of the Hooghly, is little industrialised and mainly an administrative and commercial centre. Across the river is the industrial core of Howrah ($\frac{1}{2}$ million people in 1951). Joining the two towns is the giant Howrah Bridge, a cantilever bridge with a central span of 564 ft. which carries an eight-line traffic road of 70 ft. and footpaths.

A general view of the Howrah Bridge, Calcutta

Before 1941 when the Howrah Bridge was completed, the famous pontoon (bridge of moored boats) crossed the river.

In Howrah are engineering workshops, iron foundries, sugar mills, India's largest chemical factory, her most productive paper mill, cotton mills, automobile works and railway workshops using Jamshedpur steel. And here, too, are 90% of India's jute mills lining the river banks up to Hooghly town. The mills are close to the river, for much of the raw jute is brought from the growing districts by country boats along the canals and rivers. The first jute mill was opened in Calcutta in 1855 when George Acland brought spinning machinery from Dundee. Four years later power was applied to the making of jute goods. Partition severed Calcutta's supply of raw jute for many years, but now intensive planning and investment has brought India's internal jute supplies to a satisfactory level. In the great mills along the Hooghly the jute is cleaned, spun and woven into hessian, canvas and sacking on spindles and frames just like cotton equipment.

167

Greater Calcutta has a large and growing population and here are the world's worst industrial slums—the "bustees". Calcutta is a city where masses of migrants come, and at the time of Partition thousands of Hindu refugees fled into Calcutta from East Bengal looking for homes and employment. Few houses were available so they swelled the ranks of the bustee livers. The bustee is a hut, rarely larger than 10 ft. square and with one room only, built in any open space and of any scrap material. Most are shelters of rags, foul matting or petrol cans beaten flat and tied to a flimsy framework. Hundreds of these crowd into available spaces in the Calcutta suburbs and have open drains running between the rows. Somewhere nearby, there will be an open cesspool and a drinking and washing stand-tap. Mortality rates are high because of the ravages of disease encouraged by lack of sanitation. Much of the industrial working force is housed in brick-built houses or flats, but the bustees of Calcutta are sores on the city's skin.

Transport and Communications Calcutta was originally on marshy land and all roads and railways have had to be built on raised banks and ridges. Its connections with the rest of India and the world are from the airport of Dum Dum, 7 miles east of the city, and from the Howrah railway terminus for western stations and the Sealdah terminus for areas east of the Hooghly. But transport within the city is of more interest.

The roads of Calcutta have been built haphazard and are for the most part narrow lanes and streets ill-suited for automobiles and a great population. Until the mid-nineteenth century there were no metalled roads in the city and the monsoon rains churned them into mud seas. The problem that the engineers had to face was how to surface new roads to withstand the heavy wear and tear of bullock-cart wheels. "Khoa", or broken bricks, were used in the early attempts.

Within the city there are a number of means of transportation. In 1867 the Calcutta Tramways Company started operations and the city's trams are the most efficient and comfortable in India. There are 'bus companies and taxis operating in the Calcutta streets and the cheap carriers—rickshaws. The latter give the quickest ride in congested and narrow thoroughfares where cars

Making fuel-cakes from cow dung. The dung is patted
into shape and then placed in the sun to dry

and 'buses cannot move. Most of the rickshaw pullers come from
Bihar.

For carrying merchandise and food in the busy centres and
bazaars of Calcutta, human labour is the most common, the
bundle being balanced on the head. In the suburbs the bullock-carts
do most of the fetching and carrying. These carts amble through
the streets causing long and frustrating traffic jams by their slowness. Pedestrians, too, add to the general confusion. Pavements
are narrow and the traffic heavy, so many walk in the road. This,
combined with the average man's complete lack of traffic sense,
leads to many accidents.

The number of bullocks and cows wandering through the
streets of Calcutta must exceed that of any other city. They squat
in the road unmolested; they pasture in the large Maidan Park
in the city centre under the care of the "doodh wallah", or milk-
man. They are efficient pack animals, but they also give full time
employment to those people who collect their dung from the
streets. These strange scavengers wander through the streets and
lanes scooping the dung into baskets which they carry on their

heads. When they have a full load they take it to their pitch in an alley, mould it into cakes and plaster it on the wall to dry in the sun. When dry, these cakes are sold to poor people for fuel. This practice of burning cow dung is common to all parts of India and prevents the dung from being used as valuable manure. Indians do not think cow dung dirty as we do in Europe for the cow is to them a sacred animal. They clean their houses with cow waste.

One sight never to be forgotten is pay-day at the mills. The Pathan moneylenders wait outside the mill and as the workers file out with their small handful of rupees they pounce on their debtors for repayment. Even the poorest labourer or farmer will borrow heavily to give a lavish party for an occasion such as a wedding or a birth, and this may cripple his finances for many years to come. One of the most serious problems facing India is the indebtedness of its people and the large proportion of their weekly income that is taken, at very high rates of interest, by harsh moneylenders.

BANARAS

Four hundred miles up-river from Calcutta is the holiest of al Hindu cities—ancient Banaras. Sprawling for 4 miles along the Ganges banks, Banaras is a town of festivals and sacred buildings, from primitive painted stone shrines to wonderful temples. When the Muslims conquered northern India they destroyed the city they found at Banaras because of their hatred of all idol-worshippers. Most of the temples, therefore, are of recent origin, built by Maratha princes who restored Banaras' glory in the eighteenth century.

First founded about 1200 B.C., Banaras is also called Kasi which means "Ever resplendent with Divine Light". It is Lord Siva's city, and the most holy building in this most holy place is the temple of Vishwanatha, Siva's temple. Its spires are plated with pure gold which shines in the sun.

The city stands upon a terrace of the river Ganges. Rising up from the level of the waters to the streets and temple yards are flights of stone steps. Here are the "ghats" where the faithful bathe before offering their prayers to Lord Siva in his temple. On the ghats, too, the bodies of Hindu dead are burned according to

Hindus burn their dead. Here a funeral pyre is being built on the Burning Ghat at the holy city of Banaras

ancient custom and the ashes scattered upon the flowing Ganges. One of the ghats at Banaras is particularly sacred for here Brahma sacrificed ten horses; another is where Parvati, Siva's wife, lost her ear-ring. Behind the temples which face the river is a network of cramped alleys with overhanging houses, and shrines are found at every corner.

Banaras is a city of religious celebrations—she has 400 festivals every year. It is said:

> Strange is the life that Kasi leads,
> In seven days nine festivals feels.

The citizens stay up half the night catering for the pilgrims. By flickering lamp-light shopkeepers sell milk, sweets, betel, tobacco and food from their stalls and stores in the bazaars. The temples rarely close their doors except to non-believers, and Siva's bulls wander through the crowded alleys reminding passers-by that they are in his city.

Of special significance in Banaras is Siva's Night. At this festival the worshippers fast during the day and offer milk, betel and holy water from the Ganges to Siva's image in the Vishwanatha temple. Then, as the sun goes down, they start their night-long parades through the city singing the god's praises.

Local craftsmen make saris, famous throughout the whole world for their quality and beauty, brassware, brocades and toys for sale to tourists. A favourite spectacle in Banaras is the local wrestling match, for the people of Banaras excel at this sport and are trained in it in well-run gymnasia from an early age. Banaras is also an ancient centre of Hindu learning and teaching. Its Hindu university takes students from all over India and has a fine collection of Hindu books and writings in its libraries. Also, behind the temple of Vishwanatha is the Well of Knowledge serving, perhaps, a less practical function than the university.

Five miles north-east of Banaras are the ruins of the ancient city of Sarnath. Here, 2,500 years ago, Buddha preached his first sermon in the Deer Park. Ruins litter the site of Sarnath and much careful digging by archaeologists has uncovered the remains of buildings of past glory, thus adding to the knowledge of India's pre-history.

THE SIKHS

Most of India's 6 million Sikhs live in east Punjab, but they are found as minority communities throughout the whole Union.

The Sikhs are a religious sect founded in the fifteenth century by Guru Nanak. Nanak rejected Hinduism and its rigid caste system and the religious intolerance of the Muslims. The name "Sikh" is taken from the Sanskrit word "shishya" which means "disciple". Sikh greets Sikh by saying "Sat siri akal", meaning "Truth is eternal".

Nanak founded the religious community of the Sikhs, but Guru Gobind Singh gave them their distinctive habits and customs and their common name—all Sikhs are called Singh. He lived from 1666 to 1708 and, in face of Muslim persecution, welded the Sikhs into the militant race of valiant warriors who later were to defy the might of the British armies.

The magnificent 'Golden Temple' of the Sikhs at Amritsar in the northern end
of the Ganges Plain near the Pakistan border

It was Guru Gobind Singh also who gave the Sikhs their "five
K's". These are the distinguishing marks of the Sikhs. They are:
(1) *Kesh:* unshorn hair. The commandments of the Sikh religion
forbid the cutting of the hair of the head. The long flowing locks
of the Sikh are wound into a knot (called "chignon") on the top of
his head. It is then covered with a turban. The Sikh also allows his
moustache to grow long and twists the ends just like a sergeant-
major. He also has a long beard which he encases in a black
hair-net held in place by an elastic cord over the head.
(2) *Kangha:* This is a small wooden comb thrust into the hair-
knot on the top of the head.
(3) *Kirpan:* a short sword which the Sikh is expected to wear in
accordance with the commandments. In the modern world this is
not strictly obeyed.
(4) *Kachh:* a pair of shorts worn by a Sikh.
(5) *Kara:* This is a flat iron ring worn on the wrist. Sikh warriors
of the last century wore another ring, the chalikar, about 10 ins.

in diameter, suspended from the loose ends of their turbans. These they ground as sharp as razors on their outer edges and used as effective weapons. They spun the ring about their finger or a stick and let it fly at their opponent. So accurate was their aim and so heavy the iron ring that the unfortunate adversary was often beheaded. In the last century these Sikh soldiers formed a regiment called the Acalees and they gained a reputation for great bravery and daring in battle. In fact, the Sikhs were the last of the major peoples of India to be conquered by the British.

But the spirit as well as the body of the Sikh is strong. While I write, Tara Singh, the leader of the Sikhs, is on the twenty-fifth day of his fast-to-death ordeal in trying to force the Indian Government to establish a separate Punjabi-speaking state in the Union.

SNAKE-CHARMERS OF NORTHERN INDIA

In the Punjab live the Kom Jogis, a tribe of professional snake-charmers who make their living by wandering from city to city along the Ganges, pitching their cotton tents in open and waste places and giving spectacular shows in the streets. The favourite snake of the crowd, who throw small coins for the performance, is the cobra, especially the king cobra which may reach 12 ft. in length.

The uninterrupted music of the charmer's gourd-pipe taunts the cobra into taking an upright position, the only position from which it can strike, and into spreading its hood. The cobra has a great fear of all sounds and keeps the pipe in its sight and sways with it until it decides to strike—but the charmer is too quick and pulls his gourd-pipe away from the fangs. The charmer continues to irritate the snake much to the amazement of the spectators. Every action of the charmer and his assistant emphasises the risk that is being taken in toying with the cobra. Some of the Kom Jogis tribe are so accomplished that they charm the snake with their swaying knees and even their hands.

The Kom Jogis catch and train their own snakes. Let us see how they manage the cobra, the most dangerous and poisonous of all snakes.

The wandering snake-
charmer stops to give a
way-side show

Rats form a major part of the cobra's diet and one of the places where the hunter looks for his prey is down a rat hole. He digs down into the hole until his instincts, inherited from centuries of snake-charming ancestors, tell him that he is very near the snake. He then thrusts a long stick into the hole. Underground, the cobra strikes with full force at the interfering stick and its fangs become embedded in the wood. Feeling the snake on the end of the stick, just like a fisherman with his line, he pulls the stick out with the trapped cobra dangling from it. He is then reputed to make a whispered deal with the freshly captured cobra to treat it well and free it after two years' good service.

The cobra is placed in a flat wicker basket and left without food or drink for some days. By the end of this time it is weak with hunger and thirst and may be handled with safety. For hours the charmer holds the cobra by its tail and when it rears its head upwards he flicks it down again. This completely exhausts the snake and now its fangs may be extracted with pincers and the poison-sac removed.

For weeks afterwards the charmer trains the cobra in his ways with the gourd-pipe, his hands and his wavering knees. The flicking treatment continues so that the cobra's spine is stretched, which makes its movements and its strike slower. Eventually it is fully mastered and fit for public display.

The charmer feeds his cobra on milk. This is not the natural diet of the snake, which prefers frogs and rats, but these are difficult to supply when travelling the road giving shows. At first the charmer has to feed the milk down the cobra's throat through a straw, but later it takes to its new food so well that it will lap it from a bowl just like a kitten.

The skill of the Kom Jogis charmer depends upon his quickness of hand and his instant reactions, but he himself attributes much of his power over snakes to secret words and spells, told him by a magician, that he chants to the snake while it is performing. Despite their ability to control the cobras, the Kom Jogis are very superstitious about them. They will not let one die whilst in their possession. If one gets sick they will free it, for they believe that if it dies they will be bitten by a cobra in the bush—which would be just as fatal for the Kom Jogis as for anyone else. The cobra injects enough poison through its fangs in one bite to kill a human in a matter of minutes. But, contrary to common belief, the cobra is very reluctant to strike when disturbed for it produces only a certain amount of venom daily and prefers to keep this for hunting its food. Further, for poison to flow from the fangs into a wound the cobra must twist its neck sharply and this is not always possible when an arm or leg is withdrawn quickly.

VI

NORTHERN INDIA (HIMALAYAS)

PHYSICAL FEATURES

LIKE the huge rampart of some natural fortification the Himalayas rise into the clouds to cut off India from Central Asia. This complex of mountain ranges, stretching roughly in an arc from the Indus bend in the west to the Brahmaputra bend in the east, contains the world's highest peaks. For the purpose of our studies, this region also includes the Assam Hills, uplands associated with the Himalayas and raised by the same forces. (See map on p. 147).

The rocks of the Himalayas are mainly sedimentary and it is strange to realise that these, the highest mountains on the earth's surface, were once the flat bed of the ancient Tethys Sea. Great and sustained southward pressures from the Tibet area pushed and buckled the crust of the earth against the rigid block of peninsular India, thus forming the giant folds of the Himalayas. Some of these are still rising!

Three parallel main mountain ranges, separated by high valleys (e.g. Kashmir) and plateaux, are recognisable in the Himalayan system. Rising immediately from the northern edge of the Indo-Gangetic Plain are the Siwaliks which are most clearly marked in the west. This low range is made up of material eroded from the higher ranges in the north and can, therefore, be regarded as the off-spring of the Himalayas proper. Across a wide valley-trough are the Lesser Himalayas, the middle range of the system. These are really a series of ranges more complicated in the west than the east, with an average height of from 12,000 to 15,000 ft.

After traversing another but higher valley-trough, the Great Himalayas are reached. Up here where the pillars of Everest (Nepal

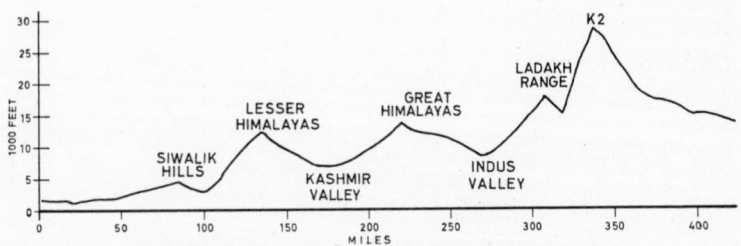

Cross section of the Western Himalayas through K2 and Srinagar

Himalayas: 29,002 ft.), Kanchengunga (Sikkim Himalayas: 28,146 ft.) and K2 (Karakoram Himalayas: 28,250 ft.) support the sky, is a bleak world of ice, snow and bare precipitous rock faces. Up here the god Siva lives with his wife, the daughter of the Himalayas. These mighty frost-shattered peaks have very steep southern (Indian) faces, but slope more gently to the high Tibetan plateau in the north. So rapidly does the eastern section of the Great Himalayas rise from the south that Everest and Kanchengunga can be seen by the plainsmen only a few miles away.

On these higher ranges are found the largest glaciers outside the poles. Fed by the great snowfields—these peaks rise well above the level of permanent snow—they in turn feed the mighty Indus and Ganges with their melt waters. The Baltoro Glacier of the Hunza valley (Gilgit, Kashmir) is 38 miles long with an ice-depth of 400 ft. Much of the surface of the Himalayan glaciers is covered with morainic materials (soil and debris brought down by glaciers) so that Kashmiri shepherds often take their flocks of sheep and camp on them in summer.

It takes brave men to travel from India into the secret land of Tibet for the only communication routes across the Great Himalayas are high and wild passes (about 17,000 ft. above sea-level) that are open only during the short summer months. These notches have been cut by the rivers which are older than the mountains themselves. The rivers cut into their beds faster than the mountains were being raised so that the river system bears no relationship to the shape of the land. Deep, steep-sided gorges replaced normal valley shapes. Some of these are fantastically deep; at Gilgit the Indus flows through a narrow gorge with sides more than 17,000 ft. high.

The Pir Panjal range which separates the valley of Kashmir from the plains of northern India. The forests covering the lower slopes look like dark shadows in this aerial photograph

It is possible to give only a scanty sketch of weather conditions in the Himalayas for two reasons: most of the area has still to be investigated scientifically, and secondly, it exhibits features of most of the world's climates. In short, there is no "climate" as such, but a variety of micro-climates depending upon situation, aspect and elevation. Every little valley has its own climate. There is the intense, malarial heat of the foothills ("Terai") in the east, the frozen wastes of the peaks, and between them is the transitional zone with a myriad of climates. The undulating foothills are hot, swampy and exhibit the climatic features of the Indian plains. This region has the well-marked monsoon seasons with total rainfall varying from 40 ins. in the west to 100 ins. in the east. At the other end of the scale are the peaks with their Arctic climates. Here temperatures never rise above 50°F. even in the hottest months and precipitation is mainly in the form of snow. Lower down the slopes have tundra (land with frozen subsoil) and Alpine weather with short warm summers and long cold winters. For most of the year (October to April) the ground is covered with snow.

It is in the intervening valleys, between the higher slopes and the foothills, that climate varies much with aspect. The monsoon brings most rain in June and the heat of these summer days in the valley bottoms is very oppressive. The summer nights are cool and pleasant. Between 5,000 and 10,000 ft. the climate of the temperate oak predominates. It is common practice in summer for herdsmen to take their animals up the slopes to alpine pastures.

Perhaps the most pleasant spots in the Himalayas are the hill-stations perched on the southern side of spurs of the Lesser Himalayas. They were founded by the British, who felt the need for a "change of air" from the summer heat of the plains. These stations, Ranikhet, Almora, and Dalhousie to mention a few, have climates very similar to that of a warm English summer and it was to them that the British state governments moved to conduct their business. Simla, one of the most popular resorts, has an annual maximum of 70°F. in June and a minimum of 39°F. in January. Annual rainfall is about 63 ins.

ASSAM

Assam lies in the north-eastern corner of the Indian Union and is bordered by Tibet, China and Burma. For many centuries Indians called it Kamakhya, "the magic land", and today much of it is still practically unexplored. It is a land of mystery, wild animals, damp forests and secret hill paths. Here, in the Sylhet district, is a variety of paddi which can grow 6 ins. in a day; here at Cherrapunji in the Khasi Hills, is the wettest place in the world having 500 ins. of rain per annum; here, on the island of Majuli in the Brahmaputra river, are priests so holy that they must never put their feet on the ground; here, on the swampy fringes of the rivers, are grasses which stand 20 ft. and more.

There are two distinct regions in the state; the narrow, flat and marshy alluvial valley of the great Brahmaputra pushing towards the north-east; and the surrounding hills and mountains, separated by deep valleys, looping around this lowland. In the north these mountains are part of the Himalayan system, in the south they are lower (4,000 to 10,000 ft.), but still Himalayan in origin.

The people of the valley differ little from the people of the rest of India and they wear dhotis and turbans. They live in scattered

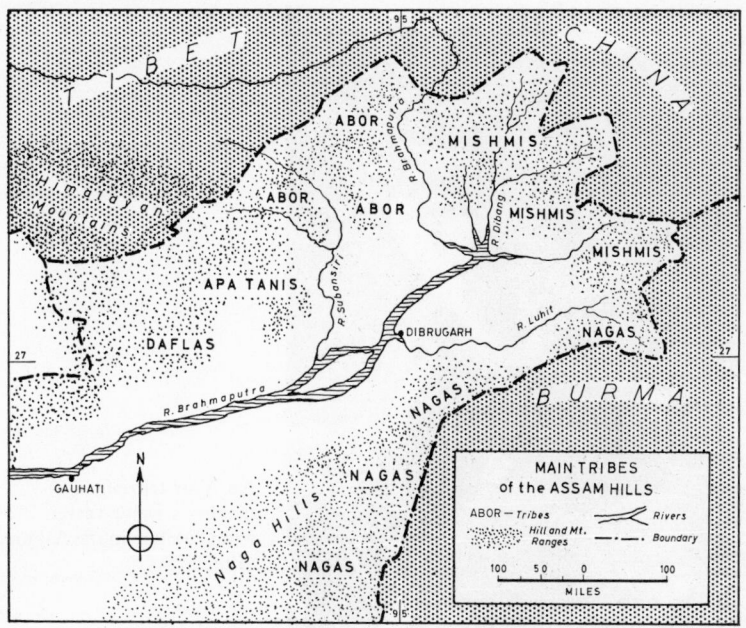

villages of thatched houses away from the river which floods in the monsoon, and grow rice, bananas, mangoes, palms and vegetables in their plots. Many areas once settled have now reverted to jungle because "kalazar", a very deadly malaria, has driven the people away. Making handloom silks is the most common industry in Assam and "eri" (white) and "muga" (yellow) silks find ready markets in the rest of India. Communications with the other states of India are good and cater for tea, Assam's main export, coffee and rubber shipments. Progress is finding a welcome in the valley of Assam. But the people living in the rain-soaked semi-tropical forests of the hills, with elephants, tigers, boars, cobras and pythons for neighbours, are as they were centuries ago.

In this forgotten land, aflame in season with wild roses, azalias, orchids and rhododendrons, Hinduism, Buddhism (mainly on the Tibetan margins) and Christianity, first brought by the American Baptist Mission in 1836, have made many converts, but still the majority of hill tribes are animists, worshipping and fearing nature. For men of commerce the forest hardwoods, especially teak, are

An Abor tribesman
making a water vessel
from bamboo in the Assam
Himalayas

economic assets, for the hillmen these trees, together with stones, rivulets and caves, conceal spirits that have to be placated with sacrifices and rituals.

The hill peoples live in tribal villages, flimsy houses made of bamboo, easily built and rebuilt, that can be disbanded when attacked or when the surrounding land becomes exhausted. For these people the bamboo is the equivalent of our iron, bricks and cement. It is used for building, woven into walls, for making traps, knives, snares, spear-heads and a host of other things. It produces fire when a thong of it is rubbed through a slit in a bamboo board; it is used as cooking vessels, rice being put into a section and dropped on to a fire. The rice does not burn for it is cooked before the fire evaporates the natural sap of the bamboo. Tender bamboo shoots are dried in the summer sun and stored as food for the winter. But the season when the bamboo seeds ripen is an unhappy time for the tribes. Swarms of rats leave their hiding places to eat the falling seeds, and when these are finished they often turn to the village crops. Bamboo is a variety of grass and the king of all is the 80 ft. Giant Bamboo.

Daflas are a tribal group living in the hills to the north of the Brahmaputra. They are warriors who terrorise the more peaceful tribes, especially their neighbours the Apa Tanis, by their aggression, cattle-rustling, raiding, kidnapping and even murder. The men wear heavy homespun tunics covered with body-armour of cane hoops, helmets of woven cane with colourful bird feathers attached, and because they are archers, heavy wrist guards. Their weapons are flat, broad swords brought over the mountains from Tibet by traders, long lances (often 30 ft. long) and bamboo bows with fibre strings that shoot arrows with feather flights and stone or metal heads. Male children are tutored into expert use of the bow by making them practise shooting at logs rolled along the ground. Their few fields, contrasting with those of the Apa Tanis by their neglect and low productivity, are tended by womenfolk and slaves (prisoners from battle or victims of kidnapping). A Daflas counts his wealth by the number of his "mithans", a unique breed of cattle found only in Assam. These mithans are found in all villages of the Assam Hills and are used for eating, sacrifice and often for trading.

In the foothills of the Lohit province, the cul-de-sac of Assam, live the Mishmis, a group of tribes that count their wealth in cattle and wives. They make rare visits to the lowlands to trade their animal skins and musk for salt and rice. The warriors wear coats woven from bark fibre mixed with human hair, which is said to be effective enough to deflect arrows. These coats are made only by men who alone can impart the necessary magic. Their weapons are flat swords, the nobility having two slung across their backs, and long lances. Mishmis take more trouble over raising their opium poppies than they do over growing food. They are all addicted to opium. Their food crops are small and poor, but they will find room for their poppies even if it means sacrificing millet fields. Mishmis will eat almost any flesh including lizards, snakes, frogs and grubs caught beneath stones.

Women cut open the pods of the poppies and wipe off the running juice with a rag. This rag is dropped into a pot of boiling water which is left to evaporate. In the bottom of the pot a yellow deposit is left which, when mixed with strips of tobacco leaves, is

A Naga chief

smoked in bamboo pipes. Among the Mishmis there is a legend of an Abominable Snow-woman who eats men. She has one leg only and is always smoking a pipe. Might she come from the opium dreams?

Nagas, the name being variously interpreted as meaning "hill people" and "naked people", are the most notorious of the hill tribes of Assam. They live in the hills bordering Burma. In the past they were headhunters and it is certain that the practice still lingers in some of the more remote hills. To capture a head meant that the Naga took possession of the victim's strength, soul and magical power. This gory trophy gave the Naga youth prestige in the village and the status of a full warrior. Before he could marry, before he could build a house in the village or till fields or wear the uniform of a warrior (hornbill's feathers, a necklace of boar's tusks and a tail of human hair), he had to return from a raid with a human head. To fail brought lasting shame.

The coming of any calamity, disease or famine was blamed upon a failing stock of village magic. The young warriors were called

The centre of a Naga village

upon to remedy the position by bringing back heads from a raid upon a nearby village. The haul from the raid was buried near the village "hazoa", the sacred stone. Today the drums sound for the headhunting dance in Assam, but only for the benefit of rich tourists.

Because of the widespread practice of headhunting and raiding, each village did its utmost to make strong defences. Naga villages are still built upon hilltops and are surrounded by wide trenches, thorn-bush ramparts or high stone walls. The village gate is a large wooden structure with heads, horns and warriors carved upon it. At either end of the village were, and still are, the "morungs". The morung is the bachelors' house where all unmarried men live a communal, barrack-room life under the charge of an overseer. They form the village army and must be prepared to fight at any time of the day or night—they even sleep with their weapons at their sides. Boys leave their parents to enter the morung at about twelve or thirteen, and for the first three years of their stay there they act as "fags" for the older youths. After this period they take a step up the ladder of seniority and the newcomers "fag" for them (see table in Appendix at end of chapter).

185

There are seven Naga tribes, whose villages are scattered over the hills. Each village is ruled by a council of elders whose mark of authority and prestige is that they have their heads shaved at the sides leaving a ridge of brush-like hair standing in the centre.

Nagas, like all the hill tribes, cultivate jungle clearings with hoes for they have not discovered the technique of ploughing. They keep pigs, poultry and "mithan" cattle, the latter for meat and sacrifice.

The feeding habits of the hill tribes are interesting and entirely controlled by their environment. Take the Abors of the northern hills as an example; their name means "unknown savage". In their jungle clearings they raise millets, rice, pumpkins, vegetables, yams, onions and chillies, and from the forest they collect leaves for vegetables, honey and fruit. Meat is supplied by hunting and trapping. Wild boar, deer, squirrels and other animals are speared or shot with bow and arrow; field rats, often eaten smoked, are caught in traps set in the brush surrounding the village. Fish also forms part of the diet; they are caught in cane traps and often by poisoning streams and collecting the disabled fish floating in the shallow water. The poison, made from juices of jungle plants, does not make the fish unsuitable for human food. Pigs and chicken also roam about the village and are used as food, but eggs are not eaten. They are kept for special ceremonies; for example, they are broken to the ground when making promises or contracts.

The hill tribes boil or roast their foods, but they use no oils of any sort for cooking. A typical meal is boiled rice and green vegetables with boiled or roasted fish or meat. The liquor of the wild tea tree is a favourite drink with the tribes. Much goodness is added to the diet of the hill peoples by millet beer. Each person drinks about a pint per day.

Generally, the diet of the hill peoples of Assam is superior to that of their brothers in other parts of India, but diseases, especially goitre, malaria and T.B., still take their heavy tolls on life.

KASHMIR

Kashmir is a large state, but the area of practical importance is only a fraction of its total; 90% is unusable and uninhabited. The heart of the state is the Vale of Kashmir, 85 miles by 25 miles, and 6,000 ft. above sea-level, through which lazily flows the Jhelum

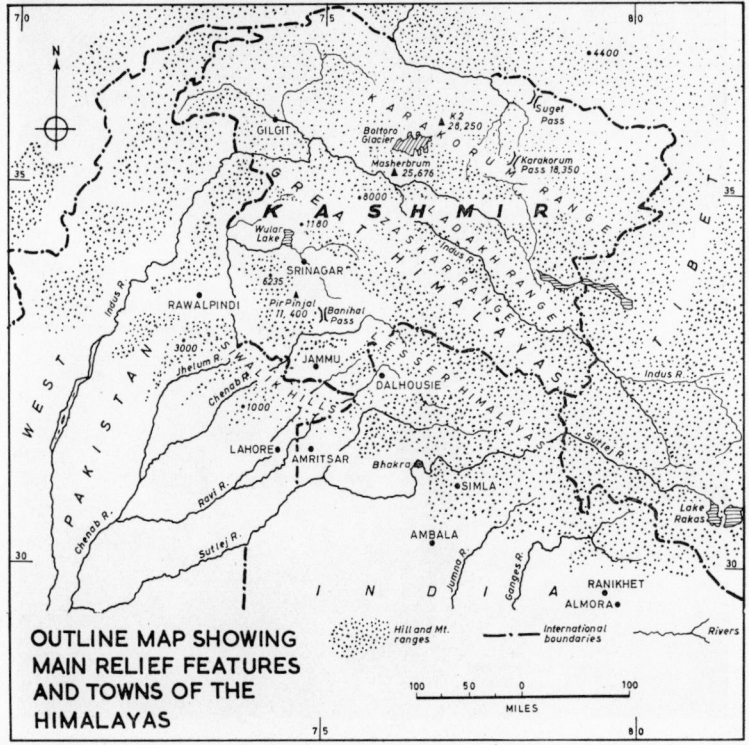

OUTLINE MAP SHOWING
MAIN RELIEF FEATURES
AND TOWNS OF THE
HIMALAYAS

river. Enclosing and surrounding this large and beautiful valley
are the Pir Panjal range in the west and south, and the Great
Himalayas in the north and east.

The Vale of Kashmir is in the south of the state, the northern
and eastern parts being occupied by mountains permanently
covered with snow. The only other inhabited parts are the Gilgit
valley and the Indus gorge to the north of the Vale. Access to the
Vale is through high passes; the Banihal Pass (9,000 ft. above sea-
level) through the Pir Panjal range from India, is snowed up
during the winter months and the road is impassable; the Balakot
Pass leads from Pakistan, and the Karakoram Pass from China in
the north. People usually travel to Kashmir by air, or by the
tunnel which now makes the pass usable in all weathers.

Travellers come down from the Great Himalayas into the Vale of Kashmir. Valleys, like this one at Amarnath, were once the only way into the Vale. In this photograph we are looking northwards into the great, uninhabited wilderness of the Himalayas. The huge rocks were dumped by the retreating glaciers

The Vale of Kashmir is about the size of an English county and is a beautiful land popular with tourists. It has been described poetically as "an emerald set in pearls". In winter it is cold (about 30°F.), but summer temperatures never rise above 75°F., making the climate healthy and bracing. Most rains come from June to September and precipitation in winter is always in the form of snow.

Many lakes fill hollows in the floor of the Vale, the largest being Lake Dal, and besides the Jhelum there are innumerable small

This little Kashmiri boy looks very much at home in his boat on Lake Dal

streams, frothing over their rocky beds, that bring ice-cold waters through minor valleys from the snow-capped mountains that ring the Vale. Kashmir's Vale is a land of trees; in the marshy soils of the Jhelum's flood plain, graceful willows bend their branches to the water; higher up are the walnut trees and farther still, the thick forest belt of birches. Timber is an important export and cricket bats are made from willow logs.

Most Kashmiris are farmers. Near the rivers and larger streams are the ubiquitous paddi fields; on higher levels up the valley sides rice is grown on terraces, but maize is more important; even farther up where neither could survive, a hardy breed of Tibetan barley is raised. Irrigation is necessary for growing rice, and spread over the landscape like a great spider's web is a network of "kuls", channels, leading from streams to the paddi plots. All rice is transplanted from nurseries and the farmer's time after planting is taken up with weeding out grasses that look almost exactly like paddi shoots.

Farmers of the Kulu Valley harvest their grain crop

Other important crops are fruits, vegetables and tobacco. "Demb" lands are used to grow these. This land is reclaimed from the riverine marshes by planting willows and filling in the intervening spaces with branches, weeds, turves and silt. Even more astonishing are the "floating fields" of Kashmir where grow tomatoes, tobacco, melons, cucumbers etc. A flat raft is woven from reeds and on this is piled sods, rotting vegetation and mud. This is then moored at the shallow edge of the lake and is tended just like other fields. Only where land is scarce and labour cheap could this sort of intensive horticulture pay dividends. Besides the fruits of the moored fields, the lakes also give food for humans in the form of lotus roots and delicious water-chestnuts (these taste like small apples).

Kashmir is also famous for her delicious fruits. In the Vale's temperate climate apricots and apples and wine-grapes and walnuts grow well. Minor products are saffron from crocuses (used as a dye for caste marks in India), and opium from poppies. Walnuts are eaten as food, but oil is also extracted from them to be used locally as fuel for wick lamps and for cooking.

A little Kashmiri girl. Note the heavy and ornate metal
ear-rings she wears. The pot she holds is for collecting water

Besides cropping his arable lands, the Kashmir farmer keeps
herds of cattle and flocks of sheep. In the winter these animals live
in a stable which forms the lower level of the farmer's house. The
coldness of winter and lack of pasture because the land is snow-
covered, make this necessary; but it also helps the farmer, for the
warmth of the animals' bodies keeps the living rooms over them
warm, and the accumulated dung is used as manure for the
intensively cultivated fields. Weeds dragged from lakes, dried
willow and iris leaves form the fodder given to the stock.

In summer the farmer hires a professional shepherd to take his
flocks to the rich summer pastures that lie high up the mountainside. This man is usually a hardy hillsman and his characteristic

A Kashmiri shepherd at
rest. The heavy and
coarse blanket thrown
over his shoulder keeps
him warm in the cool
nights on the mountains

garment is a heavy blanket which protects him from the cold of
mountain nights. He takes the animals up through and beyond the
belt of birch forest to the Alpine pastures that lay covered with
snow during the winter. Farther up reign the snow and ice. As
summer wanes and winter approaches, man and sheep turn down-
hill and work to the valley bottom, grazing on patches of grass as
they descend.

The animals provide skins and wool and meat and milk.
Kashmir is noted throughout the Himalayas for its leather goods,
especially belts, straps and harnesses, which are of great importance
here where all transport is by pack animal (see section on Himalayan
trade). But it is the wool from sheep that gives more than a
$\frac{1}{4}$ million Kashmiris opportunity to make goods for sale. Blankets,
rugs, carpets and shawls are produced industrially in Srinagar, the
capital, and in many of the scattered cottages. The heavy, hand-
woven Kashmir carpets compare with the more famous Persian
in quality and design, and the dyes used are made locally from
plants and earth pigments. A unique rug, the "gabha", is made

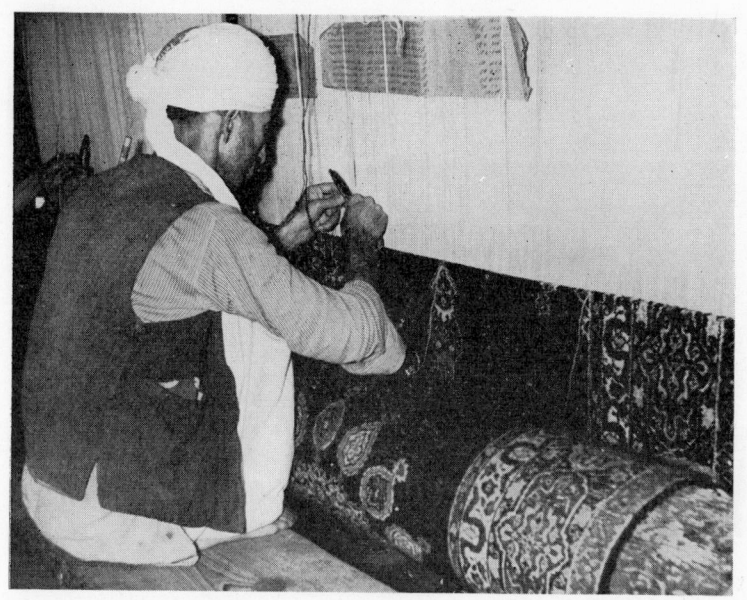

Kashmir is famous for the quality and beauty of its carpets. Here a cottager is hand-weaving a thick-pile wool carpet with the distinctive 'Persian' design

from scraps of wool discarded from carpet manufacturing. It is light and has a felt texture. Gabhas are cheap and attractive with an off-white base and a tasteful floral pattern worked in dark green or brown. It is particularly useful for floor coverings in bedrooms where it will not encounter heavy wear.

Silk making is another craft practised in the Vale of Kashmir. Fine embroidery is also produced—by men only. In workshops in Srinagar, bowls and vases are made from papier-maché composed of waste paper mixed with rice flour. The worked article has designs painted on and is then covered with a clear varnish.

The artistic nature of the Kashmiri is also expressed in wood. Walnut, a wood with rich graining, is the speciality and is carved into figures, boxes and tables. Metal-workers produce by hand silver-coated lampstands, rose bowls, egg-cups, paper-knives, ashtrays and condiment sets, all beautifully engraved with floral designs. Kashmir craft products find ready markets in many parts of the world today.

Wood-carving is a flourishing cottage-industry in Kashmir. The products, like this beautifully fashioned table, find ready buyers the world over

Srinagar, the capital of Kashmir, is a miniature but rather dirty Venice. In the overcrowded old quarter of the town three- and four-storied buildings, made of wood and sporting carved façades and lattices, back on to canals. Along these canals "shikaras" ply, carrying the trade of the city. A "shikara" is a flat-bottomed boat of shallow draught about 50 ft. long and able to carry 30 tons of cargo. Most heavy transportation in Kashmir is by boat. Other smaller boats act as travelling shops and taxis. Kashmir's cool, invigorating climate and her magnificent scenery have made the Vale popular with tourists. Her sports include golf, skiing, hiking and walking, hunting, mountaineering, fishing (the record trout is 14 lb.) and camping.

The Dispute over Kashmir   Upon this land a political bomb exploded when independence came to India and Pakistan in 1947. Both new nations laid claim to Kashmir: India because the rulers of Kashmir were Hindu; Pakistan because most of the people are Muslims (almost 80%). Further, Kashmir is of vital importance

Boat-taxis, called 'shikaras', carrying passengers on Lake Dal, Srinagar. In the background are houseboats

to Pakistan because it holds the key to her irrigation and power projects—the headwaters of the Indus and Jhelum rivers.

Fighting broke out and the Pathans came from their hills to support the Muslim cause. The United Nations arbitrated by declaring a cease-fire line through Kashmir leaving the Vale in India's portion. Whilst both nations are pursuing their aims in the state, the people of Kashmir remain unimpressed, but not unaware of the political troubles their land is causing.

TIGERS AND OTHER ANIMALS

Animal life of this region is as varied as the climate and natural vegetation. In the cold deserts of the Tibetan border are found wild sheep, goats and asses; in the wet, tangled forests of Assam and the eastern foothills live the tiger, buffalo, rhinoceros and fruit-bat; ascending the high mountain peaks the last creatures to be found are the world's most primitive species—spiders.

Near the snow-line in the regions of the Indo-Tibetan frontier live the animals found on all steep mountainsides, sheep, goats and deer. They feed on the high pastures where Arctic hares bound over the springy turf. All have one thing in common—they must be certain of foot and step to prance over the loose rocks and steep slopes. The Blue Sheep, or Bharal, lives amongst the rocks and scree of the mountains. Its blue coat blends perfectly with the grey and bluey-black of the bare rocks amongst which it lives. The long fleece of the Tahr, hanging to well below its knees, does not restrict its agility and this animal never wanders far from the precipices and crags. The clown of the Himalayan goat family is the Serow. It has a head much too large for its body, its legs are thick and short and it has ears that stand erect. Despite its ungainly appearance, it is a very agile beast. Beauty and savagery are matched in the Ounce, or Snow Leopard. This attractive animal lives in the snowy regions and preys upon the sheep and goats mentioned above. The ounce is a very elusive creature and is to be seen only very rarely.

The Himalayan Black Bear reaches a height of 7 ft. and a weight of 400 lb. It has sharp hearing and keen eyesight. Although primarily a vegetarian, it will attack and kill sheep, cattle, goats and dogs, and will maul humans. Despite its great bulk and weight, the black bear will climb trees to collect a favourite food, especially acorns, and one of the warnings given to hunters is never to shoot at a bear in a tree. The farmers of the hills hate and fear this bear. It will uproot and despoil carefully tended crops of maize and millet, ravage fruit trees and kill stock. Where a bear makes itself a particular nuisance, the irate villagers organise a hunt, corner it and beat it to death with heavy clubs.

When attacking a single human the bear always aims its heavy paw-blows at the face and head. Such attacks are fierce and sometimes fatal for the victim. One method of escape practised by the hillmen is to run down a steep slope. As the bear follows in pursuit its long hair falls over its face and eyes and hinders its progress sufficiently for the hunted to escape. But what if there is no convenient slope nearby? Women of the Danpur district defend themselves with great courage and ingenuity. They thrust a forked stick into the mouth of the advancing bear and, whilst it is trying to extract the stick, they hack at its throat with a knife or harvesting sickle.

The Great Indian Rhinoceros, the "tank" of the animal world, was common in parts of India until the last century, but is now

Bear cubs in a zoo at New Delhi

Rhinoceros at Kaziranga Sanctuary, Assam

in danger of becoming extinct. It may not be shot for it is protected by Indian law. It is now confined to the wetter jungle and
grassland areas and game reserves of Nepal and Assam, especially
at Kaziranga Sanctuary in Assam where the rhino population has
been estimated at 250.

The Indian rhino reaches 6 ft. at the shoulder. It looks like a
nightmare relic of pre-history with its skin of armour-plating. Its
horn is smaller than that of the African species. Contrary to
popular belief, this cone of congealed hairs is not used as a weapon.
The rhino fights with its teeth—and, of course, with its great,
speedy bulk.

The tiger is found in all parts of India except the dry western
deserts, but the writings of Major Jim Corbett about his adventures
with man-eaters in the foothills of Kumaun make it a natural
choice for this section of northern India. A male tiger will reach
9 ft. in length and a female 8 ft., but those of the Himalayas are
generally larger than the tigers of southern India.

Tigers live in grassland and forest areas where they can find
water, leafy glades for their daily rest in the shade (rarely can they
stay in one spot for flies bother tigers very much), and food. A
tiger will eat almost any animal, even rotting corpses, and it is

A Royal Bengal Tiger

everyone's enemy, even that of fellow tigers and panthers. Cattle, buffaloes, boar, deer and bears are normal fare, but human flesh is the staple diet of some. The forest and grass also give it cover for its skilful stalking, using its sight and hearing rather than its poor sense of smell. It is the killer *par excellence*, being able to break a bullock's neck with one blow of its great paw, and most of its hunting is done in the still of the night. A tiger will establish its mastery over an area of the forest where it reigns absolutely.

The tigress teaches her cubs to hunt and kill at the age of six months, even to the extent of disabling an animal herself and allowing her cubs to come and make the final kill. Unlike the panther which drags its kill into cover, the tiger carries its prey, and Major Corbett saw a tiger carry a fully grown cow in its mouth for 4 miles. Tigers can climb trees when the need arises and are accomplished swimmers.

Tigers also sometimes become man-eaters. In 1949 a tigress was killed that had eaten 400 people in the Lucknow region. Most man-eaters are females who, having found difficulty in getting food for their cubs, turn on man in desperation. Old tigers with worn claws, broken teeth and less powerful, slower legs, will also take man for food. Wounded or maimed tigers will turn on man, the slowest and feeblest of creatures. Whatever the reason, once having killed man the tiger loses all fear of him and will come and carry him off in broad daylight. Corbett mentions a case where the people of a village stayed in their huts for five days because a man-eater was terrorising the area.

Fear of the tiger has led to a tiger-cult amongst some Indians. Teeth, claws and bones of the tiger are worn as amulets for protection against him. Other parts of his body are used for medicinal cures and charms: his fat will get rid of aches; his whiskers are brewed into poison and love potions; eating his liver will give great strength. At the place where a human has been killed by a tiger the villagers build up a pile of stones which they paint red. Here they pray so that the same fate may not overtake them.

Tiger hunting is a sport filled with hazards. Queen Elizabeth took part in a "beat" hunt in Nepal in 1961. An area of grassland was encircled and "beaten" by an army of men, and as the circle closed the tiger rushed into view to be shot by the hunters seated on elephants. In forest areas a platform is built high up in a tree where the hunters watch for the tiger to come for the bait, a tethered bullock or goat, on the ground below.

The Tourist Traffic Branch of the Indian Ministry of Transport offers the following warnings to tiger hunters. These points give some idea of the dangers accompanying tiger shooting:

(1) If the tiger shows signs of life after being shot, shoot again.
(2) Do not follow a wounded tiger or descend from the machan at night.
(3) Throw stones into all bushes and cover.
(4) Have your rifle always ready and carry plenty of ammunition.
(5) If charged, wait until the tiger is at close range before firing.

EVEREST

At 11.30 a.m. on 29th May 1953 two men scrambled up over the last slippery slopes to stand where no man had set his foot before—the summit of mighty, stubborn Everest—and to gaze down at the shattered peaks of Nuptse and Lhotse below them. They raised a small Union Jack, stood for a moment looking more like spacemen in their Arctic suits, giant's boots and huge mittens, with

An aerial view of the North face of Everest

oxygen cylinders strapped to their backs, and then patted each other with delight at their feat. Their names, Edmund Hillary, a New Zealander, and Tenzing, a Sherpa, were soon to be heard by all the world. They had conquered the highest mountain on earth. The shadows of past Everest climbers applauded with, perhaps, a slight feeling of envy.

Eight attempts to reach the summit, all sponsored by the Alpine Club and the Royal Geographical Society, had been made before 1953. The first (1921) and subsequent parties moved from the Tibetan (northern) approach until Nepal was opened up. Then Eric Shipton's small party made the first exploratory approach from the south in 1951 to pave the way for the successful assault of two years later. A number of climbers, notably Norton (who reached 28,100 ft., the highest pre-1953 level) in 1924 and Smythe in 1933, got within striking distance of the summit by climbing up along the north-east ridge. But all were driven down again from the base of the final pyramid by gales, unfavourable snow conditions and exhaustion.

In 1924 Mallory and Irvine moved up into the mists from their camp at 28,000 ft. on the north-east ridge, to vanish for ever in that cold and angry world. Nine years later Mallory's ice-axe, a pathetic relic of brave men, was found by members of the 1933 Everest Expedition. Did Mallory reach the summit? No one will ever know what happened to him: an ill-considered footstep and a fall of thousands of feet? crashing down into a snow-covered chasm? perishing from exposure or fatigue? buried by a roaring avalanche? The possibilities are too numerous.

If Everest claimed man as its victim, the courage of man eventually defeated Everest. The beginning of the end came after the Second World War when the northern route was closed by Chinese domination over Tibet; but at the same time the southern approach, which was to prove more "possible", was made available when Nepal, until then a secret, forgotten land, opened her window to the world. Further, the 1953 expedition led by Brigadier John (now Sir John) Hunt, was the most carefully planned and best equipped of all expeditions. But what factors had frustrated the superhuman efforts of those who had tilted at Everest for thirty-two years? Those who have been on the mountain declare that its terrain of rocky slopes, ice masses and snowfields is less difficult than that of many of the lower, already-conquered mountains of the world. What then are the hazards that the Everest climber has to face and overcome to give him a sporting chance of success.?

Everest is the highest mountain in the world, and high altitudes have strange effects upon the human mind and body. Experienced climbers have heard music and voices, and one even talked to a person who he believed was walking next to him. On high mountain-tops the air is rarified and this lack of oxygen slows physical movement, mental processes and nervous reactions. At very high points the content of oxygen falls so low that human life is impossible. The critical level appears to be 23,000 ft., above which the body deteriorates rapidly. At very high altitudes climbers find sleep difficult and lose their appetite so that they do not get the rest and nourishment necessary for the strain of mountaineering. And on Everest it is over the last 2,000 ft. that the rock faces are most difficult, and here, because of atmospheric conditions, the climber is least fit for the attempt.

To overcome these effects all Everest expeditions ascend the mountain by stages, staying at each camp long enough for the party to acclimatise itself to the different conditions. Oxygen equipment, too, is a standard item for all attempts on Everest. It was first used by Finch in 1922. But such equipment must be so light that the benefit of a supply of oxygen is not discounted by the extra effort needed to carry heavy cylinders up the mountain on the back. The 1953 expedition supplemented this individual equipment with devices that gave oxygen in the sleeping tents at night thus ensuring deep and refreshing rest, an essential prelude to a day's gigantic effort in ascending the mountain.

Weather conditions also present difficulties. The great cold and high winds (about 80 knots) in winter on the peak have to be met. The soft blanket of snow brought in the monsoon season makes climbing risky and dangerous (hard snow is the best for gripping) and increases the possibility of avalanches. So the only practical time for making an attempt on Everest is during the short period between the end of winter and the start of the monsoon—not long for the vast job in hand! Even at this time temperatures in the high regions are Arctic for there is a fall of 3°F. for every 1,000 ft. rise.

It was with these conditions in mind that much attention was paid to clothing during the planning of the 1953 expedition. From a light and tough cloth which gave protection against winds up to 100 miles an hour, protective clothing was made with hooded Arctic smocks and leggings. This padded suit was proof to – 40°C.

Under these outer garments the climbers wore pullovers and jumpers.

Special climbing shoes had to be made for the final assault; these had a 1 in. layer of kapok lining the uppers, and kid and waterproof layers over the rest of the boot. The soles were made of micro-cellular rubber. Protection for the hands presented a problem. It was not enough to provide bulky gauntlets, for many of the party had delicate jobs to do whilst climbing, taking photographs, scientific measurements etc. Each climber had a pair of silk inner gloves over which was a woollen mitt, and over this again was a glove of windproof cotton. It was possible to remove the bulky outer coverings for brief periods without running the risk of frostbite. All the above articles had to be light as well as warm. For instance, the total weight of the protective clothing per man was only 17 lb., and the high-level climbing boots weighed only 4 lb. 4 oz. per pair despite their great bulk.

The tents carried by the party weighed 15 lb. each. The sleeping bags had two layers of nylon-encased down. Mattresses were of the inflatable type.

Besides all this "personal" equipment, the party carried special primus stoves adapted for high altitude cooking (all water was obtained by melting snow), stocks of food (see note below), ice-axes, sectional ladders, rope ladders, thousands of feet of strong rope, photographic equipment, medical supplies, radios and much more.

All this was carried to the base camp at the foot of Everest by pack-animals, but on the trek up the mountainside the loads, care-fully balanced and apportioned, were carried by Sherpas. These are strong, hardy little men, able to carry very heavy packs for long periods up steep slopes with the agility of mountain goats. Without the assistance of a small army of Sherpas, no Everest expedition would be possible.

Note on Feeding of the 1953 Everest Expedition

The Army supplied special cartons of ready-packed man-day meal units to the 1953 expedition. This saved time when sorting, made distribution easy and avoided the danger of food running out. The meals for Friday were:

Breakfast and Lunch	Main Meal
Oatmeal biscuit	Salmon
Bacon	Peas
Butter	Tinned fruit
Jam	
Marmalade	
Cheese	
Chocolate and Sweets	
Salt and matches.	

CHILDREN'S GAMES

Do you like to race your best friend around the block on your bikes? The youngsters that live in the deep, cool valleys of the Himalayas hold races, but they hurtle down the mountainsides on peculiar toboggans. Their "slide" is not snow or ice, but the thick layer of shiny, slippery, glossy-green pine needles that lie like a blanket on the slopes. Their toboggan is a bundle of the same needles.

Many of these boys tend their father's sheep high up on the bright summer pastures, so it is natural that they should call their game of hide-and-seek "sheep and shepherds". The "shepherd", a boy chosen by lot—or the toady of the gang—has to round up his scattered flock, all the other boys and girls, who have hidden away. And what exciting hides there are in these high valleys: massive piles of round boulders stacked up in bygone ages by green rivers of ice (the "giants" of the Himalayas), deep gulleys, shadowy oak and pine forests and dark, secret, forgotten corners where only the highest midday suns can penetrate. But the "sheep" must take care not to become too isolated, not to wander beyond shouting distance of the village, lest they meet an ill-tempered bear or a hungry tiger—or sit on a bees' nest!

TRANS-HIMALAYA TRADING

Over and through the high and wild passes that straddle the Indo-Tibetan border in the Himalayas, traders drive their herds of sheep and goats laden with goods. Peoples living near the frontier,

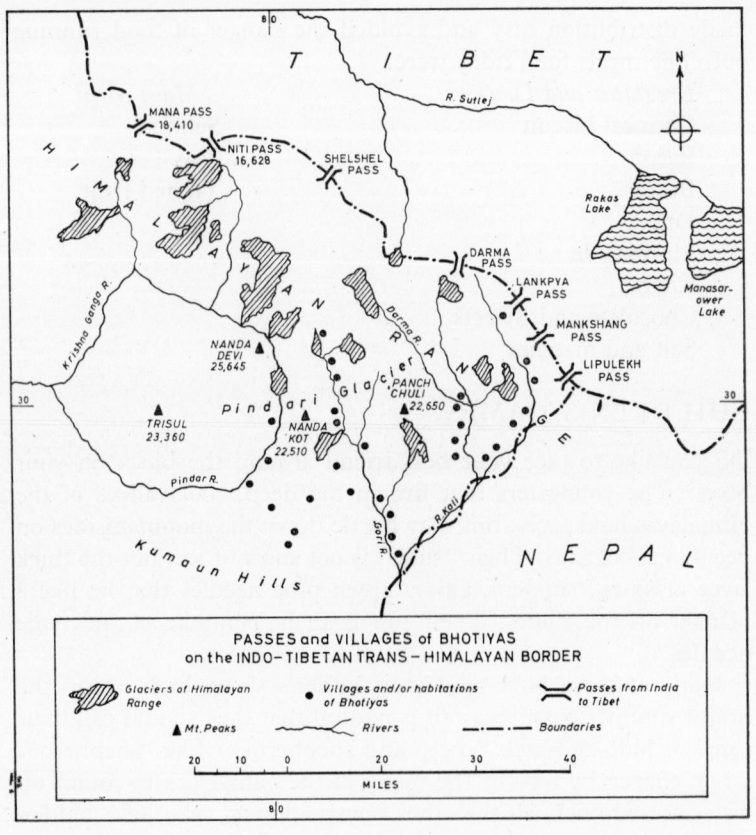

PASSES and VILLAGES of BHOTIYAS
on the INDO-TIBETAN TRANS-HIMALAYAN BORDER

like the Jadhs, Bhotiyas and Zoms, hold a monopoly of this international trade for they alone know the secret trails of this snowbound, dreary world and have beasts capable of carrying loads along them, and they alone have good contacts in Tibet.

Each trader has an agent in a Tibetan town, perhaps two weeks' journey into Tibetan territory, who collects goods ready for when he comes over the mountains in summer. A bond of recognition, usually a stone broken in two, one half being kept by the trader and the other by his agent, is formed between them. The trader brings with him goods and luxuries from the rich towns of the Indian plains which he barters for the Tibetan produce. Rarely does money change hands.

These Jadh traders have just returned from Tibet. Soon they will leave this, their summer home high up the mountains, for it will be snow bound. They go to their winter home lower down

The passes are free from snow and open only from June to October of each year. The caravans coming from India reach the frontier passes in May, but before the traders and their herds of pack animals can cross the border into Tibet they have to wait for the arrival of a Tibetan envoy. He is the representative of the "dzongpen" (local official) through whose territory they will pass. When he comes certain formalities have to be observed and taxes paid—such as sunshine and grazing taxes. The leader of the trading party has to assure the envoy in writing that no man or beast is bringing disease. To support his word he gives the Tibetan a large stone; if any of the traders or their beasts do take disease into Tibet they must pay gold equivalent to the weight of the stone to the Tibetan Government. When the official has given his permission then, and then only, may the herds of sheep, goats and yaks move into Tibet carrying their packs.

The strange animal being milked here is the 'dzo', a cross between a cow and a yak

What do they carry in their packs? In the winter when the passes into Tibet are closed by snow the traders leave their hills for the prosperous towns of the Indian plains. Here they exchange the goods brought from the last visit to Tibet for articles, mostly foodstuffs, which will find buyers in Tibet when they go there in the summer. Cloth, tobacco, sugar, wheat, rice, barley, tea, matches and metal goods form the bulk of exports from India. When they return from Tibet at the end of the summer they take back to the towns of the plains Tibetan goods that are in demand: high-grade wool, drugs, carpets, borax, gold-dust, precious stones, furs, skins and hides, yak tails, salt and ponies.

These Himalayan traders have two homes. Their summer village lies high up the pass very close to the frontier—the closer the better, for it is from here that they make their expeditions into Tibet and it is to this village that they bring goods as to a depot.

Their winter village is lower down the mountains, partly because the severe winters cover the summer home with snow, but also because it, like the frontier village, acts as a trading depot for the Indian side of their business life. The trader's expression for going to the plains is "eating sunshine."

Such is the pattern of life followed by the traders of the Himalayas, but what of the means of transport used by them? Up here the roads are mere wild-goat tracks and trails. Bridges are ropeways slung over the torrent or across the ravine. Paths turn and twist, rise and fall, skirt precipices, hug chasm walls and sometimes disappear under landslides. The bulky bullock carts of the plains are useless along these routes for no form of wheeled transport could get very far. All goods, both for Indo-Tibetan trade and for commerce between local markets, are carried by pack animals or by porters.

Sheep and goats are the cheapest beasts. They move in herds, with saddle bags thrown across their backs, and are led by a herder and protected by a fierce shaggy dog. Such a dog has been known to kill a leopard in defence of the herd. Most of the animals have bells hung round their necks so that the trader can keep a check of their whereabouts, and a herd makes very pleasant music as it goes on its way in the mountains. The caravan moves in the cool of the morning, with breaks for rest and grazing in the shadows during the hot hours.

Tibetan ponies are shaggy and, like the sheep and goats, are very surefooted on the steep and slippery mountainsides. They are not used as pack animals but are reserved mainly for riding. They are not shod, but they too have bells round their necks and the leader wears a red fringe about his forehead as a mark of distinction.

To look at the Yak, a large animal similar to a bullock with a shaggy coat, you would think him a very clumsy animal. He is far from it! His hoofs are as large as the feet of a camel and he can negotiate the most difficult paths with the delicacy of a ballet dancer. He is the most efficient beast of burden in the mountains, with the exception of his cousin the Jibu. Wild yaks live in the high valleys of Tibet. They are caught and sold or bartered to the traders on both sides of the border. One peculiar thing nature has given the yak is a hook-like protruberance on his tongue

Carrying men and kit across this rushing mountain stream calls
for a sure foot and a steady nerve

which enables him to probe the eternal snows of his home country
and pull out the underlying grasses by their roots.

It often happens that whilst two herds of pack animals are
passing each other on a narrow mountain-path, one animal is
pushed over a precipice. By the unwritten laws of the mountains,
the owner can claim compensation from the other trader for his loss.

All these animals, surefooted, confident and brave on the
dangerous paths, carry heavy burdens of trade. But man himself
also helps. The porter, male and female, of the Himalayas is a
strong little human. All he wears is a coarse homespun blanket
draped over his body and fastened with iron pins. His load-basket

("doka") he slings on his back and it is held in place by arm-straps and a band over his forehead. In this 3-ft.-high basket he can carry loads of 60 lb. and more for long treks in the mountains well above 12,000 ft. Sometimes he will even carry a full basket—and a person squatting on top of that! His only personal equipment on a journey is his "tasla", a small iron bowl which he uses for boiling, frying, washing, drinking and as a pillow at night. His "matta" is another essential item. This is a T-shaped stick on which he rests his basket whilst having a "breather". This saves him from taking his load from his back. Often even these tough characters feel the weight of their load. When it begins to drag on their backs they put large stones on top of the basket and trudge on carrying this extra weight. After a while they discard the stones and their original load seems less heavy.

The "ghat-men" have little to do with Indo-Tibetan trade because they operate in the lower Himalayas, but they deserve mention. They are professional swimmers who carry goods and people across rapid streams. To help them and make their work less perilous they float upon inflated goat-skins or buoyant gourds.

FARMING

As height increases so the weather gets colder, the soil thinner and stonier and farming more difficult. In very elevated places where the ground is covered with snow from October to April there is only one crop of hardy plants (wheat, barley, turnips and cabbage) and even this is won only with great human labour. The soil is strewn with boulders so the hoe is the most convenient implement, but the plough is used and is pulled by men, not animals. A man is tied to the plough just like a bullock and he pulls it over the rough and sloping ground with the help of a walking stick. When the crop is ripe it is harvested, in the case of a grain, by the women who use a kind of bamboo scissors to clip the ears of grain from the stalk. The crop is then threshed by beating it with a short plank of wood very similar to a cricket bat.

Most of the sunny, south-facing slopes of the Himalayas are terraced. These terraces rise up the mountainsides like great staircases. Stones are dug from the soil or collected by the women and children from the stream beds in the valley-bottom and the men build these into walls. The ground behind the wall is levelled by shifting the soil in baskets from place to place. A terrace might cover an area of from 60 to 200 sq. yds. and there are often more than 500 terraces in a flight. This whole ladder represents many years of human effort, but the rewards are crops of millet, rice, wheat and chillies.

Animal husbandry is the same in Kashmir, Nepal and Indian Himalayan states. From the wool of the sheep the men spin coarse yarn, whilst weaving is the work of the women. Spinning is done whilst the herdsman is tending his flocks; he spins on a small spindle as he walks.

NEPAL

Nepal, famous for having Mount Everest within its territory (it was shared between Nepal and China by treaty in 1961), is a small kingdom nestling high in the Himalayas. Most Nepalese live in the Vale of Katmandu, thought to be the bed of an ancient lake, where they farm the land. The vale is surrounded by mountains and broken country; a few roads lead into it from India, but only high passes and tracks lead northwards from it over the Himalayas into Tibet.

In the Vale of Katmandu are the large cities of Nepal: Katmandu, Patan and Bhatgaon. In these towns the buildings are most attractive with their rafters and façades of richly carved timber. Here, on the frontier of India and Tibet, the Hindu and Buddhist religions meet and mix. Buddhist stupas* and Hindu temples crowd each other in the cities. But our interest lies not in the cities of Nepal, nor her farmlands, but in two world-famous peoples— the Gurkhas and the Sherpas.

Gurkhas

In the hills of western Nepal there is a village called Gurkha on a tributary of the Trisuli river. It is from this village that the name of the Nepalese royal family and the fighting men of Nepal is taken. When the Rajputs were preparing for their successful assault on

*Monument built to house relics of Buddha or at a place associated with him.

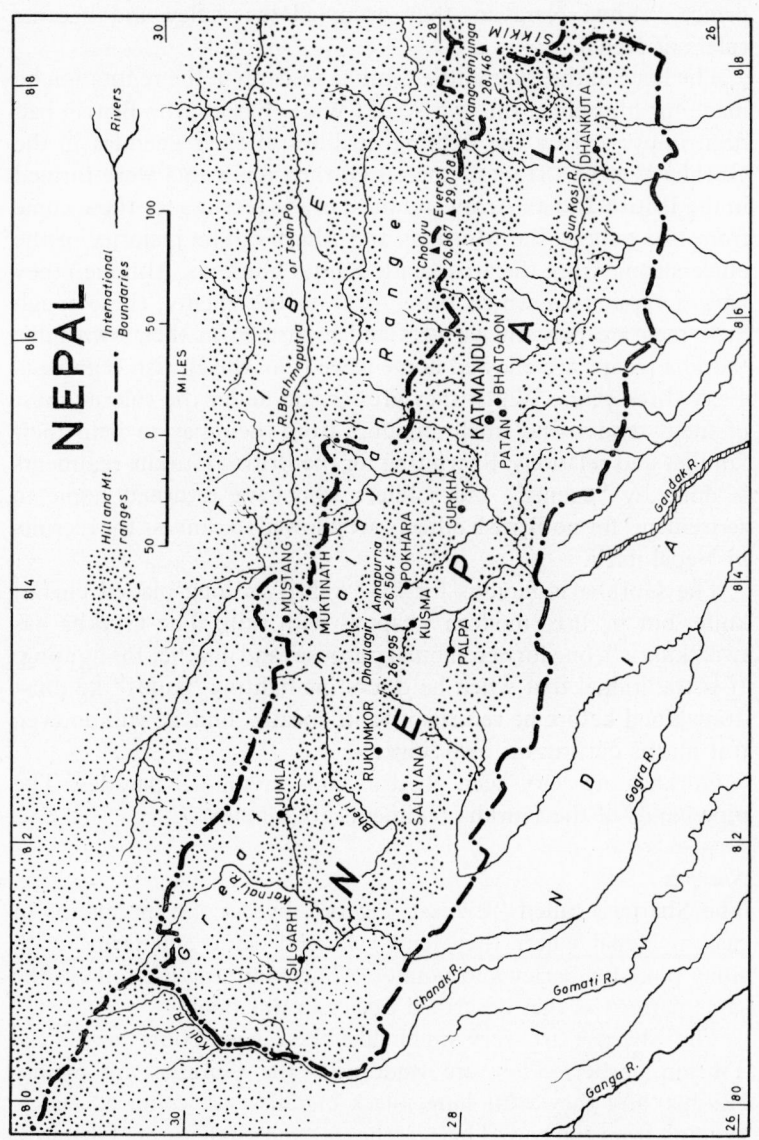

the whole of the Vale of Katmandu they used Gurkha as their base for attack. In 1769, under the leadership of the Gurkha prince Prithwi Narayan, they occupied the valley and became rulers of Nepal.

The fame of the tough little Gurkha rests upon the reputation he made for himself in the two World Wars. Earlier, the British had been impressed by the fighting qualities of their enemies in the Gurkha War of 1814-15. Special Gurkha regiments were formed in the British Indian Army and most of the recruits for these come from two tribes—the Morungs and Magars. The majority of the officers come from the aristocratic Rajput Gurkhas. Although they have a reputation which brings fear to the enemy, these tough little men are peaceful farmers and herdsmen in their own hills. Gurkha troops are allowed home leave from the British regiments every three years. Whilst they are serving under the colours most of them send home small amounts from their pay to help their families and relations. Recruiting for the British Gurkha regiments is done by "agents", old soldiers who have returned home to retirement, for no British officers are allowed to canvass for recruits in Nepal itself.

The Gurkha is famous for his "kukri", a long-bladed curved knife, but he uses modern weapons with skill. The Gurkha has two "kukris", one for ceremonial purposes and another for fighting. It is traditional that when he draws his fighting "kukri" he must draw blood before he returns it to its sheath. This he will do even if it means cutting his own finger.

Gurkhas are very keen on drill and ceremonial parades. The pipe bands of the Gurkha regiments are famous.

Sherpas

The Sherpas, called "Everest Tigers", live in the mountains of eastern Nepal where they tend yaks and cattle and farm small, stony plots for barley and potatoes. Their farming life follows the same pattern as that described earlier in this book.

The Sherpas are very much like their neighbours across the Tibetan border. They are Buddhists (the Gurkhas are mainly Hindus) and they wear long, black pigtails with coloured tassels hanging from the end. Their clothes are the same as the Tibetan's: they have a great coat tied round the waist, long baggy trousers,

The famous Sherpa,
Tenzing

large cloth boots with thick skin soles and colourful designs embroidered on them, and caps with fur flaps to keep their ears warm. Their houses are built of stone with stone roofs and heavy timber doors and windows. Like the hill houses of the Kashmiri shepherds these houses have a lower storey used as a barn and animal stall, and an upper storey where the family live. Access to the upper living space is through the stall and up a ladder. Sherpas, besides looking after the yaks in the stone-wall pens, do much trade with Tibet and the goods are carried over the mountain-passes on the backs of the yaks. But it is not as traders or pastoralists that we know the Sherpas but as the valiant carriers of the many expeditions on the Himalayas.

They are sturdy little men who will convey heavy loads up and over the steepest and most dangerous slopes. The leader of every Everest expedition has paid glowing tribute to them. The Sherpas first made contact with the early explorers of the mountains at

Darjeeling. They went there to find jobs as labourers and rickshaw pullers. Many were employed by the mountaineers, who were so impressed with their skill and endurance in the mountains that the Sherpas gained a great reputation and a monopoly of the porter jobs on the expeditions. Their skill is born of their love and knowledge of the mountains.

Sherpas are a very happy people who enjoy practical jokes. One of the favourite pranks is to put heavy stones into a pack which a friend is going to carry up the mountainside. Sherpa women enjoy many rights among the men that would make Indian women envious. They too act as porters with endurance almost equal to the menfolk, but one of their main tasks is to spin, weave and dye the woollen cloth that keeps out the cutting mountain cold.

APPENDIX

On entering the morung at the age of twelve, the young male Ao Naga has the following stages ahead of him, each lasting for three years, to rise up the tribal social scale.

Group's name	Duties	Privileges
"Unripe gang"	Sleep in morung Fag for elders	None
"Ripening gang"	General village work Carry messages	Waited upon by new Unripe gang. May sleep outside morung. May marry.
"Morung leaders' gang"	Headhunting	Leaders of morung
"Pig's leg eaters"	Headhunting	Given pig's legs to eat at morung feasts.
"Clan leaders"	Villagers of high standing.	Leave morung.
"Load carriers"	Supply men to carry loads at sacrifices	Get share of councillors' meat.
"Councillors"	Organise and rule village affairs.	Get largest share of meat.

When the young Ao Naga enters the morung at twelve, thereby becoming a member of the "Unripe gang", he has a hard life of service, slaving for the older warriors and with little time for play; but he knows that he will, one day far into the future, have the position of "Councillor" and be a ruler of his village.

VII

PAKISTAN

PHYSICAL FEATURES

PAKISTAN is unique in the modern world. The state consists of
two units separated by over 1,000 miles of the Indian Union. The
larger of the two units, West Pakistan, is bordered on the west by
Iran and Afghanistan, and on the east by India. East Pakistan is
surrounded on the west and north by states of the Indian Union
and meets Burma on its south-east boundary.

In almost every way East and West Pakistan are contrasts.
West Pakistan has many deserts and mountainous areas and
has an average population of a little over 100 persons per sq. mile.
East Pakistan, a land of surface water and intensive farming, has an
average population of nearly 700 persons per sq. mile.

East Pakistan (East Bengal)

Nearly 45 million people live on the flat land of East Pakistan,
little of which rises higher than 50 ft. above sea-level. The excep-
tions are Sylhet and the Chittagong Hills where high ridges,
varying in height from 500 to 2,000 ft., alternate with deep valleys.
In the extreme south of East Bengal are the tidal Sundarbans,
tropical forests hiding deer, crocodile and the famous Bengal tiger.

The region is a vast flood plain and delta built up by the Padma
(Ganga), Jamuna (Brahmaputra) and Megha rivers that drain
northern India and the Himalayas. So huge is the river system here
that at Chandpur, 70 miles from the sea, the mingling rivers are
17 miles wide. The southern part of the country is formed by the
still active delta of these rivers, and the agricultural
prosperity of the peasants depends largely upon the renewal of

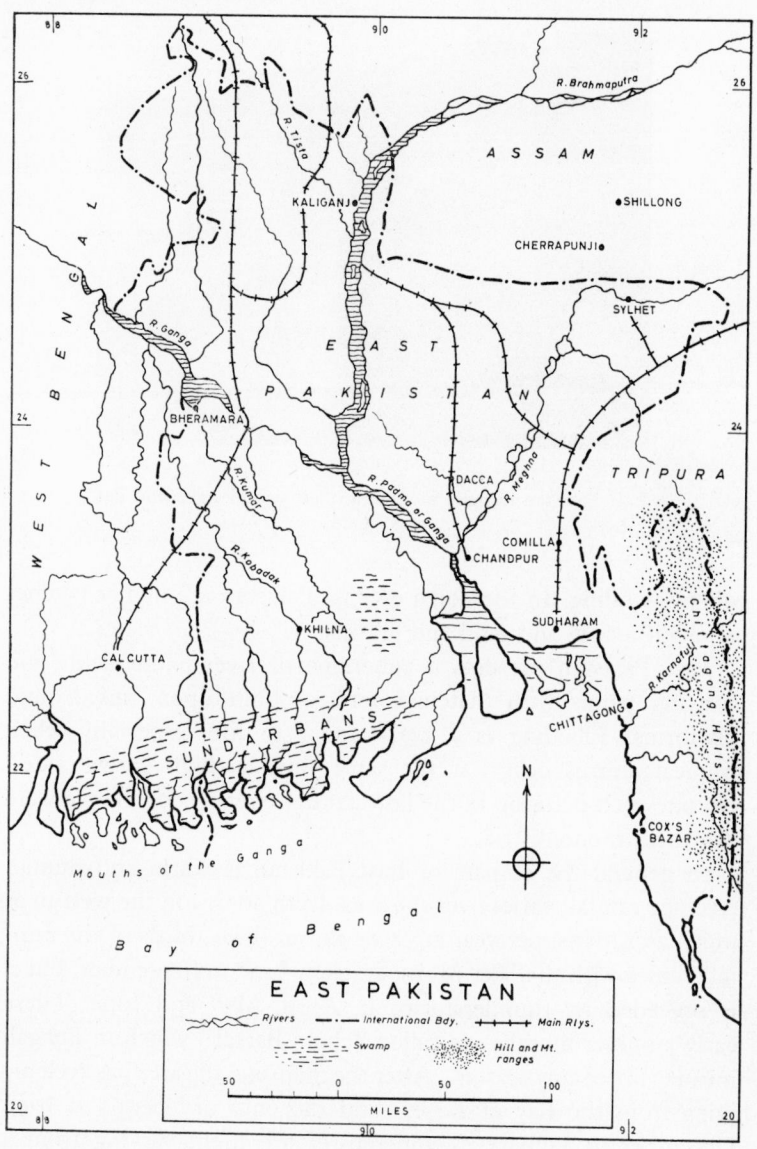

EAST PAKISTAN

Rivers — · — · — International Bdy. ┼┼┼┼ Main Rlys.

Swamp · · · · Hill and Mt. ranges

```
50        0        50       100
```
MILES

East Pakistan farmers ploughing their waterlogged and flat paddi fields

silt by flooding. In the north of East Pakistan are higher patches of old alluvium and sand and gravels.

East Pakistan presents a panorama of rivers, jute fields and swaying palms with thatched cottages built upon raised mud platforms. Flooding is a real danger to life, especially when tropical storms occur at the same time as high spring tides. On one such occasion in the last century over 74,000 people were drowned in one district.

In general the climate of East Pakistan is warm and humid. Average rainfall varies over the area, from 50 ins. in the west to as much as 140 ins. per year at Cox's Bazar. Two-thirds of the rainfall comes with the Wet Monsoon from June to September, but it is preceded by thunderstorms in April, May and June. These early summer months are called "chota Barsat" which in Bengali means "little rainy season". After the monsoon the area has cyclonic rains from the Bay of Bengal and the only dry period is from December to January. Temperatures are high, varying from a mean average of 75°F. in the north to 79°F. in the south. January, besides being a dry month, is also the coldest although the annual range of temperature for East Pakistan is under 20°F. High temperatures and heavy rainfall give a humidity of never less than 70.

West Pakistan

Two distinct regions make up the state of West Pakistan. On the borders to the west and north are the high and mountainous regions of Baluchistan and the North-West Frontier Province. Forming the heartland to the east is the vast, flat plain of the Indus and its tributaries. The highland of the Baluchistan plateau, clearly marked off from the Indus valley by the sharp Kirthar range and the Hindu Kush mountains, was raised up when the sedimentary rocks, formed at the bottom of the sea, mainly limestone and sandstones, were buckled and folded by pressures from the west. The hills, separated by more fertile and sheltered valleys, have a northwest-southeast trend, and communications through the North-West Frontier are possible only along deep valleys and gorges such as the Khyber Pass. The mountain-slopes of the North-West Frontier are densely forested and villages nestle down in the valleys. Baluchistan is an eastward extension of the Iranian plateau and presents a dreary landscape. There are fertile rock basins, but most of the plateau is a barren, wind-eroded surface with sand-drifts, salt ranges and deep gullies that have been carved out by the infrequent rains. Unlike the North-West Frontier, much of the region is bare rock with desert vegetation in some areas.

The peoples of these marginal lands are hardy, tough and independent tribesmen who, in recent history, terrorised the settled people of the plains.

Over geological ages the Indus has built up a vast plain almost 3,000 ft. thick by flooding and depositing material eroded and transported from the Himalayas. The Punjab, meaning "Land of the Five Rivers" (Indus, Jhelum, Chenab, Ravi and Sutlej) is a broad plain of old alluvium which they water.

Sind, the area adjoining the coast between the Thar Desert in the east and the Kirthar range on the west of the Indus river, is the land of the Indus delta. It is built of new alluvium and is still subject to flooding except where man-made canals drain off excess waters. Only where irrigation has been introduced are

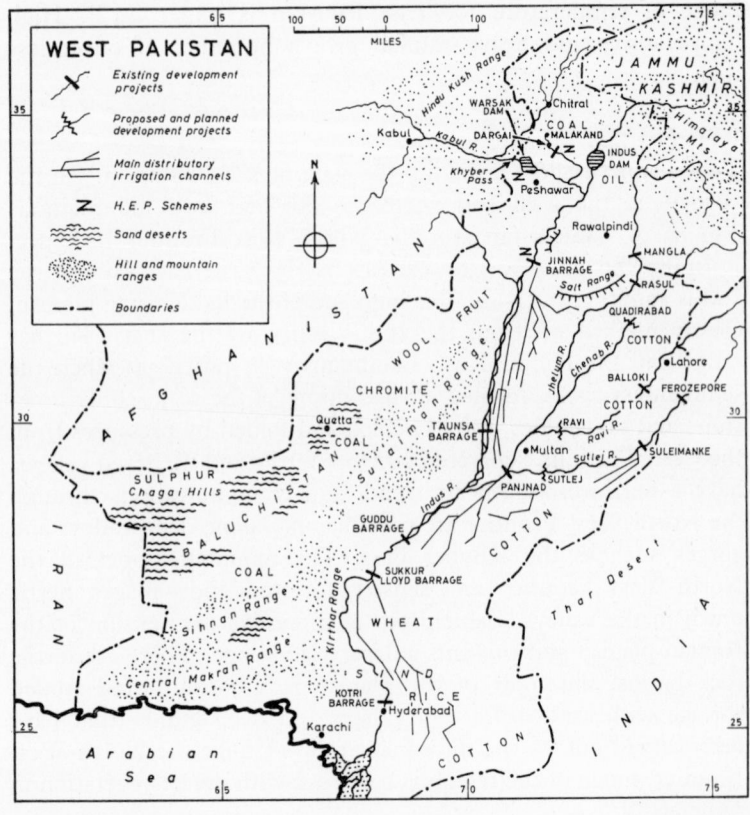

agriculture and settlement possible. Eastern Sind peters out into the sand of the Thar Desert.

West Pakistan is a land of scanty rainfall, hot summers and cold winters. Most of the year's rain comes during the monsoon period, 15th June to 15th September, and averages 16 ins. on the plains and 60 ins. over the hills.

Baluchistan is an arid land for the rainfall is slight and erratic, for instance, Quetta, the capital, has only 10 ins. per annum. When it does come the rain falls in heavy, sharp downpours that flood the dry courses that are like the Sahara wadis. Summer temperatures are very high and scorching winds, heavy with dust from the Iranian desert, sweep from the west. In winter these winds

A West Pakistan farmer ploughing his land by the centuries-old method. His plough is merely a heavy bent stick or branch. Compare this photograph with that of the farmer ploughing in East Pakistan

are freezing cold. Except in the valleys in spring, only thorn scrub and semi-desert vegetation can survive this climate. In the North-West Frontier Province climate varies with height. Most of the rain falls in winter although the Summer Monsoon does influence the southern margins of the region. Again, there is a wide range in temperatures. Chitral, situated in a valley bottom, has known temperatures as low as 5.4°F. and as high as 108°F.

In Sind the pattern of heat and aridity applies again. Temperatures of 100°F. have been experienced at midnight at Shikapur. A local Sindi proverb runs: "O Allah, having created Sewistan,* why bother to conceive of Hell?" Rainfall is irregular and scanty, varying from 5 ins. in upper Sind to 10 ins. in the southerly parts. It comes in violent torrents that overflow the dry river-beds. Karachi, the capital city of Pakistan, has received 12 ins. in twenty-four hours. Except for irrigated farmlands and forest near the Indus banks, thorn scrub is the common vegetation. Most of the great Punjab plains get from 10 to 15 ins. of rain per annum, but

*SEWISTAN: a district of Sind.

223

The marble domes of the famous Badshahi Mosque at
Lahore. It was built during the seventeenth century
and is the largest mosque in the world

the mountain foothills have up to 30 ins. Great varieties of temperature are the rule and Lahore has temperatures in the low
fifties in winter and the middle nineties in the summer. Dust
storms and heavy showers are common.

THE PEOPLE

Political separation from the Indian Empire in 1947 created the
largest Muslim state in the world, Pakistan. Minority groups of
Hindus, Christians and Buddhists are respected, but more than
85 % of Pakistan's people are devout Muslims and every town and
village has its mosque, some being humble but clean and colourful
buildings, others among the most beautiful places of worship in
the world. It is from the mosque tower that the "mullah" calls the
faithful to morning and evening prayers.

A man from the arid Sind

The majority of Pakistanis belong either to the Aryan racial group (in West Pakistan), or the Mongolian (East Pakistan), but here unity ends for each district enjoys its own traditions, customs and dialect. The two main languages are Bengali in East Pakistan and Urdu in West Pakistan. Urdu, the official state language, was brought by the Moguls who invaded northern India in medieval times. English is still widely used in official circles, commerce and education.

The Sindi and Punjabi wear clothing that affords protection from the climate. They will have either a wool cap or a "pugri" on their head. The pugri is a strip of cloth 6 to 7 ft. long wound round the head in the form of a turban. Their cotton shirt will hang outside their baggy cotton pyjama-type trousers. In winter they will drape heavy, greasy, camel-wool blankets about their

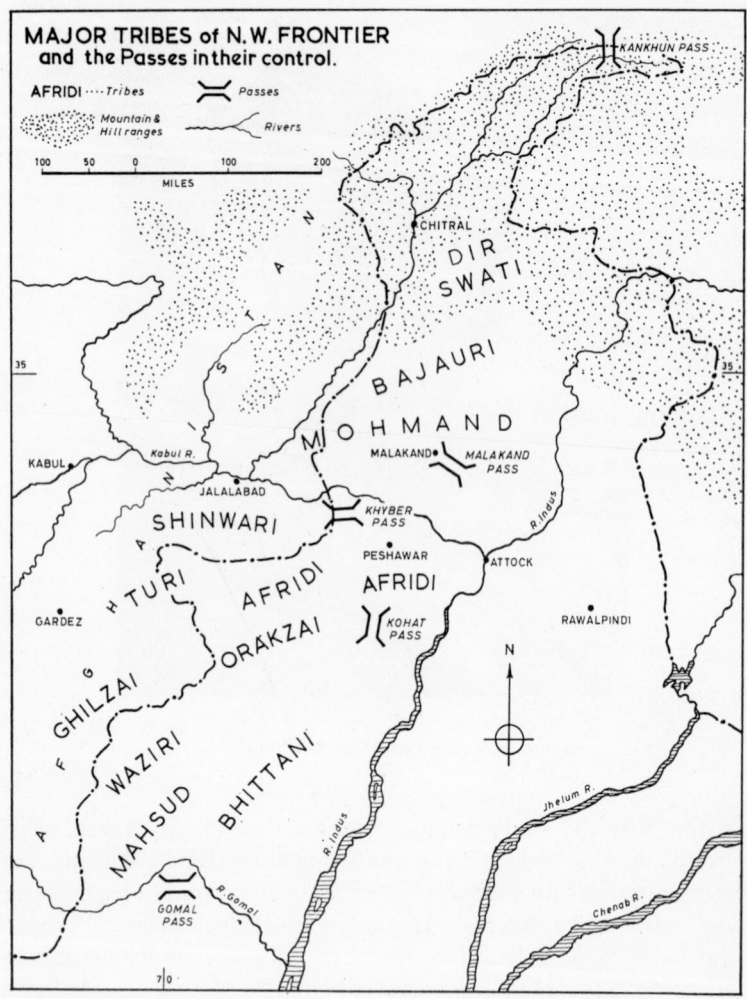

MAJOR TRIBES of N.W. FRONTIER and the Passes in their control.

AFRIDI ···· Tribes
Passes
Mountain & Hill ranges
Rivers

100 50 0   100   200
MILES

chests and backs to keep out the cold winds. Because the climate he lives in is hot and humid, the Bengali wears a single loincloth tucked in at the waist and no shirt or upper garment.

The waves of invaders coming from Asia and the Middle East have each contributed to the complex culture and society of Pakistan. A full description of her people is, therefore, impossible, but mention can be made of some interesting groups.

A bird's eye view of the historic Khyber Pass showing the zig-zag road twisting through narrow, rocky passages

West Pakistan

The Powindas of Afghanistan are tribes that make annual visits to Pakistan whose government shows great consideration in allowing these people to continue their ancient migrations without passports and frontier inspections. They come to escape the cold Afghanistan winters and spend from November to April on the warmer plains. The long camel trains begin to arrive in October bringing sheep to pasture, donkeys, geese, tents, "charpoys" (beds) and goods—blankets, carpets and coats—for sale. As May approaches the Powindas drift home, for summer on the plains is too hot for them; they take with them their purchases: wheat, sugar, flour and matches.

More notorious than their West Pakistan brothers are the Pathan tribes, the proud, brave warriors who live among the hills, valleys and ravines of the North-West Frontier Province. The Pathans are herdsmen who graze their sheep and goats on the barren hills that support only a few edible plants and roots amid the thorn bushes and cacti. Some fruits, especially peaches and

227

A noble Pathan from Chitral. He is holding his hunting
hawk

walnuts, and crops of wheat, sugar-cane and potatoes are grown
on irrigated plots in valley bottoms. Near to the fields are the Pathan
villages, walled for defence and with high watch towers. Life in
such a harsh and challenging environment has made the Pathan
lean, hardy and independent.

Pathan is the group name for all the tribes who have their
origins in Afghanistan, among whom are the Afridis who held in
their territory the gateways to India, the Khyber and Kohat
passes. All tribes speak dialects of Pushtu and are fanatical
Muslims. Each tribe is split into clans under their own chiefs, and
each clan into families, but a man's first loyalty is to himself. The
rule of the tribe is democratic as decisions are taken at the tribal
assembly where each adult male has an equal say in debate.

There is a saying that peace comes to the tribes only in war time. This apparent contradiction is explained by the fact that all tribes and clans are divided by feuds and vendettas. Any insult to the family must be paid for in blood. Any unpaid debt of honour, a burden which is passed from father to son, brings contempt upon the head of the family. These age-old quarrels are forgotten only when some outside danger threatens the Pathans' beloved liberty or religion.

As an enemy the Pathan is cruel and ruthless, as a friend he is gracious and generous. He will kill his last sheep and bake his last flour for a guest, and will feel that he himself, his family and his hospitality have been insulted if his guest refuses.

Pathan dress is simple and suited to the climate. They wear shirts and loose, baggy trousers tied at the ankles; above this are a waistcoat and shawl.

Favourite sports of these hill peoples are shooting (for they are great marksmen), hunting and hawking, and putting trained fighting rams against each other. Folk-dancing and singing also help to occupy the Pathan's leisure, with flutes, drums and bagpipes providing the music.

Pathans are courageous and skilful fighters. Britain was at war with the tribes from 1849–88, from 1897–98 and as recently as 1937–43. These wars were merely a series of expeditions sent from British India to ferret out the tribes from their hills. All had one thing in common—they failed, owing to the supreme ability of the Pathan to use his hills for guerrilla warfare.

The Pathan cares for his rifle like a brother and he will never be without his bandolier of ammunition even when watching his sheep. His old-style rifle was the "jezail", a flint-lock with a very long and ornately carved and inlaid barrel. He now has modern rifles and even automatic weapons. Many of the weapons are made in village workshops of the Adam Kitel clan of the Afridis by copying rifles stolen from the British. Often the Pathan would join the British forces on the frontier to get his hands on a modern rifle and then desert back to his hills. These village-made weapons are exact copies down to the smallest detail, and considering the lack of precision tools in this remote part of the world, these feats of skill are to be marvelled at.

East Pakistan

Inhabiting the dense tropical forests of the Chittagong Hills in East Pakistan are a number of tribes related to the Burmese. They have mongoloid features and, unlike the mass of Pakistanis, they are Buddhists. All of the ten tribal dialects are closely akin to the Burmese language.

The largest of the tribes is the Mogh. The name was given by the English as a corruption of "mug", a term of derision for they were pirates in the eighteenth century.

Moghs, in common with most of the Chittagong hill tribes, are "jumyas". This name refers to their method of cultivating "jums" which are clearings burned from the jungle. The steep hill slopes make normal plough-farming impossible, so the Moghs burn the soil as preparation for cropping. With his long-bladed knife, used also for digging and building, the head of the family fells the vegetation over an area large enough to provide crops to feed his family. This clearing of the jungle is done at the beginning of the year so that during February and March the sun can shrivel the leaves and twigs. In early April this dry, dead vegetation is burned leaving ashes on the soil as fertiliser. Rarely is this clearing a difficult task for, after bearing a harvest, jums are left fallow for at least three and often ten years to prevent soil exhaustion. There are, therefore, many old jums covered with low brush that can be used anew.

In late May paddi, mustard, cotton and cucumber seeds are mixed together in a large wicker basket. Using the utility dao as a dibber, women make holes in the soil and place a few of the mixed seeds in each. The coming of the rains in June heralds the start of intensive vigilance in keeping the jum clear of weeds that grow very quickly. July and August are tiresome months for the adult Moghs. They leave their homes in the village to live in a bamboo and thatch hut at the jum where the work of weeding takes all their time and attention. The watch huts are built upon stilts to give protection from wild animals, especially the tiger. Spiced fish, rice and bamboo shoots collected from the jungle are the only foods of the workers at this time.

The weeks spent at the jum are lonely for the father and mother, for the children have to be left behind in the village in the care of the old folk as the parents can spare no time to attend to them. Their only neighbours are those who are tending jums in nearby areas. On occasion, communal sacrifices for the success of the harvest will bring them together. For long periods communication is limited to shouting news across the jungle at night. This also helps to keep wild animals at bay. At harvest-time neighbours help one another and the Moghs are in a gay mood and dance and sing. Back at the village a "new rice" ceremony is held when all the household, including any servants, eat a meal made from the fruits of the harvest.

Winter is the time when the family is together. The men repair the houses, make baskets from split bamboo and gather indoors smoking home-rolled cigars and chewing betel-nut. Women do the household chores and spin and weave the cotton crop into clothing. But these tasks are light and the family is united and happy.

Mogh children are much affected by the twofold life of their parents. In winter they have the love and protection of the adults, but when the adults are at the jum they are left to their own devices in the care of older brothers and sisters. The mother hangs an amulet about her child's neck before she leaves to ward off illness and animals whilst she is away. This long period of separation makes the children independent and brings them to an early maturity. While quite young they have all the forest lore and practical skills of the adults, and they adopt the habit of smoking cigars from as early as four years. Only the old and maimed adults are in the village in summer and the children play with their parents' hookah, a bamboo tube pipe filled with water with a bowl attached containing mixed tobacco and molasses.

Mogh children have improvised a number of games to entertain themselves during the lonely weeks. "Konyon" is a game in which the pods of a giant bean are used as discs. Two teams of players have to hit the pods of their opponents by throwing their discs at them. "Gyang" is a top game where the players have to stop their opponents' tops by spinning their own at them. Another favourite pastime is enticing insects to fight in a small trench.

Older Mogh children attend boarding schools at the nearest Buddhist monastery. Here they are taught Burmese writing and Buddhist prayers and general subjects like arithmetic. For any misbehaviour the monks write unkind words and names in soot on

Pakistan women love their jewellery. Here are fine examples of favourite
heavy bracelets

the pupil's shaven head or make him carry heavy stones on his
head. Only larger villages can afford to have a monastery, for the
people of the village have to keep the monks in food, so children
of the smaller outlying villages often have to walk many miles to
get to their boarding school. Monastery schools are for boys only.
Girls get little education for they are too helpful in the home to be
allowed to spend time in learning. Girls of the poor are sent as
servants in the larger homes and are often adopted by the family
they serve.

THE EAST PAKISTAN VILLAGE

The delta region of East Pakistan is a densely populated land ($\frac{1}{2}$ acre
of cultivated land per person) where settlement and the siting of
villages are determined by one dominant factor—water. It is a
land of rivers, lakes, islands, jute fields and trees. Each year, from
June to October, the mighty rivers of north India bring floods that
leave swamps and lakes on the land throughout the ensuing months.
No village in East Pakistan is more than a mile from water of
some kind.

In a sense there is no village, for houses can be built only upon
land which stands above the normal annual flood level. During
the season of inundation the small groups of houses stand upon

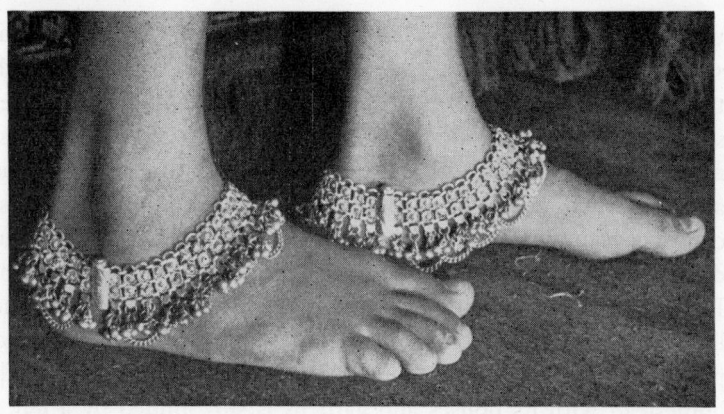

Pazeh or anklets

tree-fringed islands separated by swollen rivers and streams; in the dry season they are separated by mud and sand coursed by shrunken streams. But in some years contrary nature plays a sly trick upon the Bengali and in 1954-5 the flood-waters reached 45 ft. Much damage was caused to crops and livestock, and many villagers only saved their lives by sitting upon wooden platforms built above the floors of their houses.

Many of the smaller ponds and lakes have been deepened by man. For centuries the peasant has dug soil from the depressions and dumped it on to higher land; this process has lifted the level of his crops higher above the floods and has given the soil a yearly renewal of fertility. He has, by moving the soil, made a series of terraces about his raised home that have special significance for his farming. The highest land platform is untouched by all but the most severe floods and it is here, therefore, that he builds his house.

The Bengali house accommodates the undivided family and is often built in the form of a rectangle about a central courtyard. But even the poorest have a number of buildings for sleeping, cooking, and living. Those that own cattle have in addition a rough kadjan shed for their beasts. All houses stand upon mud platforms and have floors of hard-packed earth. Roofs have to be high-pitched and steep to allow the heavy rainfall to run off easily. Materials used in the construction of the house vary from the traditional split-bamboo or reed woven walls and palmyra palm leaf thatch to the still infrequent cement and corrugated iron. Every homestead is surrounded by trees that supply fruits, coconuts, bananas, mango, guava and papaya, and give shade from the sun. There is also a garden patch where the farmer raises ginger, brinjals, cabbage, cauliflower, chillies and potatoes which he sells to dealers in large urban areas like Dacca, the capital of East Pakistan. In the dry season (winter) these crops have to be irrigated by the laborious method of carrying pitchers of water from the doabs and pouring them on to the soil via corrugated iron sluices. Each homestead with its houses and gardens is surrounded by a fence or hedge.

The peasant's main item of diet, paddi (rice), is grown on the next highest terrace, "bhoret". "Jaula", the lowest of all the terraces immediately next to the doab, is the least useful as it is too marshy for crops and merely supplies rough grazing for the farmer's few cattle—and buffalo if he is rich enough. The two great cash crops of Bengal are grown on the "nal" terrace. Double cropping, first potatoes (sown in October after the floods have subsided, and dug in January), and then the commercially omnipotent jute (sown in March and cropped, often from boats riding the flood waters, in July), ensures that the peasant gets maximum value from this terrace.

Clever combining of crops is a feature of the intensive farming of East Bengal. An example is the growing of potatoes and tobacco in the same field. The livestock will not eat the tobacco leaves which therefore protect the potato plants.

The value of land varies with its height above the water. The highest land is the most expensive to buy and the cheapest is that which lies nearest to water-level. Within paddling distance of the scattered homes are the amenities necessary for communal life. These also are found on high land and usually include shops, a post office and the only local brick buildings, the school and mosque.

Such is the Bengali peasant's environment. Let us take a look at the daily routine on his little plot of land which would rarely exceed 5 acres. After praying at sunrise in answer to the call of the mullah from the mosque tower, he attends to the feeding and milking of his poor cattle before he himself has his meagre break-fast of boiled rice. The rest of the morning is spent grazing his cattle, after which he returns home to a bathe and a mid-day meal of boiled rice, vegetables and fish. In the afternoon he labours in his rice or jute fields or the vegetable plot with plough, spade, sickle, harrow or "mugri" (an implement for breaking up hard soil), according to the time of the year and the state of his crops. If it is husking time for the rice crop then he will pool his animals and tools and work in co-operation with his neighbours. When it is his turn to have his rice husked, he will borrow the bullocks, tie them in a line to a stake in the middle of the treading floor where he has laid his crop, and supervise the animals as they walk round and round treading the grain with their hooves.

The peasant's wife attends to the children, of which there are many, cooking three meals of rice a day and doing general house-hold chores. If her husband cannot borrow oxen from neighbours she may have to husk the rice by trampling it with her feet. Much of her time is taken in fetching and carrying water from the nearest doab or well. This water is very muddy and salty and is usually polluted for when she goes for water she washes the clothes, herself and the children before she draws water for drinking. The doabs are essential to life in Bengal for they yield water for irri-gation and domestic use, fish, mud, clay and water-hyacinth which is used as cattle-fodder when fresh and fuel when dried.

A WEST PAKISTAN VILLAGE

The Sindi and Punjabi, like their East Pakistan brothers, are primarily farmers and live in villages. These are either of tightly packed houses centred upon a well or are strung along irrigation channels. The West Pakistan village is self-sufficient in food and everyday needs are provided by artisans, blacksmiths, potters, carpenters, open-air barbers and tailors and the letter-writer. It has its own ruling council of elders. Some villages, like the planned, Government-sponsored colonies, are recent; others are so ancient that the village stands above the level of the land on the ruins of its predecessors. Surrounding the village are the fields and beyond them the edge of the barren land, where there is no irrigation and only goats may find food such as the roots of dry scrub.

235

A modern village in the Thal area

Local materials are used in the construction of houses—mud, stone or reed-thatch according to the climate and geology. Mud is the most common for it is cheap, stands up well to the hot, dry climate and keeps rooms cool in summer and warm in winter. In the semi-desert areas where the soil is sandy, mud will crumble easily so rough stone blocks or thatch are used for walls. When the Indus floods the flat land each year the water washes away the lower portion of the walls and women and children have the job of fetching mud from pits and repairing the damage.

Each peasant home has two units, a single storey mud house and an open yard surrounded by a high mud wall cutting the dwelling off from the lanes. The house is square with a flat mud roof supported by wooden beams or a layer of thatch. On this roof the farmer may keep his cattle fodder or he may sleep there on hot nights. The house may have one or more rooms according to the wealth of the owner, but all have small windows and only one door leading in from a verandah of thatch roofing supported by wood posts. The one door makes it easier to keep out thieves and hot summer winds. The West Pakistan peasant's house bears a marked resemblance to those of Jordan and Israel.

The walled yard is very important to the farmer for he likes his privacy. Here he keeps his farming tools, a heavy wooden plough

A family resettled in the Thal. In the background are the new living quarters.
Cattle and seed are supplied by the Government under special loans

("desi") which has changed little since the Aryans brought it 5,000
years ago, hoes, spades, his country bullock-cart, fodder and the
cattle, sheep and a camel. Fodder is all-important in West Pakistan
for farming land is so scarce that cattle cannot be allowed to
wander freely, so they have to be stall-fed. Besides being a barn
and a stable, the yard also contains the mud-brick hearth where
wheat is baked and large mud bins where it is stored.

Like the Bengali, the West Pakistani starts off for his fields very
early in the morning after saying his prayers. Much of his day will
be spent in supervising the bullock- or camel-driven "Persian
wheel" which raises irrigation water on to his fields. His plots of
land will amount to a very small holding, usually not more than
an acre of irrigated land, unless he share-crops with the rest of the
village and just has enough to support his family. By Muslim law
land passes from a father to his sons and over the centuries this
has led to subdivision of farming lands into smaller and
smaller plots. The Pakistan Government is easing the land problem by making it unlawful for one person to own more than 500

237

acres of irrigated land. This law should bring more land to the small, land-starved peasants.

The Pakistani's farming techniques are traditional and poor for he has not the education or money to improve them. When he ploughs, his camel or bullock enables the plough merely to scratch the ground. The farmer's main crop is cool-season wheat which he grows on irrigated land and the best of his dry land. It is harvested with a hand sickle. His irrigated plots will also give him crops of rice, a very minor item of diet in West Pakistan, vegetables and sugar-cane. His cattle give him milk and butter, his goats milk, his long-eared sheep wool for making cloth and blankets, and his camel is a pack animal. He labours in the fields by day and takes his rest for meals, for worship and, in the evenings, talking to his neighbours over a "hookah" (pipe).

In the more remote villages his wife will be forced to observe strict "purdah" (isolation) in the house or yard out of sight. Her jobs are cooking the curries and "chapatties" (unleavened pancakes), looking after the children, washing the clothes by pounding them on flat stones at the village well (when she goes out for this she must wear the "yashmak" or veil across her face) and preparing fuel for the oven by mixing cakes of cow-dung and grass and drying them in the sun. Because she has to spend much of her time indoors, she is more liable to attack from diseases like cholera and T.B. than is her husband.

The smallness of his land holding often means that the peasant will have time to spare at certain seasons. During the slack periods he will often turn his hand to making craft goods from local materials as an extra source of income. Date-palm leaves are made into baskets, matting and ropes; camel skin is pounded into a type of papier-maché and then moulded into vases, bowls or opaque lampshades; oilskins and bedding are also made from the skin of the camel; in areas where wood is plentiful he will carve furniture; blue, green and pink glazed pottery in the Persian style is made at Multan; dye-embossed silver and copperware are other favourite cottage industry products.

THE AGRICULTURAL BASIS

In Pakistan most of the people are engaged in raising food crops. Irrigated West Pakistan is the great granary where wheat is the

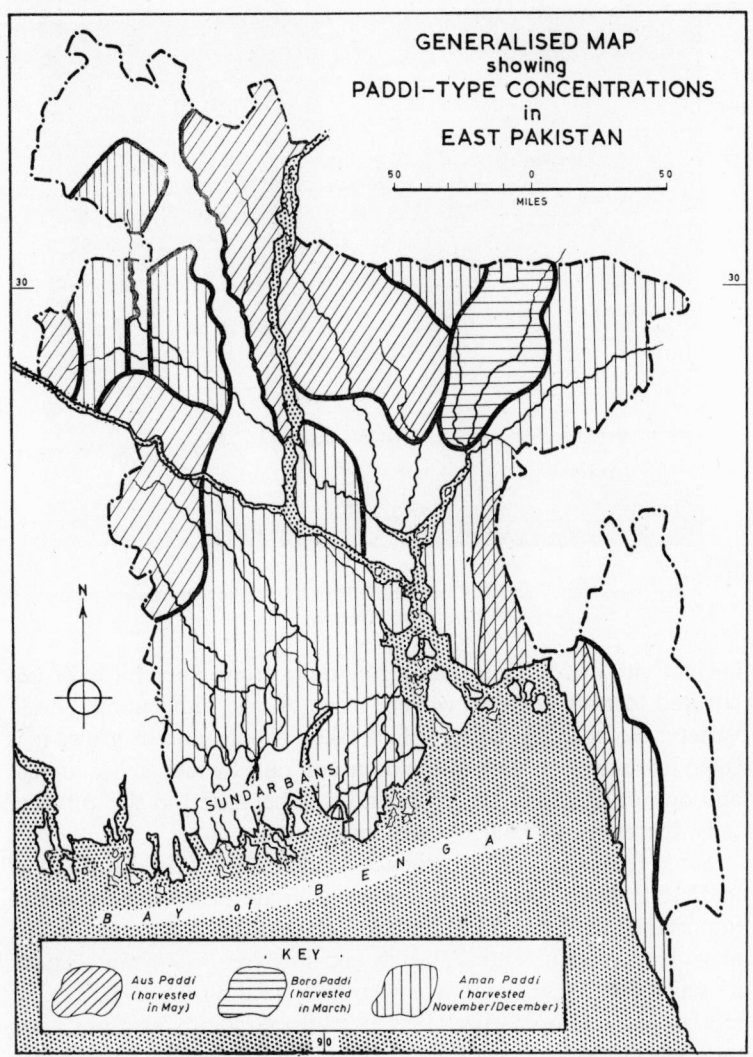

GENERALISED MAP
showing
PADDI-TYPE CONCENTRATIONS
in
EAST PAKISTAN

50 0 50

MILES

30 30

N

SUNDARBANS

B A Y of B E N G A L

· KEY ·

Aus Paddi
(harvested
in May)

Boro Paddi
(harvested
in March)

Aman Paddi
(harvested
November/December)

staple food. Wheat depends upon irrigation for it is grown as a
"rabi" (dry season) crop. It is sown after the monsoon rains are
over and is harvested in March. More than 12 million acres are
given up to wheat, but much is double cropped with cotton.

Cotton, the peasant's cash crop of West Pakistan, has been grown
in Sind and Punjab since prehistoric times. Excavations at the

This sugar-cane crop has been raised on a once barren stretch of the Thal Desert

ancient city of Mohenjo-daro, 266 miles from Karachi, have un-covered cotton textiles woven from Asia's indigenous "desi" variety. Because the cotton plant takes a long time to grow, it is sown just after the start of the monsoon rains, which are moderate and do not endanger the crop, and it is harvested in the autumn. It is, therefore, a "kharif" (wet season) crop.

Some rice is grown on irrigated lands in lower Sind for export to East Pakistan. Maize and sugar-cane are other food crops of importance in West Pakistan. Rice, the potato of the East, is the main food crop of East Pakistan and jute (see following section) its chief cash crop. Rice is a wet crop needing 60 to 80 ins. of rainfall and a temperature of 75°F. whilst growing; conditions are, therefore, ideal in East Pakistan. The farming year is divided into three seasons: "rabi" (dry season) lasting from October to March when rainfall is light and erratic; "bhadoi", or "kharif" of north India, is the wet season from April to August; and overlapping the other two at times, "aman" from June to November. The main rice crop, almost 75% of the total, is grown in the last season and is called "aman".

Dry rabi crops, mainly vegetables, wheat, peas and beans, rely upon irrigation from the creeks and lakes and water left in the soil from the monsoon rains. "Bhadoi" crops are the quick-growing paddi and jute. Much rice is sown broadcast in seed, but the main "aman" crop is transplanted as seedlings from nurseries at the beginning of the monsoon rains (May). This is back-breaking work for each small shoot has to be planted individually; it is done by women.

JUTE

A little over 200 years ago the East Indiaman *Streatham* brought to England the first shipment of what was then called "Indian grass". This was jute, which had been in use in India for over 2,000 years for making coarse cloth and twine. Today, jute is known to the world of commerce as the vegetable fibre used in making hessian, ropes, canvas, tarpaulin, carpet bases and a host of other goods. To Pakistan it is the mainstay of her economy for she exports jute to provide over 75 % of the world's yearly needs—and it all comes from East Pakistan. There it is grown as a cash crop by the peasants who also carry out the preliminary preparation of the fibre before taking it to market. More than 10 % of the total cultivated land of East Pakistan is devoted to jute. It is an annual grown from seed each year, and matures within four to six months into a single-stemmed plant with no twigs or branches.

Conditions in East Pakistan are ideal for raising jute. It is grown in flooded fields and often the harvest has to be cut from boats riding upon water 2 or 3 ft. deep. Jute needs constant high temperatures not falling below 70°F. or rising much above 90°F., and, because it is a "wet "plant, a total of at least 40 ins. of rainfall during the growing season. The jute plant makes heavy demands upon soil fertility, but the annual inundation of water in the Bengal delta region ensures that goodness is replaced by deposits of silt.

Jute seeds, kept over from the previous year's seed plants, are sown broadcast over ploughed plots from March to May, just before the coming of the monsoon. Anything from 8 to 12 lb. of seed are used per acre according to the soil and the quality of the jute. After four months the plant is up to 10 ft. or more and has reached the fruiting stage when the fibre is at its best, soft and strong, and now is the time for cutting. If it is cut later the fibre

Cultivators carrying jute away to be retted

will have become hard and poorer in quality. Between June and September the Bengal jute fields are dotted with squatting farmers cutting the jute low to the roots and wearing straw hats to shade them from the sun.

The cut stems are bundled and left in the sun for some days while the leaves wither off the stems. Later, the bundles are submerged for ten to twenty days in clear, running water for the fibre to be "retted". In this process the water dissolves the soft pith leaving the fibres free so that they can be separated by beating with a mallet. The farmer's next job is to clean and squeeze dry the fibres and hang them on bamboo frames in the sun. His labour over, the farmer piles the bundles of jute into his boat and takes them to the nearest village or riverside market where he sells them, at a very low price, to a middleman who delivers them in bulk to the jute mills.

Partition and the Jute Industry When India and Pakistan became separate sovereign nations in 1947 the jute industry of the Indian sub-continent faced a disastrous prospect. All the existing jute mills were situated on the Indian side of the border in the Calcutta-Hooghly industrial area, but more than 80% of the raw

Washing jute fibre in East Pakistan

jute supply came from East Bengal, part of the new state of Pakistan. This situation led to a severe disruption of the industry and when trade stopped between the two states for six months in 1949 the outlook for jute was bleak. Such political rivalries made little sense to the peasants of East Pakistan who continued to sell their jute in the Calcutta area by smuggling it across the border, until the Pakistan Government stationed soldiers along the frontier.

Since then India and Pakistan have made great efforts to balance their respective jute industries, Pakistan by investing capital in jute-mill construction, India by increasing her jute acreage. Both have met with considerable success considering their initial difficulties. In 1959 India grew enough jute to keep her mill capacity satisfied and is now launching a campaign of extension and modernisation. Pakistan, through her Industrial Development Corporation, has now fourteen jute mills working with a total loom capacity of 7,750 units.

DEVELOPMENT PROJECTS

Since independence Pakistan has started and completed many development schemes in her drive for more farming land and further industrialisation. Some of these projects are for irrigation only or for the generation of electricity, others combine the two in multi-purpose projects.

East Pakistan   The river Karnafuli, flowing from the hills to reach the sea at the port of Chittagong, has been harnessed for a number of purposes. More than 10,000 locally recruited labourers, with bulldozers, tractors and elephants, were used to build a 140 ft. high dam, a generating station and pump installations. When the project is fully complete it will supply electricity to cottages in Bengal, drain flooded land in the monsoon season and irrigate parched land in the dry season. Already, the large paper factory at Karnafuli draws its electric power from the generators.

Though still in its early stages, the Ganges-Kobadak Irrigation Scheme has already succeeded in increasing rice yields on sections of Bengal land where experiments have been tried. The object of the scheme is extensive and will cover all East Pakistan west of the Kumar and Passur rivers. Although the area gets an average of 60 ins. per annum, the rainfall varies greatly from year to year and from November to March of each year crops need irrigating. The scheme will give irrigation when needed, as well as flood control when the monsoon rains gorge the rivers and streams over their banks. Further, a main north-south trunk canal is projected and with the material dug from this a raised road will be constructed. Water for this scheme will be drawn from the Ganges at Bheramara. The main benefit of this scheme to the Bengali peasant will be that with water in the dry season he will be able to cultivate more land, and will increase the yield and variety of his rabi crops.

West Pakistan's problem is one of getting water to arid lands. The Indus valley is a great, flat plain with a southward gradient of only 1 ft. drop per mile, so the construction of high dams holding back great reservoirs is impossible. But the rivers draw a perennial flow of water from the monsoon and the melting snows of the Himalayas. Irrigation is therefore possible by feeding water

The Kotri barrage, West Pakistan

through canals leading from barrages built across the river. West Pakistan has a greater proportion of her land irrigated than any other country in the world. Since Mogul times canals have been built in the Punjab and today there is a vast and complex network supporting the colonies of farmers in the Land of the Five Rivers.

In 1932 the world's greatest single irrigation work was opened on the Indus, at Sukkur in upper Sind. The barrage, over one mile long and having river gates that weigh 40 tons each, spans the Indus and holds back the waters so that they may be diverted to more than 6 million acres where rainfall is less than 3 ins. per year. Leading from both sides of the barrage are 36,000 miles of canals taking water to fields of wheat, cotton and rice where once was arid, barren land. Similar to Sukkur is the Lower Sind Barrage at Kotri which irrigates 3 million acres between Hyderabad and the sea.

The Thal Development Project For centuries the great Thal Desert between the Jhelum, Chenab and Indus rivers was a desolate sandy waste scantily peopled by a few poor cultivators and a barrier to communications except by trains of camels. Sand drifts, summer temperatures of 120°F., winter temperatures below freezing, rainfall of 8 ins. a year at the most, drought and scorching dust storms all combined to keep man away.

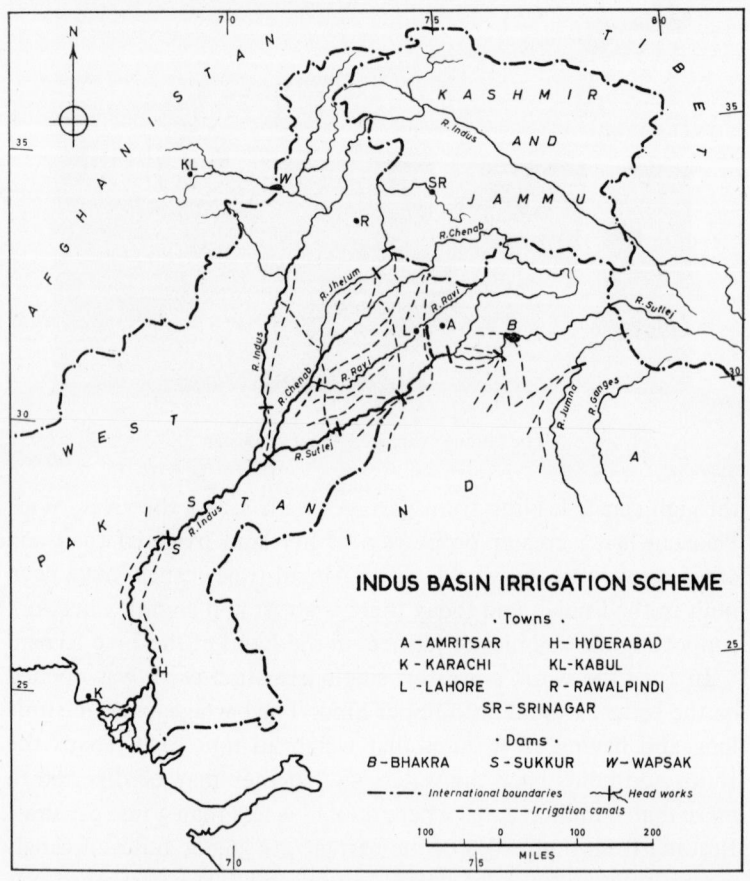

INDUS BASIN IRRIGATION SCHEME

· Towns ·

A – AMRITSAR   H – HYDERABAD
K – KARACHI   KL – KABUL
L – LAHORE   R – RAWALPINDI
SR – SRINAGAR

· Dams ·

B – BHAKRA   S – SUKKUR   W – WAPSAK

—·—·— International boundaries   ⊥ Head works
— — — Irrigation canals

100   0   100   200
MILES

Today, under the Thal Irrigation Scheme begun in 1939 but suspended during the war, 1½ million of the desert's 5 million acres bear crops and support villages. Over the lonely camel routes have been built miles of modern roads.

After Partition in 1947 hordes of Muslims fled from India into Pakistan seeking land and homes. They built elephant-grass huts and mud shacks where they found room, but pressure on existing cultivated land became a serious problem. To accommodate these extra millions and ease the congested areas the Pakistan Government revived the Thal Development Project to open the desert for colonisation. The project has two aspects; the laying down of a network of canals leading from the headwaters at Jinnah Barrage, Kalabagh on the Indus, to the desert; and settling colonists on the new lands. The first section has been completed and the colonisation and development section is progressing rapidly.

Before the colonists could plant the soil it had to be prepared. Fleets of bulldozers, earth-moving machines and tractors were bought to level the sand-dunes and break up the hard soil surface. Irrigated estates of trees were planted to stabilise the soil, increase air humidity and to act as wind-breaks.

The new villages built in the Thal are called "chaks". Houses are of a good and uniform design and are built around the traditional compound. Surrounding the villages are strips of common grazing land where the animals roam, and beyond these lie the irrigated plots. Besides the chaks, five "mandi" (market) towns have been built where the farmers may sell their produce. These are larger than the chaks and have all facilities for serving the population: schools, post offices, banks, hospitals and cinemas.

Each family is given on arrival fifteen acres of land, a house and a loan with which to buy agricultural tools, seed and bullocks. They agree to pay for these over a generous period of time, but such has been the success of the scheme that many of the first settlers have earned enough money to pay their debts.

Crop yields per acre are still small in the Thal, but great strides are being made towards improvement. The farmers receive practical advice from experts on crop types and the best methods of growing them. The main "kharif" crops are maize, cotton, sugar-cane and millets; "rabi" crops are wheat and oil-seeds. Fruit trees are thriving on the new Thal lands and give harvests of oranges, limes, mango, date and pomegranate. In short, the success of the Thal Development Project has proved that man can turn a barren desert into a fertile place.

Power

Hitherto Pakistan's programme of industrialisation has been handicapped by her poor power resources. She has few and small reserves of low-quality coal in Baluchistan and the Salt Range and, despite intensive surveys, she is able to supply only a small percentage of her oil needs. A number of hydro-electricity stations have been built in the hills of West Pakistan to supply her expanding industrial centres. Within a few miles of each other two generators have been installed on the river Swat at Malakand and Dargai. The latter was built with labour from a Pathan tribe, the Mahsuds. At Warsak the project gives electricity and irrigation.

Discoveries of vast natural gas reserves at Sylhet in East Pakistan and Sui in West Pakistan have enabled Pakistan to reduce her coal and oil imports. The Pakistan Petroleum Company reached the gas at Sui whilst drilling for oil in 1952. The reserves are estimated to equal 96 million tons of coal and are 90 % methane (an inflammable gas—fire damp). By 1963 it is hoped to tap more than 100 million cu. ft. daily and pump it through pipe-lines to industries at Karachi, Hyderabad, Multan and Lahore.

The discovery of the gas at Sylhet was of major economic importance to East Pakistan. Gas first escaped from drillings in 1954, but a spark from a worker's kitchen fired it in May 1956 and it burned itself out. Drilling was resumed a month later to 9,000 ft. and another reserve was found. This is 95 % methane and is piped to the thermal plants at Dacca where they have replaced oil and coal converters.

MANUFACTURING INDUSTRIES

Although still primarily an agricultural country, Pakistan has expanded her industry through the guidance of the Industrial Development Corporation. A great variety of new industries have been established, from ship-building at Karachi and Khilna, foundry and engineering works at Lahore, to cement, light metal, electrical goods, cigarettes and food. One of Pakistan's traditional manufactures, leather goods, is now being exported to England in the form of footballs.

Textiles Pakistan's cotton industry is fed with raw materials by her peasant farmers. Women and children pick the cotton and it is carried to market by camels, donkeys, bullock-carts and trucks. Karachi is the centre of the industry, but mills are found throughout West Pakistan. Only certain types of cotton goods are produced by the mills for Pakistan wants to preserve her handloom cottage industry. The textile mill at Kaliganj, East Pakistan, has 50,000 spindles working to supply the cottage weavers with yarn.

Sugar Both the refined white sugar and the local "gur" are essential items of the Pakistani's diet. Pakistan now has the largest sugar-refining mill in Asia at Mardan. Further growth of this industry will come when sugar-cane, a peasant grown crop, is produced with higher yields and quality. Experiments with sugar-beet have been successful and the acreage under this crop is increasing. Gur, the indigenous brown molasses-sugar, is made in all villages in Pakistan. The cane is crushed in a primitive bullock-driven press and the juice is collected and boiled in tin cans to extract the sugar.

Paper Great strides have been made in the effort to make Pakistan self-sufficient in paper goods. The Amangarh mills in West Pakistan use local grasses for high grade board and the Sethi mills, also in West Pakistan, use the straw from rice and wheat harvests for making board and wrapping paper.

In 1953 the bamboo handling and cutting machines of the Karnafuli mills, Chittagong, began to operate. Karnafuli will ultimately produce more than 100 tons of writing, wrapping and printing paper per day. The inexhaustible bamboo resources of the Chittagong forests are easily able to supply the mill with its annual requirements of 90,000 tons. In the lush and damp environment the bamboo grows at a rapid rate, up to .6 mm. per minute has been known, hence the local saying, "Never sleep under a bamboo bush". The bamboo is cut in the forest and floated down-river to the mill in raft convoys.

Three thousand people are employed at the Karnafuli mill and all of the technical and engineering posts are filled by trained Pakistanis. To house this labour force a colony was built with schools, hospitals, mosques and playing fields.

TRANSPORT AND COMMUNICATIONS

The two wings of Pakistan are connected by an air-route on which a Super-Constellation makes the Karachi-Dacca trip five times weekly. Ships sail round the Indian peninsula from Karachi to Chittagong, the major port of East Pakistan, carrying goods and passengers. The railways of Pakistan are state-owned and link the large cities.

I

Karachi, the capital city of Pakistan, has many fine buildings. Some are shown in this photograph of the Mereweather Tower on Bunder Road

A variety of colourful vehicles move along the network of roads in West Pakistan. Bullock-carts and donkeys move at a slow trot to be overtaken by 'buses full to overflowing with passengers. It is normal in the modern city of Karachi to see camel-drawn floats parked next to glittering automobiles.

River Traffic in East Pakistan   East Pakistan has few roads and railways. During the monsoon floods all communications and transport are by boat along the river highways. The Bengali is not only a good boatman, he is also a boat-builder whose designs are dictated by need and tradition. The art of boat construction was introduced into Bengal over twenty-five centuries ago by the Austries, migrants who came from the Indo-China region.

Bengal country boats are of varied styles—large and small, sailed, rowed or punted—but they all have the "chhai" in common. This is a bowed shelter made of bamboo-thatch sections or corrugated iron to protect passengers and cargo from the hot sun. It covers the middle or stern of the boat. The "kosha", the smallest

A Kosha

of these country craft, may be compared with a bicycle. Its main use is for "getting about" and for carrying goods to riverside markets. Its other uses are for fishing, cutting jute on the floods and gathering water-hyacinth for cattle food. The kosha is punted by the boatman with a "loggi", a straight, sturdy bamboo about 12 ft. long and 2 or 3 ins. thick.

A popular medium-sized boat is the "dinghi" whose stern curves upwards to a greater height than its bow. It is mainly used for ferrying passengers just as a taxi or 'bus does. It may be manned by one, two or three men according to its size, but the larger dinghis need two men rowing with a third working the "baitha", or tiller, in the stern.

The "ghashi" is so large that it may use only the wider and deeper channels. It can be driven along by oars when the wind is unfavourable, needing five or six men pulling at long-handled paddles, or by two large rectangular sails hung from a single main-mast. Its chief use is for transporting heavy goods and large cargoes.

A Dinghi

A Gaina

The ghashi is built by constructing the shell first and then the frame is added. The design of the ghashi is very similar to that of the great boats of the Pharaohs of Egypt.

Many of the native country craft have been displaced by motor launches and British-built paddle-steamers on the larger river channels of East Pakistan, especially for transporting the raw materials of modern industries and for operating scheduled, main-line passenger services between the larger towns. But there are strong objections from the farmers in some districts to the use of motor boats, for their swell tends to wash away the laboriously banked crop lands.

INDIAN BIRDS

A complete survey of the bird life of such a large area as the Indian sub-continent would take a large book in itself. Here there is room to give thumbnail sketches of only a few of the many kinds. In India are found varieties of many of the birds that may be seen in the British countryside: tits, swallows, crows, larks, owls, robins, sparrows, magpies—not very different from their British cousins. The following are some of the more unusual birds.

The Adjutant Stork   This large member of the stork family (he stands about 5 ft. tall) and looks like an old man. His bald head, large eyes and long, thick beak give him a very comic look. He lives in marshy land and on the edges of ponds and lakes. His name was given to him because of his walk; he struts about with a very stiff, military step raising his legs high into the air. The Adjutant is a very clumsy looking stork, but except for a great deal of noisy fuss and flapping when taking off, he is very mobile and agile in flight. His food is mainly frogs, reptiles, fish and insects, but he will gobble at anything soft enough to eat. Before Calcutta city was equipped with efficient sanitation, the Adjutant, along with vultures and kites, wandered freely about the outskirts feeding upon the rubbish dumps.

The Cattle Egret   This fine looking white bird (about the size of a slender village hen) is a common sight amongst the paddi and pasture fields of India. The egret follows the buffaloes and cattle as they graze on grass and stubble; it perches on the animal's back, darts in an out through its legs and struts by its side. The cow does not mind its visitors, for they peck off blood-sucking parasites like ticks and snap away the hordes of flies that buzz round its eyes. It welcomes the egret's attentions for the comfort they bring. Other food comes the egret's way as the trundling animals disturb the long grass of the fields. Insects like grasshoppers, and frogs and lizards are frightened from cover to be eaten by the birds.

Peafowl   In this bird family, the male, the peacock, wears the fine clothes and the female is dressed very drably. The peacock's beautiful "tail" (it is not a tail really but very long back feathers) has made the bird famous. It was sought after by the Pharaohs of Egypt and has been given religious significance in some areas of India. Peafowl have exceptionally acute hearing and sight and are the first animals of the jungle to sense the approach of the large and dangerous cats. They utter screaming alerts to all the other jungle animals. Their heavy trains make them reluctant to take to the air even when frightened, but once they are in flight they are very competent.

The Tailor Bird   Of the smaller species in India the tailor-bird is one of the most interesting because of its ingenious nest. It actually sews one or more leaves into a cone which hangs from a twig. It bends the leaves over and, using its beak as a needle, and cotton or vegetable fibres as thread, it sews its nest. Once the stitches are in place it ties a knot in the loose end of the thread so that it will not slip out.

The Red Jungle Fowl This is the ancestor of our domesticated fowl and is therefore of special interest. It looks very much like the fowls that scratch about farmyards, but it lives in the wild jungles. Jungle fowls are very shy of man and if disturbed will rush away with a great noise of cackling and fluttering. They are very good fliers, unlike their tame cousins who have almost completely lost the use of their wings. Their food is mainly grain and seeds and they particularly like bamboo seeds. The cocks crow like our farmyard cocks, at a slightly higher pitch, at sunrise and sunset.

The King Vulture Scavengers are very important creatures in hot countries where rotting carcases will spread disease and pestilence. The vulture is a scavenger. Like all of its kind, the King or Pondicherry Vulture is very ugly and menacing looking; it is also very large and powerful, but, contrary to popular belief, it is not an aggressive bird. In fact it will hang about the fringes of the crowd of vultures and other scavengers pecking at a carcase; occasionally it will scurry in, rip a gobbet from the bones and rush off to swallow it. This vulture, which is black with white patches on the chest usually goes about alone or at the most in pairs.

Kestrels and Hawks, Eagles and Kites There are a great many birds of prey in India, ranging from the drab Pariah Kite to the delicately grey Pale Harrier. Indian farmers usually kill them whenever possible, for they carry off their poultry. Other items of their food are carrion and rats. It is as killers of the latter that these birds give great service to humans. All tropical countries are plagued by rats; they eat the rice as it stands in the fields, they eat it from bins in the homes, they scurry over floors whilst people are asleep, and carry diseases that are fatal to man.

Rats breed very fast. It was calculated in India that a single pair of rats, following normal breeding habits, *could* multiply into

940,369,969,152 rats in five years if there were no deaths at all. This shows what a signal service is done for man by the hawks, kestrels, eagles and kites, for if one pair of rats is killed by one of these birds, it means that a possible increase of 880 rats in one year has been prevented.

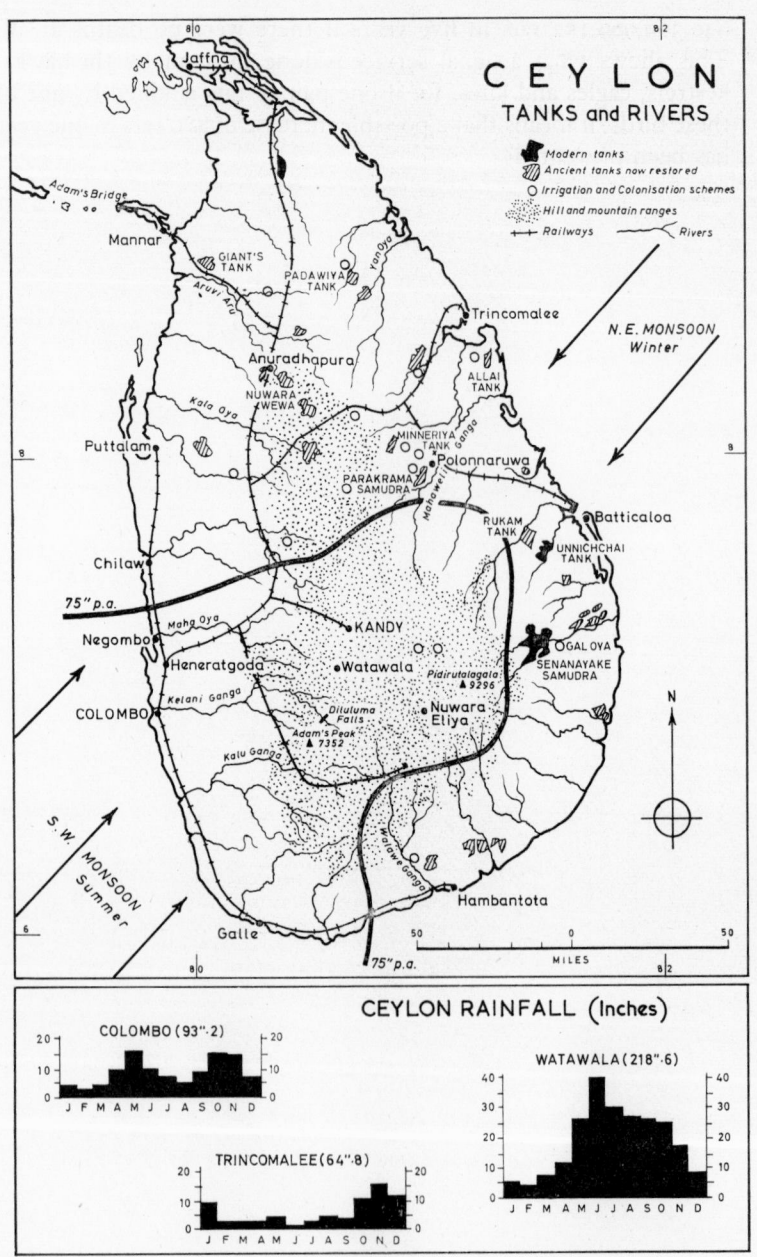

CEYLON

TANKS and RIVERS

- Modern tanks
- Ancient tanks now restored
- ○ Irrigation and Colonisation schemes
- Hill and mountain ranges
- ┼┼┼┼ Railways   ～～ Rivers

N.E. MONSOON
Winter

Jaffna

Adam's Bridge

Mannar

GIANT'S
TANK

PADAWIYA
TANK

Anuradhapura

Trincomalee

NUWARA
WEWA

ALLAI
TANK

Aruvi Aru

Kala Oya

Puttalam

MINNERIYA
TANK

Polonnaruwa

PARAKRAMA
SAMUDRA

RUKAM
TANK

Batticaloa

Chilaw

UNNICHCHAI
TANK

75" p.a.

Negombo

Maha Oya

KANDY

Heneratgoda

Watawala

Pidirutalagala ▲ 9296

GAL OYA
SENANAYAKE
SAMUDRA

Kelani Ganga

COLOMBO

Diluluma Falls

Adam's Peak ▲ 7352

Nuwara
Eliya

Kalu Ganga

S.W. MONSOON *Summer*

N

Galle

Walawe Ganga

Hambantota

50   0   50

MILES

75" p.a.

CEYLON RAINFALL (Inches)

COLOMBO (93".2)

WATAWALA (218".6)

TRINCOMALEE (64".8)

VIII

CEYLON

PHYSICAL

TAKE a 'plane from London Airport and within thirty-six hours you will be on the pearl-shaped island of Ceylon off the tip of southern India. Its ancient name was "Lanka", but it has been called at various times "Isle of Gems" by the Chinese, "Isle of Delight" by the Moors and "Isle of the Lion Race" by the Sinhalese themselves.

At some stage in geological time there existed a vast continent that stretched from Malaya to Madagascar. This land sank beneath the sea leaving remnants above the surface, and one of these is Ceylon. Hard, crystalline and very old rocks form the core of the island. On the lowlands they have been overlaid with soft rocks called laterites. These are the results of tropical weathering of the structural rocks.

The heart of Ceylon is the mountain massif of the south-central part of the island from which radiate all the rivers. From 3,000 to 7,000 ft. in elevation, it is a land of beautiful scenery and exciting waterfalls (e.g. Diluluma Falls, over 600 ft. high). In its forest live panthers, leopards, ill-tempered bears, strange and exotic birds, leeches, monkeys, centipedes and thousands of different insects. There are deep valleys and pockets of country still unexplored by man. Higher peaks jut to the sky above the general level, the highest of all being Pidirutalagala (8,296 ft.). Adam's Peak, the world's holiest mountain, is a place of pilgrimage for Buddhists for here is an imprint of Buddha's foot.

Surrounding this central core is a plateau from 1,000 to 3,000 ft. high which drops down to the plains. The latter are wide in the north, but narrow in the west, east and south. The flat regularity of the plains is broken in places by ridges and isolated outstanding masses of granite. One such is the brooding Sigiyar (400 ft. high) which was made into an unassailable fortress-palace by Kasyapa, villain-king of Sinhalese history who murdered his father and brothers.

In the north the limestone Jaffna Peninsula is almost land-linked to India by Adam's Bridge. Sinhalese myth-history tells that it is the remains of a bridge built by Hanuman, the monkey general, over which he helped Rama to rescue his wife from her captor Ravanna. In fact it is a series of sand-banks deposited upon coral by the coastal currents.

The climate of Ceylon is similar to that of southern India. Temperatures are high (about mean 80°F. on the plains) because the island lies only 6° to 10°N. of the Equator; but they are not as high as this position might suggest for oceanic influences modify them. Lower temperatures are also experienced in the hills because of their altitude. For example, Nuwara Eliyas, a hill-station 6,200 ft. above sea-level, has a mean annual temperature of 60°F., whereas Colombo on the coast has a mean annual temperature of 75°F.

The monsoons have the biggest effect on the rainfall and divide Ceylon into two regions with distinct rainfall patterns. From May until September the South-West Monsoon brings heavy daily rains to the south-western parts of the island. This is the "Wet Zone", some hilly areas of which get as much as 200 ins. average in a year and 50 ins. per month during the monsoon. Whilst this area is being soaked, the "Dry Zone" over the mountains is arid. The "Wet Zone" has some rain all the year round.

The North-East Monsoon, blowing from November to January, comes from across the Asian land mass and is less heavily laden with moisture when it reaches Ceylon than is the South-West Monsoon coming from across the oceans. Rainfall is experienced in the north-east of Ceylon, especially on the hill-slopes, and is heaviest in December and January. Nevertheless, the "Dry Zone" (north, east and south-east) gets little rainfall in the year, often less than 40 ins. Anuradhapura gets an average of 118 drought days per year. It was in the "Dry Zone" of northern Ceylon that the great and finely balanced irrigation civilisations of Ceylon were centred on the cities of Polonnaruwa and Anuradhapura. So aware were these peoples of the terrors of low rainfall that in the chronicle *Mahawansa** the invasion and looting of the Tamil chief Magha was likened to "a fierce drought".

THE PEOPLE

Nine million people live in Ceylon. They are all called Ceylonese, but they are not all of the same race. There are Sinhalese, Tamil, Malay, Moorish and European communities.

The Sinhalese, totalling two-thirds of the population, are the true people of the island for they are the descendants of the Aryan migrants from India. They were the people who created the great ancient civilisations and who retreated to the hills as successive waves of Tamil armies came and went across the Palk Straits. They have their own language and their culture is a reflection of their Buddhist faith.

The Sinhalese themselves are split into two groups: the Sinhalese of the lowlands and the Kandyan Sinhalese. There was an independent kingdom centred on Kandy and defying the British until 1815. The many military expeditions sent by Governor North in the early nineteenth century failed to subdue this realm until 1815, when the king was captured with the help of treachery on the part of his chiefs.

The vast majority of Sinhalese are peasant cultivators.

Tamils are of two types: the Ceylon Tamils and the Indian Tamils. They are practising Hindus and speak the Tamil language. The Ceylon Tamils have been on the island for over 2,000 years and they are concentrated in the Jaffna area. At times Ceylon has been ruled by Tamil kings (e.g. Rajendra A.D. 1014–44) and they have had their own state alongside the Sinhalese kingdoms of the hills. Most Tamils are cultivators. It is interesting to note that their coming to Ceylon drove the Sinhalese into the Wet Zone whilst they themselves took to growing rice in the Dry Zone, using a fine system of irrigation.

*The Mahawansa is important as it marks the beginning of Sinhalese "history", with the landing of the Indian prince Vijaya and his followers in the sixth century B.C.

The Indian Tamils are mainly contract labourers on the tea and rubber estates. They come from southern India to earn enough money to return home rich and they still regard India as their home even if they do not go back. The Sinhalese did not like working on the estates so the planters imported the Indian Tamils who have made a vital contribution to Ceylon's prosperity. A profitable sideline for boat owners of south India is smuggling Indians across the narrow Palk Straits into Ceylon where they can find work and higher wages. Traders from other parts of India and Pakistan also come to the island. Baluchi moneylenders are unpopular but do good business. Cloth trading, shopkeeping and food trading are occupations in which Indians are well represented.

The half-million Ceylon Moors are farmers and traders. The gem trade of Galle is their monopoly. The Portuguese gave them the name "Moors", but they claim descent from early Arab traders. Another Muslim group are the Malays who first came to Ceylon as soldiers in the pay of the Dutch and British.

CEYLON AS A CENTRE OF WORLD COMMUNICATIONS

Ceylon is a cross-roads of trade routes. This was realised by traders in the ancient world. The Arabs or Moors sailed their dhows to Ceylon and southern India to buy the goods brought westwards by Chinese, Malayan and other traders. The Arabs then took the goods to Africa and the Mediterranean to sell to European merchants. No wonder the Arabs did all in their power to keep their monopoly of Orient trade safe against the competition of Europeans who made their appearance in the sixteenth century!

In 1505 the Portuguese first landed in Ceylon. They were seeking trade and converts. Their ships pressed on to the Spice Islands farther east and a station was founded at Malacca in Malaya. Like the Arabs before them, the Portuguese used Ceylon as a staging point where their ships could stock with fresh foods and water for the long voyage round the Cape. Malacca was the source of goods; Ceylon was the stepping-stone on the homeward journey. When the Dutch challenged the Portuguese in the East they took Malacca in 1641 and Colombo in 1656. The long-standing influence of the Dutch in Ceylon may be seen in the

Colombo, Ceylon's capital and a great international port, seen from the air

Burghers, the descendants of mixed marriages between the lowland Sinhalese and the Dutch settlers. They are one of the most enterprising and active of all the Ceylonese communities.

It was not until the British came that any real interest was shown in the interior of Ceylon. Colombo and Galle, ports on the west coast, provided the Europeans with their paramount need: ports catering for ships carrying on trade between Europe and the Orient.

Even the most modern forms of transport have not diminished the great importance of Ceylon as a communication centre. Colombo, with its magnificent harbour, is one of the greatest trading ports in the world; and from Colombo goods flow through the Suez Canal to Europe. They come from Australia, Singapore, Malaya, Indonesia, Hong Kong and Japan. Along these routes there is also a return eastward flow of manufactured goods coming from Europe.

COLOMBO CITY

Colombo is the capital of Ceylon. Here is the seat of Government, the university, museums, banks, the great trading houses, foreign

261

consulates, etc. Colombo is one of the cleanest cities in the East. Many of its public buildings are fine examples of western and eastern architecture. Buses, just like the double-deckers found in any English town, carry passengers on their journeys. The population of Colombo has increased fourfold over the past seventy years. To accommodate this increase the city has had to grow. It has spread southwards along the coast, for inland and to the east are precious paddi fields and swamps that prevent expansion in this direction.

As a city of some size and importance Colombo is only about 200 years old, and for all but the last sixty of these she was overshadowed as a port by Galle, which was very much a Dutch settlement. All the bulk of trade came to Galle until the harbour at Colombo was built. Now this can give shelter to the largest of modern ocean-going ships. The city soon surpassed Galle and earned for itself the titles of "Gateway to the Orient" and "Crossroads of Asia". Now it is only challenged by Singapore as the greatest port in Asia.

BUDDHISM

In the fourth century B.C., Mahinda, the son of Asoka the Emperor of India, "flew" to Ceylon on a carpet, according to legend, and in the Minhintale Hills converted the Sinhalese King Tissa to Buddhism. Tissa ordered the teaching of the new religion to be spread throughout Ceylon and soon it displaced the more ancient Hinduism. A shrine holding the ashes of Mahinda now stands on that peak where the meeting took place and it is venerated by Ceylon's 5 million Buddhists who climb the 1,840 steps to worship there. Buddhism is Ceylon's national religion. It claims to be the oldest religion in the world for the present Buddha is the twenty-fifth, and his period of veneration will last from his birth in the seventh century B.C. to the coming of the next Buddha in the forty-fourth century A.D.

Gotama, the reigning Buddha, was born to a chieftain's wife in northern India. He married young and lived in great luxury, but at the age of twenty-nine he tired of riches and, renouncing the world and its desires, he became a hermit. He studied under religious teachers for six years and, one day, after twenty-four hours of deep meditation under a bo-tree, he attained "Nirvana"

A 'pandal' telling stories of episodes in the life of Lord Buddha

(enlightened peace). For forty-five years he wandered about teaching his faith, and died at the age of eighty. Buddha paid three visits to Ceylon. On the third occasion he came to attend a feast after which he ascended into the air to fly home to India. As he rose his foot touched Adam's Peak and the imprint as of a giant's bare foot is there to be seen to this day. It is a sacred object and pilgrims toil to the top of the high peak to worship and be cured of ills.

Besides Adam's Peak there are fifteen other holy places in Ceylon and every Buddhist tries to visit all of these in his lifetime. Apart from pilgrimages, the Buddhist worships at his local temple at the four quarters of the moon. Bearing offerings of colourful flowers (these are essential to Buddhist worship and one temple in Anuradhapura used 10,000 each day in its ceremonies), he visits the room containing the serene image of the Buddha ("vihara"), the bo-tree in the courtyard and the relic room, to recite sacred stanzas in each.

The Octagon of the magnificent Temple of the Tooth
at Kandy

The monks of the temples have no set duties. They have dedicated themselves to a life of poverty and meditation in order to
reach "Nirvana". Occasionally one will officiate at a special
family ceremony, for which service he is presented with a cloth or
food. Buddhist monks have shaven heads and wear saffron-
coloured robes. A custom dating from the early days of Buddhism
is attached to these robes. Anada, the Buddha's favourite disciple,
was given a fine robe by an admirer. As a gesture of his faith that
worldly riches had no meaning for him, Anada cut the robe into
thirty pieces and sewed them together again. All Buddhist monks
do this to their one and only robe to this day.

Buddhism is a difficult religion for the Western mind to understand. It teaches that Buddha was not a god, but a man who found

The splendidly decorated elephants in the Kandy
Perahera

peace of mind by renouncing all worldly desires. Buddhists
believe, with Hindus, in transmigration of souls, that is to say,
each person is born a number of times, his status in the next life
depending upon his conduct in the present. Buddhists have a set
of rules of conduct similar to the Christian Ten Commandments,
the most important of which is not to take life in any form. Some
of these rules are given at the end of this book.

Buddhist Festivals Comparable with the saints' days and holy
days of the Christian calendar are Ceylon's Buddhist festivals.
Each commemorates some sacred occasion and is a time of worship
and rejoicing. On these days the vendors display their cordials,

sherbet-waters, sweetmeats and betel to the merrymakers thronging the streets.

The holiest of all the festivals is Vesak, held on the day of the full moon in May. It is the Buddhist equivalent of our Christmas and houses are gaily decorated with oil-lamps and coloured streamers. Vesak commemorates four events; the birthday of Gotama in 623 B.C., the day on which he achieved Buddhahood, his death in 543 B.C., and the founding of the Sinhalese kingdom by Vijayo. Throughout the day the faithful go to worship at Buddha's images in the temples.

The coming of Buddhism to Ceylon is celebrated by the Poson festival in June. Pilgrims flock to the ancient sacred city of Anuradhapura where the first dagobas (temples) of the great religion are still standing.

Overshadowing both these ceremonies in grandeur if not in holiness is Esala, held at Kandy in August. It lasts for three weeks during which the city is packed with pilgrims and tourists. The climax of Esala is the Dalada Perahera, the ceremonial parade of the Holy Tooth Relic. Buddha's tooth was brought from India in the fourth century and is now housed in the Temple of the Tooth, Kandy. Rarely is it allowed to be seen, but during Esala it is placed in a golden casket and carried on the back of a huge and richly decorated tusker elephant. Even then it is shaded by a canopy and fanned by monks sitting beside it. Treated with great reverence, it is taken from the temple and paraded through the streets so that the crowds of the faithful may gaze at it. Accompanying the Tooth Relic in the procession are dancers; some who knock sticks together as they dance, and "Kalagedi" dancers who hurl empty pots into the air. Following closely behind are other richly dressed singers and dancers who wear masks portraying the gods who do Buddha honour.

Such is the magnificent Dalada Perahera. The Perahera of the gods, mostly Hindu, comes later and among them is Natha, the next Buddha who is at present in heaven. The Hindu element in this Buddhist festival is due to the fact that many Hindu gods have been incorporated into Buddhism. Also, the Kandy Perahera was originally a Hindu festival and remained so until some Siamese monks visited Ceylon in the eighteenth century. They immediately

The grotesque Gara Yaka mask being worn by a
Ceylonese mask-dancer

complained to the Kandyan king that it was wrong that the most
spectacular festival in Buddhist Ceylon should be for Hindu gods.
The king then proclaimed that the Tooth Relic should be carried
in the procession and should be afforded the place of honour.

CEYLON'S GIPSIES

Visits from the wandering gipsies are events enjoyed by the
Ceylonese villagers. Like our gipsies in England, they roam about
the forests, but never camp far from the villages where they give
their shows and sell their wares.

Gipsies give roadside shows with their evil snakes and clowning
monkeys. Cobras are hypnotised by the swaying of the gipsy's
body and the wail of his gourd-pipe music. These reptiles are not
dangerous for they have had their fangs and poison sacs removed,

but the gipsy is a master showman who makes his darting duet with the snake look perilous and never fails to enthral the onlookers, especially the children.

Snake-charmers are Tamil caste and legend gives the origin of their trade. Long ago, Devadatha, a gipsy, caught a cobra that happened to be a god in disguise. Devadatha trained it and made a living by its tricks. This made the gods angry and they punished Devadatha and his line by ordaining that all gipsies become snake-charmers and wanderers.

Gipsies not only bring snakes to the villages, they also take them away. Hindus worship the cobra and will feed it, and Buddhists know that on one occasion a cobra shaded Buddha from the hot sun. Therefore neither will harm the cobra, but a loose cobra is a danger to all in the village where it has made its home and must be removed. The village employs a gipsy for this. Squatting before the cobra's home, usually an ant-hill or a hollow tree-trunk, the gipsy plays his gourd-pipe. Thus charmed, the snake is removed by its conqueror. Rich rewards are given for this service; so rich, in fact, that gipsies have been known secretly to plant a cobra of their own in a village so that they might be employed to get rid of it.

Gipsies also collect money by telling fortunes, begging, dancing, tattooing and selling charms and potions. Their snakestones are popular with the villagers as they are supposed to cure bites by drawing venom from them. Medicinal seeds, sticks and roots are also sold, besides charms that keep away evil spirits or bring success in business and marriage.

From the village the gipsies return to their camp in the nearby forest. Each family—there are about twenty in a clan—lives in a low "tent" made by placing huge talipot-palm leaves over an arched framework of sticks. Such tents are easily made and suit the nomadic habits of the gipsies. They sleep and keep their pots, mats, spears, charms and cobras in the tents. Before the open end of the tent a fireplace of rough stones is arranged. Cattle, goats, donkeys and dogs wander through the camp. The wealth of the gipsy is judged by the number of cattle he owns, but neither meat nor milk is taken from the stock. They are hired out to farmers as manuring animals. The mangy dogs are kept for hunting deer, porcupine, iguana and field-rats (used for feeding the cobras).

The clan's leader, priest, chief and judge is the "Vidhana", an old man chosen for his experience and knowledge. He settles family disputes and imposes fines that are usually paid in toddy, a palm-spirit very popular with gipsies.

Gipsy dress is nothing more than a drab cloth draped around the body, but at marriage feasts they wear their best. The bride appears in a colourful cotton sari and is bedecked with bangles, rings and nose-studs. The groom puts on his best sarong and a fine silk turban. A "tamasha", a noisy celebration, is held in honour of the couple with singing and dancing to the playing of drums made from monkey skins. Liberal amounts of toddy are drunk even by the smallest children, and a meal of wild boar and "cholan-kaly" (maize porridge) is eaten. A bride's dowry to her husband will include a cobra, a gourd-pipe, a hunting javelin and a dog. This list of presents sums up the life of the Ceylon gipsies.

THE VEDDHAS

When the Indian prince Vijayo and his band of followers landed in Ceylon in 504 B.C. they found the original inhabitants of the island living in the Old Stone Age. It is thought that these people, the Veddhas, made their home on the island before it became separated from the Indian mainland. At the time, so the *Mahawansa* tells, they were divided into three tribes, Yakkas, Nagas and Rakshas, and the king of the Yakkas ruled in partnership with Vijayo. The Veddhas did not fare so well as the centuries passed for they provided the slave labour that built the magnificent cities of the Sinhalese kings. In the remote forests of north and south-east Ceylon a few of the Veddhas still live their nomadic, prehistoric lives. Their numbers have dwindled over the ages, not from disease or conquest, but because they have become assimilated into the Sinhalese way of life by intermarriage. These settled Veddhas now cultivate "chenas" (jungle clearings) and fruit gardens that surround their kadjan huts.

The remaining tribal Veddhas, like the aborigines of Australia, give an insight into primitive man's existence. They are lean and short, about 5 ft. tall, with a long growth of unkempt hair on their large heads. This impression of wildness is intensified by their shaggy beards and their single loincloth made from the bark of riti trees.

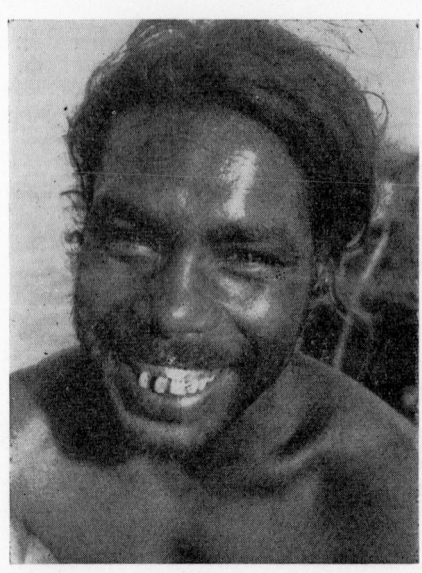

A survivor of a very
primitive race. A coast
Veddha from East
Ceylon

Veddha tribes are called "wargues" and each has its own well-defined hunting territory and fishing waters. For homes they prefer rock caves, but their wanderings make them change camps with the seasons. Their nomadic rhythm is determined by the movement of game animals, the most prized being iguana, deer and grey apes, that provide their food. In the dry season when water is scarce these creatures gather around the few remaining water-holes. The Veddhas also make their camps nearby. With the coming of the rains the animals disperse and the Veddhas are hot on their trail. Hunting is done with bows and arrows, spears and axes. Particularly useful for hunting the iguana are the hunting dogs of which the Veddhas are very fond. Veddhas have great skill in speedy tracking for they can read all the jungle signs.

The Veddhas cook their catches in one of two ways; either by roasting in the embers of a brushwood fire or by boiling in home-made pots. The meat from the hunt is supplemented with truffles, fruits, yams, berries and even flowers collected from the jungle. But there is one luxury that Veddhas will risk their lives to obtain —the honey of the wild Bambara bees. These insects form their combs on the faces of cliffs high above the jungle. Strong young

Veddhas climb to them on bamboo ladders or ropes and many have lost their lives falling to the ground hundreds of feet below. When game is scarce and they fail to secure their single daily meal, Veddhas keep away the pangs of hunger by chewing a gum made from the bark of trees.

While the men sit chatting and chewing betel, the women cook, gather fruit from the jungle and tend the children. The women of the Veddha camps have complete equality with the men even to the point of sharing in the tribal ceremonies, a rarity with primitive peoples. Veddha men are very jealous, and faithful to their women. In their cave homes special areas are apportioned to the various families that make up the clan. Here they sleep, cook and store their pots, weapons and bark clothing. They never sleep on the damp earth but on rock platforms.

The Veddhas are under the care and protection of the Ceylon Government's Backward Communities Board, set up in 1951.

VILLAGE AGRICULTURE

With the exception of coconut cash-cropping in the Negombo-Chilaw region, the 20,000 villages of Ceylon subsist on paddi and garden cultivation. Holdings are small (.8 of an acre is the average) therefore few can afford to hire labour and much farming work falls upon the wife. Paddi cultivation is so primitive in Ceylon that it has the lowest yields per acre in Asia. Two Dry Zone crops are taken in a year: the South-West Monsoon crop and the North-East Monsoon crop. On the arid north and eastern plains rice is an irrigated crop grown in fields near the local tank. Wet Zone fields suffer not from drought, but from excess flooding.

Besides the irrigated rice plots ("yaya"), the farmer of the Dry Zone has a garden, often fenced, and a "chena" (see page 272). The houses of the village are made of kadjan-thatch roofing and wattle-and-daub walls made with the straw from harvests. Rarely will the walls have windows. A rule in ancient Ceylon permitted only nobles to have these in their houses—tradition dies hard here. There will be no more than two rooms and the cooking will be done in a kadjan outhouse adjoining the rear of the dwelling. Stores of rice and millets are always kept in a small loft or in baskets raised on stilts to protect the grain from rats.

Harvesting rice. In the new farmlands of Gal Oya women have taken to helping the men cultivate the paddi fields

This is the traditional house, but in colony villages such as Gal Oya and in villages working self-help schemes under the Rural Development Society of Ceylon, it is being replaced by cooler, better ventilated plaster houses with sanitary fittings, large windows and chimneys. Such villages also have well-situated schools with desks, pictures and blackboards in place of the old improvised open-air classes. Growing between and around the tightly grouped houses of the village are coconut, papaya, mango, banana and jackfruit trees. Surrounding the Dry Zone village is a strip of cleared land which keeps forest animals from the village and makes it easier to hold back the ever-advancing jungle.

Each peasant has his "chena" away in the jungle. Chenas are cleared plots cultivated by "slash-and-burn" methods. All the vegetation, with the exception of the larger tree-trunks, is cut and burned in the dry months, and with the coming of the first showers of the North-East Monsoon the farmer hoes over the soil and throws seed on to the land. Chena crops are dry and fast-growing; maize, manioc (tapioca), sweet potatoes and bananas are the most popular. After two years the prolific jungle weeds are allowed to reclaim the chena.

Weekly markets have been established in the newly developed regions of the Gal Oya Valley. The farmers come to sell their produce and to buy food, clothes, etc.

It often happens that there is not enough water in the tank of the Dry Zone village during the drought season (South-West Monsoon) for all the rice plots to be irrigated. Then the village adopts a traditional co-operative system: the villager gives up his right to farm his own plots and only the fields nearest to the tank are used for paddi. When the harvest is home each villager receives an amount of the harvest proportionate to his holdings in the "yaya" of the village.

Cultivation methods are traditional and primitive. Poorer peasants use the hoe to turn the soil, and those with bullocks do little better, for their ploughs are wooden and have no mould-boards. If the soil within the bunds (banks around the field) is too wet for ploughing or hoeing then a team of buffaloes is driven through it to churn it up. The utility buffalo also husks the paddi by treading it on a threshing floor whilst the farmer sings songs to it to keep time.

Rice growing is a family affair. The wife helps by transplanting the paddi shoots, weeding, cutting the crop and winnowing the harvest. The son scares hungry birds away from the growing paddi by shouting or banging cans together. At night the man keeps the more dangerous wild boar, deer, elephant, monkeys, porcupines and wild buffaloes away.

All the stages of paddi cultivation are governed by custom and superstition. Every operation is begun at a "lucky hour". An astrologer is consulted to find from the positions of the planets when is the best time to start reaping, ploughing, seeding or threshing. His fee is forty betel leaves and one tobacco leaf. Before each operation starts ritual ceremonies are held and offerings made to the gods; for example, before reaping his crop the farmer bathes, puts on clean clothes and cuts three handfuls of paddi that are saved and taken to the temple as an offering of thanks for the harvest. Whilst he sows, the Ceylonese farmer holds flowers and a handful of paddi and sings sacred songs. Tamil peasants split a coconut as part of a religious rite before ploughing, sowing, reaping and threshing. One explanation given for this practice is that the farmer wants the gods to know that his heart is as white as the flesh of the coconut; the author thinks that it is a legacy from primitive practices of human sacrifice for the success of the crop— the coconut taking the place of the unfortunate victim's head.

Fear of "poothams", goblins that steal the rice, is widespread. A bow strung with an arrow is planted near the grain, or salt water is sprinkled over it (poothams hate salt water) or little squares of paper with holy writing in Arabic are put near the rice—all to scare the poothams away. At threshing time the farmer will not use his native language so that he may fool the poothams.

Why all these ceremonies and superstitions? The reasons are that the Ceylonese peasant believes in many spirits and, further, the failure or success of his rice crop means life or death to him and he wants to leave nothing to chance.

More than 60% of Ceylon's peasants work land as tenants, not owners. As payment of the rent for land they share the harvest with the landlord, the "podiar". The podiar is the richest man in the village and he wears gold ear-rings and carries an umbrella as marks of his distinction. The night before the harvest the farmer has to guard the crop from animals, and the podiar's estate manager patrols the fields making sure that all the tenants are on duty. The "puthir-koddai" (Tamil for "first-fruits") is a bundle of six measures of paddi which is taken to the podiar wrapped in a white cloth. It is presented to the podiar with great ceremony and music, and he hangs the bundles brought by his many tenants about his house. He then gives the farmers food and drink and betel.

FISHING

Along the coasts of Ceylon the fisherman takes his catch as his ancestors did ages ago. He supplies an essential item of diet, but is regarded as low caste because he takes life. Several fishing methods are used. Some fishermen stand on bamboo stilts in deep water and fish with hooks and lines, whilst others cast hand-nets into the shallows and catch small fry. The wider and longer nets ($\frac{1}{4}$ mile long) are laid by parties of men wading up to their necks. These are then hauled in from the shore—hard and tiring work if the catch is a large one. The fish are funnelled into a fine-mesh bag at the end of the net.

Some nets are taken further offshore and laid from canoes. Two outriggers set the net under the supervision of a master-fisher, an experienced, older man who can read all the signs of the sea. It is then hauled in from the shore and to keep time the happy fishermen shout and sing:

> The gods will give,
> Filled to the brim they'll give,
> Bags full of fish they'll give.

Most of the fish are small, but larger ones like rays may be trapped. A swordfish hooked by one party pulled the outrigger for seventy-two hours before it was landed.

Fishing activities are regulated by the monsoons. The season starts in August when the seas have settled after the South-West Monsoon, and ends in February in the south. During the slack season the beaches and kadjan huts of the fisherfolk are deserted for they move inland to find odd jobs.

Improvements in Fishing Aided by the Food and Agriculture Organisation of U.N.O., the Ceylon Government is operating a scheme for improving fishing on the island, and has created training facilities to teach more efficient methods. Under the Colombo Plan Canada gave forty boat engines to promote motorised fishing;

The giant turtles are safely sprawled in the boat

today, the enterprising fisherman is able to buy an engine on very favourable hire-purchase terms. Besides providing subsidised curing salt and timber, the Ceylon Government is operating welfare schemes for fishermen, building houses and auction sheds and giving loans and relief in an effort to better the lot of this poorer section of the community. An Air Sea Rescue Service is also operating.

At Mutwal, Colombo, Canadian capital and engineers have established a cold storage plant. Twelve tons of ice can be frozen to a temperature of $-30°$F. and production of ice is 10 tons per day.

Turtles On great areas of the sea-bed off the north-west coast of Ceylon grows a green marine moss. This gives the turtle-catchers their livelihood for it is the food of edible turtles (5 ft. long and about 300 lb. in weight), and hawksbills, caught for their shells. Tortoise-shell is a prized article used in making combs, paper-knives and mirror frames. The shell is taken from the turtle's back whilst it is still alive.

An average catch is three turtles and the fisherman sells these for Rs. 150 to 200 each. Apart from those females caught after laying their eggs in the sandy beaches, all turtles are caught in the water by an ingenious and simple method. A large circular net over 30 yds. in circumference with weighted ends and a buoyed middle is laid on the surface of the water. The weights sink the edges to a depth of 6 ft. and the log buoys keep the centre from sinking. When settled in position the net looks like a submerged umbrella. The turtles are feeding on the sea floor 40 ft. below. After eating their fill they rise to the surface to breathe and some find themselves entangled in the net. The more they struggle to free themselves, the tighter are their fins held in the mesh.

The fishermen, having returned to the shore to wait, are warned of the presence of turtles by a flag flying from a thin bamboo pole attached to the centre of the net. It acts like a fishing-line float and waves as the turtles struggle. At the net the fishermen noose the trapped turtles by their fins and haul them aboard the outrigger canoes. They are laid on their backs to render them harmless. On the beach the turtles are put into a palmyra-palm log enclosure built in shallow water to keep them alive. Alongside the enclosure are the kadjan huts of the watchers who guard the turtles from thieves.

Crabs In the salty lagoons of Ceylon's shores the crab-catcher plies his clever art. His net, shaped like a shallow cone, is made from coir fibre. A thin stick is bent and tied around the circular open end and a cross stick is tied to this. Bait of fish scraps is tied to this bar and stone weights are secured to the apex of the net. The recovery line is attached to the bent, handle-like stick.

As his son or assistant rows and manoeuvres the canoe, the crab-catcher lowers his nets to the lagoon bottoms. They are arranged in rows and the recovery line is kept afloat by a coconut husk. This also marks the position of the nets which flatten out as they hit the bottom.

The catcher leaves his traps and returns a little while later. His experienced eye will tell from the movement of the coconut floats where the crabs are taking the bait. He pulls upwards sharply on the recovery line and the crab, intent on his meal, falls into the rising net from the force of the jerk. Soon the canoe is piled high with crabs and he returns home with his catch. At the beach he sells them to hotels and women who market them from palm-leaf panniers to the villagers.

Tropical Fish The coral seas around the Ceylon coast swarm with small, colourful fish which are in great demand for tropical aquaria in the large cities of the world. As soon as they are caught the fish are housed in plastic bags filled with water and oxygen. Within two days they will be on sale in London.

The small group of experts who catch these fish have equipment similar to the frogman's; a face mask for underwater viewing, gloves for protection from fire-coral, flippers for speeding after the fish, and a net. If they want to dive more than 5 fathoms after the species that inhabit the lower waters they wear aqualungs. Hand-nets similar to butterfly nets are used for ensnaring the fish. The popular and colourful Moorish Idols and Butterfly Fish which are swift and darting, have to be caught at night with the aid of a flashlight which blinds them into immobility. Considerable dangers are to be met by the diver. He must be on the look-out for marauding sharks, vicious moray eels and groupers, all of which will attack him. A careless moment and he may be severely stung by a jelly-fish or sea urchin.

PEARLING

Since ancient times Ceylon has been famous for its white and perfectly round pearls. It was thought that these pearls were hardened raindrops that fell into the shells when oysters came to the sea surface for air. Modern science has found the true method of formation. Some foreign body, a single grain of sand or a worm, gets trapped in the oyster and irritates its tender flesh. Nature has provided the oyster with a protective device against this discomfort in the form of a fluid which it excretes around the intrusive material. This solidifies to form the milky-white pearl.

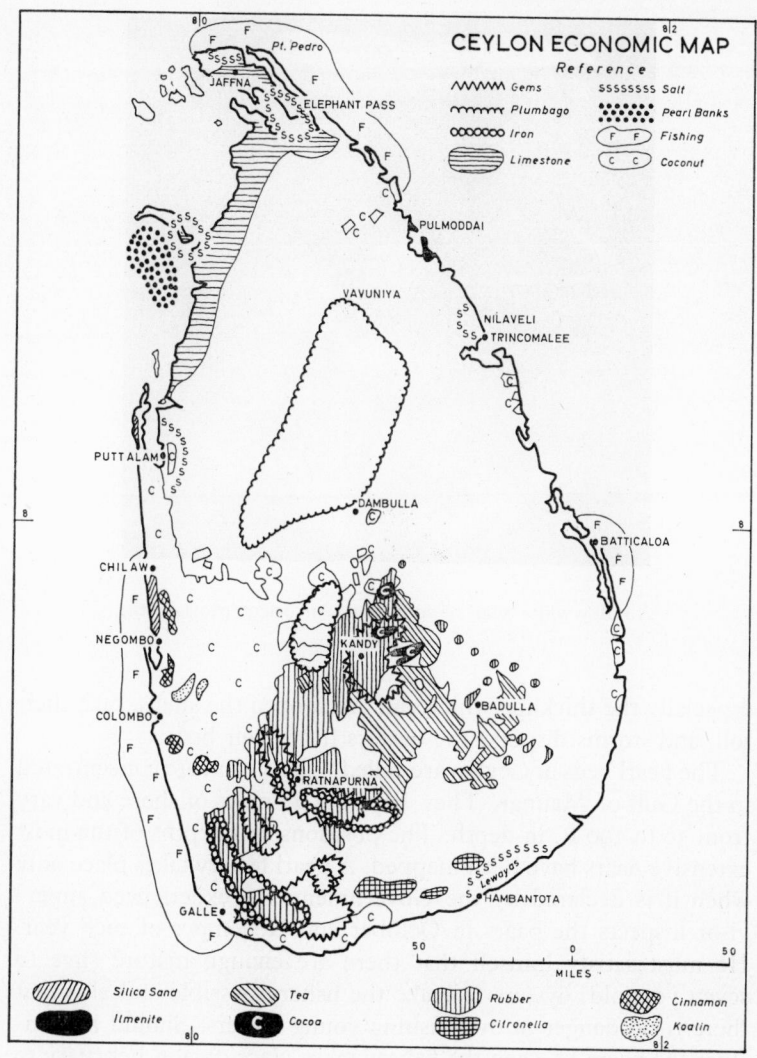

CEYLON ECONOMIC MAP

Reference

∿∿∿∿ Gems	SSSSSSSS Salt
∿∿∿∿ Plumbago	•••••• Pearl Banks
∞∞∞∞ Iron	F F Fishing
Limestone	C C Coconut

Silica Sand · Tea · Rubber · Cinnamon
Ilmenite · Cocoa · Citronella · Kaolin

MILES

Pearl fishing in Ceylon is not continuous and is strictly controlled by the Government. There have been only forty fisheries since 1800. One reason for this irregularity is over-fishing; in the 1905 fishery over 80 million oysters were raised. Certain fish, too,

279

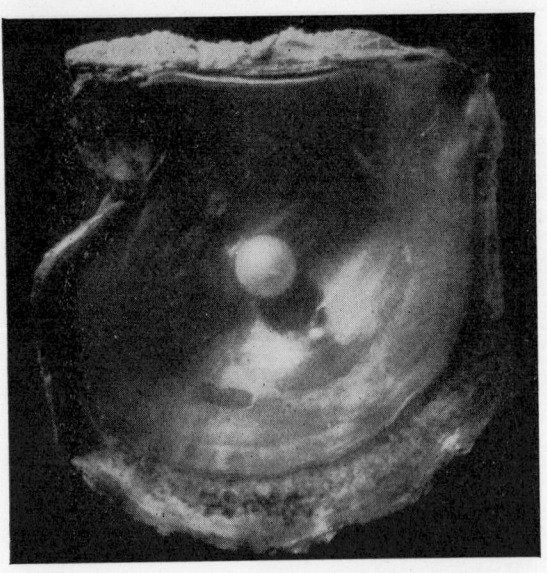

A milky white 'tear' of an oyster. An orient pearl in the shell

especially the thicklips which can crack open the shells, take their toll, and storms disperse the oysters from their beds.

The pearl beds of Ceylon are called "paars" and are concentrated in the Gulf of Mannar. They lie about 40 miles offshore and vary from 50 to 100 ft. in depth. The positions and depths of the most extensive paars have been mapped. A pearl fishery takes place only when it is declared by the Government. An experienced supervisor inspects the paars in October and November of each year. He must satisfy himself that there are enough mature (five to seven year old) oysters to make the fishery possible and also that there is no danger of over-fishing young oysters. Should he consider the paars fit, then the fishery takes place during February to April. In the 1958 survey an estimated 200 million oysters were reported on the paars.

Oysters are now raised by dredges pulled by motor boats. The dredge, a large net of steel mesh with iron framing the open end, is dragged along the sea floor and its heavy forward cutting edge tears the oysters from their hold. Each dredge takes about a quarter of an hour, after which power winches raise the bag full of oysters. The dredge cannot operate on uneven ground and cannot distinguish between young and mature oysters; therefore it is possible that the Ceylon Government may return to the traditional pearl fishery that Marco Polo described.

A Traditional Pearl Fishery "So soon as a fishery was declared it was widely publicised in Ceylon and southern India. Then the boats and canoes of all shapes and sizes began to arrive in hundreds as the start of the fishery approached. A palm-hut village sprouted on the shore, and for two months this shanty-town was bustling with activity. Amongst the crowds the divers were easily recognisable by their bulging eyes and large chests".

Only those boats and crews who were chosen in a draw were permitted to go to the paars, the rest returned home. Starting at midnight each day, the tackle and boats were checked and prepared and the paars reached by dawn. After choosing their spots the crews stood to the ready and at the starting signal, a single shot from a gun, diving began. The same signal ended the day's diving at noon. The divers worked in pairs, one diving whilst the other acted as an attendant to the lines and ropes. Each made about fifty dives in the day.

The descent was made by the diver holding his nose and dropping down with his feet on a heavy stone. At the bottom he swam clear to collect the oysters which were raised to the boat in a basket on a line. At the end of his breath the diver shot freely to the surface. Arab divers were reputed to be the best for they could stay under for 80 seconds and reach 18 fathoms. The Ceylonese could remain under for a minute. The Inspector of Fisheries reported in 1885 that an Arab diver stayed submerged for no less than 109 seconds.

Terrific pressure was built up in the diver's body, but relief was had by bubbles escaping from the eye sockets. The danger signal was when blood gushed from the ears. Other natural perils faced the brave diver. He feared most of all the large sting-ray that lay hidden in the sandy bottom and lashed out with its poisonous barbed tail. The cruel saw-fish also prowled the waters. A snake-charmer was employed to protect the divers from attacks by sharks for which service each diver gave him one oyster per day. In 1885 the Government banned him from the fisheries and with good cause for there is no recorded killing of a diver by a shark before or after 1885.

On the return journey from the paars the oysters were bagged and, on arrival, landed under the strict supervision of police and government agents. The divers took their third share of the catch and the rest were immediately auctioned in batches of 1,000. Moors and merchants from southern India were the main buyers. They took their oysters to their private yards and left them to decay. All the time they kept a vigorous watch over their purchases. The smelly heap was then searched for pearls which were sorted into sizes.

TEA

Ceylon's plantation products are rubber, coconuts and tea; it is with the most famous of these, tea, that we are concerned. The origin of the habit of tea-drinking is lost in the antiquity of the East, but a colourful account tells that the first person to taste its flavours was Emperor Shen-Nung of China. He made it a rule to boil all water before drinking it and once a few leaves from a nearby wild tea tree fell into his cauldron giving the water a delicious flavour which delighted him. Now over 800 million cups of tea are drunk in the world each day.

The industry is a newcomer to the island. In 1869 a blight completely destroyed the coffee industry of the Kandyan Hills and, in a desperate measure to make good their losses, the planters took to raising tea. It was an immediate success; within six years over 1,000 acres were being worked and by 1958 570,000 acres were flourishing.

Tea in Ceylon is grown on plantations called "estates". An estate is a holding of 10 acres and over, but in fact there are nearly 340 estates on the island larger than 500 acres that account for half of Ceylon's tea acreage. The tea tree, for it is a tree and is only trimmed to a bush for reasons of efficient production of the right leaf type, is a natural jungle hardy evergreen. Therefore it flourishes best where the climate and soil are as near as possible to jungle conditions. Most of Ceylon's tea estates are on cleared jungle land on the western slopes of the central hills, 70% of the tea being grown above 2,000 ft. Tea needs some rainfall all the year round

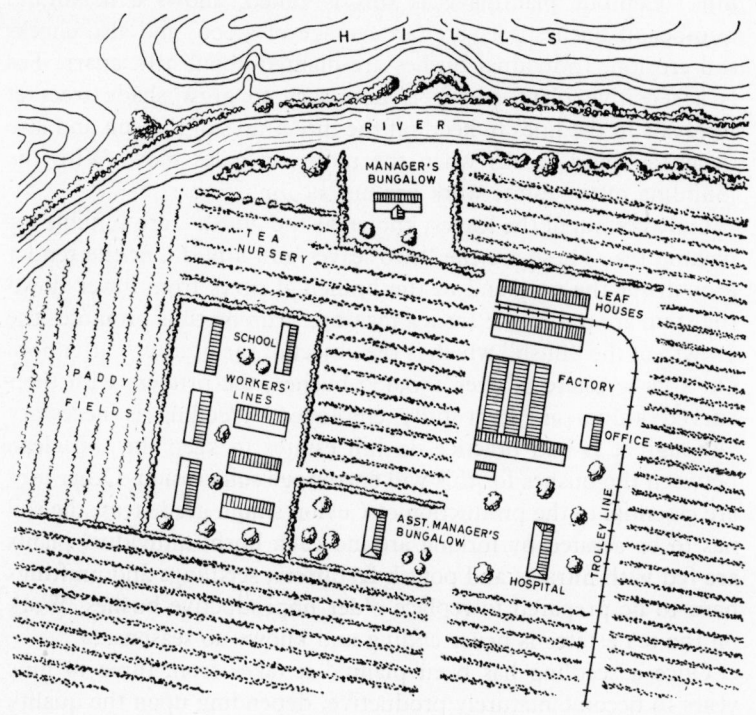

Plan of a tea estate

and an annual average of 80 to 120 ins.; moreover, it needs well-drained soils. These conditions are satisfied on the hills of Ceylon where the cleared forest land is rich in the soil foods that the tea plant needs.

A Ceylonese tea estate is a carefully planned and highly integrated unit of production. After the jungle has been cleared, drains have to be laid, roads constructed within and to the estate, quarters with garden plots and stock sheds built for the resident labour, the factory where the plucked tea is processed has to be well situated and the pattern of the neat lines of tea bushes has to be planned with great care. Most of the estates are situated on hill slopes and the lines of bushes are laid following the natural contours of the

283

hill. "Contour planting", as this is called, allows a maximum number of bushes per acre (an average of 3,000) and also checks soil erosion. Individual bushes are planted about 3 ft. apart. Tea is a sensitive plant and it is necessary to grow shade trees at intervals in the lines to keep off the direct rays of the sun and also to act as wind-breaks when the monsoon gales blow. With the founding of the estate work has just begun.

Only certain of the leaves, known as the "flush", are suitable for making tea. These are the "two leaves and a bud", or the tender growths at the very end of the branch. Leaves from lower down the stem are too coarse for tea making. Pruning thus promotes the growth of the "flush" which is the object of the plucker's attention. On a large estate of over 150,000 bushes, the pruners with their curved knives are kept fully employed. Weeding is necessary although it is bad practice on hill estates to keep the soil clean between the bushes for this will encourage soil erosion. Other jobs are essential to the production of Ceylon's high grade teas; the soil has to be aerated by forking around each bush; individual plants are fed with nitrates and potash fertilisers; seedlings and graftings have to be prepared to replace older unproductive bushes. Work on the tea estates is never ending and knows no seasons.

Once a seedling has been planted it takes from three to nine years to become maturely productive, depending upon the quality of the tea required and the altitude of the estate. Bushes on the higher estates take longer to mature because of the effect of seasons, but they give better teas in smaller yields. Bushes on lower estates mature more quickly and give larger yields but of a lower quality tea.

Plucking the leaves of the tea bush is a highly skilled job done by the Tamil women of the estate. A sure and steady hand and a quick eye are needed to select the correct leaves and the speed at which the Tamil women work through the rows of low bushes is amazing. Their practised, nimble fingers break the stems, taking care not to bruise the tender leaves, and toss them into the large wicker baskets that they carry on their backs. These baskets are held by cords around the foreheads of the pluckers.

Each bush is picked throughout the year in Ceylon, but at intervals that allow the "flush" to grow afresh. This interval varies with the altitude of the estate. Those on the lower slopes are

Women picking tea on a Ceylon estate

plucked every week, but higher plantations are plucked only every two weeks.

The filled baskets are collected from the pickers and all useless stalks and twigs are removed. After weighing, each basket is credited to the name of the picker in a tally-book. The leaf is then taken to the factory where it will be processed. Various means of transport are used to suit the layout and topography of the estate. Human labour, overhead wireways where land is rugged, trucks, donkeys and ox-carts are all used, sometimes all on a single estate if it is a large one.

Manufacture of Tea The care taken in handling the leaves whilst picking and moving them must be intensified in the processing of tea. Air that is a few degrees too hot in firing or a minute too long in the fermenting room will rob the leaf of its flavour and aroma which will lower the price it will fetch in the auctions of Colombo and London. Each of the Ceylon tea estates, like the vineyards of France, has a reputation for a certain quality of tea

285

that must be maintained. Buyers in London expect to be able to tell from which estate a tea comes merely by tasting the liquor.

Science has greatly helped in the mechanical side of tea manufacture, but it is still the responsibility of the experienced planter to supervise the processes. There are six stages in the manufacture of tea, from the green leaf to the familiar black scraps we put into our pots. They are:

Withering: During this first stage the leaves are laid evenly on hessian racks ("tats") to evaporate the moisture. Where conditions are favourable this is done by allowing the sun to work on the leaves, but more usually in Ceylon, the tats are also layered in large rooms through which hot air is forced.

Rolling: The dried leaf is placed in the tea-roller where it is twisted and rolled. This breaks up the leaf and liberates the juices.

Roll-breaking: The leaf from the rollers is passed over a coarse-mesh table to allow the finer particles to fall through. These are taken to the fermenting room whilst the leaf remaining on top is passed again through the rollers.

Fermentation: The tea-leaves are spread on concrete tables in a cool and damp room and here the process of fermentation takes place. The once green leaf emerges from this room with the familiar black colour.

Firing: Fermentation has to be arrested at this stage so that the tea will brew in the pot. The leaf also has to be dried. This is done in the automatic tea-dryer, fuelled by oil, where the tea is passed through a large chamber in which a strong blast of hot air is blowing. Care must be taken in gauging the degree of heat and the length of time, as over-firing will cook the tea.

Grading: The processing of the tea has now been completed; it has to be sorted according to the size of the leaf. Tea from the firing room is passed over a sieve surface of varying mesh. The trade arranges tea sizes into the following grades:
Leaf Grades (large): Orange Pekoe; Pekoe; Pekoe Souchong.

Broken Grades (small): Broken Orange Pekoe; Broken Pekoe; Broken Pekoe Souchong; Fannings and dust.

Such is the story of Ceylon tea, but what is the true importance of this industry to the island where the thousands who work on the estates are mostly Tamils from across the Palk Straits? Ceylon does not produce enough food crops to feed its peoples so it has to import large quantities; her exports of tea pay for this food. Over 95 % of Ceylon's exports by value come from her three major plantation commodities, tea, rubber and coconuts, but over 64 % of her total trade is contributed by the tea industry alone. The earnings from tea, therefore, help Ceylon to feed her population on imports, finance irrigation and colonisation schemes and give her economy a firm foundation.

RUBBER

In the early seventies of the last century a young Englishman called Henry Wickham managed to take out of Brazil, seeds of the *Hevea braziliensis* or, as it is commonly called, the rubber tree. The seeds were taken to Kew Gardens in London where they germinated and it was decided to send them to India for the commercial development of rubber. They did not flourish there (only in Kerala state is much rubber produced in India today), but they were shipped across the Straits of Mannar to Ceylon and planted at Heneratgoda just 17 miles outside of Colombo. The precious trees took to Ceylon's conditions well. In 1877 the first rubber trees reached Malaya where the world's greatest rubber plantations now are.

A glance at the Products map of Ceylon will show that rubber, which is grown on estates or plantations just like the tea estates of the hills, is found on the wet westward-facing foothills under 2,000 ft. above sea-level. As a native of the steaming jungles of the Amazon Basin in South America, the rubber tree requires at least 80 ins. of rainfall per annum with a temperature of not less than 70°F. throughout the year, and cannot stand drought at any season. These conditions are met in the hills of Ceylon which face the South-West Monsoon from the Indian Ocean. But rubber also dislikes waterlogging, so it needs well-drained soils; the estates in

287

Tapping a rubber tree
in Ceylon

Ceylon, and Malaya, are on the slopes of the foothills above the swampy and often flooded plains nearer the coast.

Before the rubber trees could be planted great areas of the foothills had to be cleared of jungle and bush and the ground prepared with fertilisers. Rubber saplings must be allowed to grow for seven years before they are tapped. As on the tea estates, there is much work to be done on rubber plantations; more so perhaps, for rubber tapping is done all the year round so there is no seasonal cycle. Most of the labour is supplied by "Indian Tamils" who have migrated from southern India seeking regular and comparatively well-paid employment. The following brief summary will give some idea of the processes involved.

1. *Tapping* The skilled tapper—man or woman—cuts incisions into the bark of the rubber tree to make it "bleed", using a special knife with a curved blade. Tapping is done in the early morning. The sloping incisions are never made so as to encircle the tree for this will stop the supply of plant foods coming up from the roots

and will eventually kill the tree. At the lower point of the incision a collecting cup, often half a coconut shell, is tied or staked to the tree. The sap, or latex, runs down the cut and collects slowly into the cup. Later in the day a worker comes around collecting the latex into tins or pails.

2. *Coagulating*   The liquid latex needs to be turned into sheet rubber for transporting, and large quantities of latex are exported without being processed further. Latex is put into large tanks where it is treated with acetic acid which brings about a change in its form: it coagulates or solidifies.

3. *Rolling*   The rubber is then rolled into sheets by passing it through large mangle-like machines.

4. *Smoking*   In this, the final process done on the estates, the sheets are smoked over wood fires in the smokehouse. Afterwards, the sheets are baled and transported to Colombo for export.

MINERALS

Graphite   Ceylon's graphite (plumbago) is of the highest quality and is mined in the districts of Ratnapura and of Kurunu-galla near Kandy. It is used to make blacklead for pencils and in the manufacture of munitions. The mineral is extracted from mines or pits sunk deep into the ground. Some of the larger deposits, like that at Dumbara (also near Kandy), are worked by machinery, but most mines still depend solely upon human labour. After being hacked from the dusty mine face with picks, the graphite is carried in baskets on the labourers' heads up a frail bamboo ladder to the surface. Here it is sorted and sifted for transportation.

Precious Stones   Ceylon has long been famous for its sapphires, rubies, garnets, moonstones, spinels* and topazes. Ratnapura is the centre of a large mining area and is called the "City of Gems" because of its annual Jewel Fair. The stones are mostly mined by Sinhalese, but trading and cutting is the monopoly of the Moors. By law the Ceylonese Government owns all minerals under the ground. Therefore, the prospector must seek permission from the authorities to dig and must pay them a percentage of his finds.

*SPINEL: a scarlet stone like a ruby.

The precious stones were formed in the ancient igneous mass of the Ceylon hills, but they are now found in the alluvial muds and gravels of the lower valley slopes. Digging techniques are primitive. Often it is enough merely to scoop out a hole and sift the sand with a finger. A common practice is to allow the nail of one of the fingers to grow long so that it will be a more efficient and sensitive scratcher. At other times it is necessary to dig deep into the alluvium to reach the "nillan", a layer of pebbles and gravel of an ancient river-bed, where the gems are found mixed with the loose stones. Because of the need for digging holes, mining is only done in the dry season. Each digger is obliged by law to refill his holes so that they will not become stagnant, malarial pools.

Salt Climatic conditions in certain parts of Ceylon's Dry Zone are such that they have encouraged the production of salt since earliest times. It is likely that this solar salt industry came to Ceylon from southern India.

The three working centres are at Puttalam, Elephant Pass and the ancient Hambantota Lewaya. Each of these has a concentrated but short rainy season followed by a long dry spell. Salt will form wherever the amount of rainfall is more than offset by evaporation for a long period; at each of these places this condition is satisfied.

Solar salt is the product of sea-water evaporated by sun and winds. At the end of the rains (about May in the Dry Zone) sea-water is fed into the salterns (evaporation reservoirs). A thin layer of salt will have formed after ten days. More brine is filtered into the reservoir to maintain the stock. This process is continued until there is a crust of salt thick enough for reaping with the large rakes used by the labourers. The salt is raked in to the sides of the saltern and more sea-water is fed in. Harvested salt is formed into a ridged pile and protected by a covering of kadjan so that it will not deteriorate quickly. An interesting feature of the industry is the extra allowance of money paid to the labourers to compensate for the unpleasantness of their work.

Early rainfall will ruin a salt harvest. The floods of December 1957 so diluted the brine in the salterns that it was useless.

A co-ordinated scheme for producing gypsum, potash, epsom salts and other by-products of sea-water began operations at Hambantota Lewaya in 1957.

Raking in the salt from the evaporation pans at Elephant
Pass

IRRIGATION AND COLONISATION

Vijayo and his band, coming to Lanka from India, brought with
them paddi cultivation and the practice of field-flooding. At that
time the wet south-west part of the island was clothed in jungle,
so the Sinhalese people colonised the dry northern plains by
stages of irrigation. Climatic conditions in the dry plains are such
that, despite adequate annual rainfall, rice can only be grown with
the aid of irrigation. For all but the three months from November
to January dry conditions prevail; rainfall, when it comes, runs
off the sun-baked soil surface quickly and evaporation rates are
high; all these factors mean that effective rainfall is only a fraction
of actual rainfall.

Any tourist motoring through Ceylon will, sooner or later,
discover one of the huge irrigation tanks built by the Sinhalese.
A tank (reservoir) is called a "wewa" in Sinhalese and "kulam" in
Tamil. In the fourth century B.C. the first wewa, Tissa Wewa,
was formed and, as the Sinhalese kingdom and population grew
and flourished more tanks were built until few areas of the dry

The reservoir at Gal Oya waters thousands of acres into fertility

northern plains remained unproductive. Successive waves of invading Tamils made havoc of these wonderful networks of irrigation. Tanks that were not deliberately breached in the scorched-earth policy of the retreating Sinhalese were allowed to fall into disrepair by the south Indians. When the Europeans first landed in Ceylon, centuries of neglect had allowed the jungle to swallow up these works, and enabled the malaria-carrying mosquito to breed in the marshes caused by the breaching of the dams.

A Wewa was formed by building a dam across a perennial river fed with water from the wet hills. The embankment of "Parakrama's Sea", built in the twelfth century A.D., rose to 50 ft. in height and ran for 9 miles. From the reservoirs canals were dug as feeders to the neat patchworks of rice plots below the tank. A more complex system was that of Giant's Tank where the main reservoir fed satellite tanks that in turn fed the rice plots. Labour for these vast feats of engineering was supplied by the king's tenants who received their land in return for their labour services.

Sugar cane growing in the Gal Oya valley

From 1930 engineers and surveyors were commissioned to re-discover and study these ancient works with a view to future use. The maps of the Ceylon Survey Department today show more than 12,000 known tanks. The Ceylon Government, realising how useful these tanks can be, are working state-financed schemes for the restoration of many, the clearing back of the jungle and the settlement of peasants on the lands lost for centuries. Some of the important schemes are outlined below.

Gal Oya Colony Gal Oya, flowing from the hills, used to flood the countryside near its banks during the North-East Monsoon. Today, a dam 60 ft. high holds back a reservoir from which canals feed water to paddi lands where once was jungle; 50,000 colonists have found homes, land and prosperity in this, the greatest of Ceylon's development schemes.

Padawiya Colony This colony was opened in 1957. Its basis is the ancient reservoir built in the time of King Mahasena (fourth

293

century A.D.) now restored and feeding waters to the lands from canals branching from both its banks. Every family has been given a well-designed and sanitary-fitted cottage, 3 to 5 acres of irrigated paddi land, and 2 acres of higher (unirrigated) land for gardens.

Parakrama Samudra Colony   The old break in the embankment of this twelfth-century tank was repaired in 1939. Today it irrigates 15,000 acres of paddi land to support 3,000 hitherto landless peasants.

THE ELEPHANT

Renowned in the ancient and modern worlds, the elephant is the pride of Ceylon's fauna. It can be seen in captivity working under the direction of its "mahout", pulling logs, uprooting trees and moving large stones, in festival processions richly caparisoned, or wild in the forests and game reserves at Wilpattu and Mahaweli. Ceylon's wild elephant population has been estimated at 1,000 to 3,000, a mere fraction of its past numbers. So much killing has taken place in the past that the Ceylon Government has given its elephants special protection lest they become extinct. No licences will be issued for hunting and no animals will be exported except bj the Government.

The Ceylon elephant is not, as one might expect, related to the Indian elephant. It belongs to the Sumatra family, a smaller type amongst which tuskers are rare. Only 7% of male Ceylon elephants are tuskers (i.e. have well-developed tusks) compared with 80% in south India. In the past, herds were to be found all over the island, but with the coming of the great tea and rubber estates the elephants have retreated to the northern and eastern parts of Ceylon.

Elephants are vegetarians who mash leaves ripped from trees and bushes with their large teeth. Their sight and hearing are poor, but their sense of smell is acute. They are rather timid animals, but if roused to anger or protecting their babies they can be very dangerous to life and crops. This is a description of the damage wrought by a "rogue" the most dangerous of elephants. He is an animal outlawed by his own herd and rejected by others. His lonely

Panikkars capturing an elephant

wanderings eventually turn him crazy and he kills and destroys for pleasure.

> The village huts were smashed and scattered, acres of paddi were trampled into a muddy pulp, coconut trees had been torn up by the roots, a senseless, cataclysmic force had been at work to smash, trample and ravage. Life in its first essentials had been disrupted and scattered, and the reaction was elemental. The village was a buzzing ant-heap of distressed humanity, roused to restore at once the mainspring of their existence, a destroyed agriculture.*

Villagers of the forest rightly fear the elephant. Because of the elephant they keep watch over the paddi fields day and night for if he once gets into the village he may trample paddi, huts and people into the ground. So great is the people's fear that they will not speak his name in case he appears on the scene; they call him "the old one". Shooting by peasants in defence of their paddi

*Quoted from *Ceylon; Pearl of the East* by Harry Williams (Robert Hale), pp. 122–3.

fields was a common death for elephants, but now experiments using flashlights, fire-crackers and rockets are proving successful.

Legends galore surround the elephant. One such is the belief that elephants having died of natural causes are never found. It is thought that they go to die at secret places and the peasants believe that near Anuradhapura there is such a spot. Another is the belief that by passing under and through the legs of an elephant a child will inherit its strength.

Catching Elephants The normal method of catching wild elephants in Asia and Africa is by "kraaling" them into a stockade from which they cannot escape. The Muslim Panikkars of east Ceylon use a much more daring and sporting technique. They lassoo single elephants with a deer-hide rope just as cowboys noose steers. The reigning champion Panikkar has more than 200 elephants to his credit.

Not only do the Panikkars capture elephants, they also train them. They use a mixture of patience, cruelty and humiliation to educate each animal for work. A newly caught elephant is tied to a tree for a few days for it to expend its energies and anger. In the village it is taunted by shouts and dancing and is tantalised by keeping food just out of its reach. The first principle in the six weeks' training course is to make the animal used to the smell and touch of man. It is taught to "salaam" by kneeling on its forelegs and raising its trunk high into the air. A sharp, hooked metal goad is used to discipline its movements.

Then the Panikkar mounts its back, for short periods at first, so that it will accept the mahout whose charge it will be. Specialised training in doing heavy work or performing tricks follows when the animal has accepted man's mastery.

But let us return to the exciting capture. The Panikkar hunting party sets an ambush on an elephant track, making sure to keep on the leeward side of the herd. Their ropes have one end formed into a slip noose and the other end tied in a large, heavy knot. At the ready, the Panikkars shout, light torches and fire shots as the herd passes them. The terrified elephants stampede in confusion. The nooser chases on foot after them and selects his young elephant. He slips the noose over the animals' hind leg and quickly winds the knotted end around the nearest tree. With a heavy jolt

Mechanical engineering trainees having a practical lesson at the Regional Technical Training Institute for South and East Asia, at Gal Oya

the elephant stumbles to the ground. The rest of the hunters tie its legs and neck. That dangerous limb, the trunk is tied to a foreleg lest it injures one of the party. The young elephant is free no more.

Danger stalks at every turn of this hunt. The Panikkar takes his life in his hands when he chases the huge, rampaging elephants. If the mother of the marked youngster senses the danger to her baby she will charge the Panikkar in its defence. What then is the Panikkar's reward? He will sell the young elephant at the rate of Rs. 30 (45s.) for each foot of its height; an elephant 7 ft. tall will fetch Rs. 210.

APPENDIX 1

Some rules of conduct laid down by Buddha
(1) For daily observance by all Buddhists:
>> Not to take life
>> Not to steal
>> Not to lie
>> Not to drink

(2) For observance on sabbaths and special days:
>> Not to eat after noon
>> Not to sit in comfortable seats
>> Not to sing, dance or play music, or to witness these
(3) For observance by especially devout Buddhists and monks:
>> Not to touch money
>> Not to decorate the body with fineries

APPENDIX 2

Elephant casualties and captures in the year 1958 (detected):

Captured on special licences	5
Isolated and handed to Zoo	1
Proclaimed and destroyed	0
Killed in defence of crops	17
Killed in self-defence	2
Killed by wanton shooting	6
Killed by accident	3
Found dead of natural causes	4
Reasons not known	13
Illicitly captured and handed to zoo	0
	51

(From the Administration Report for 1958 of the Warden Wild Life).

THE INDIAN SUB-CONTINENT

SOURCES CONSULTED

BOOKS

Ali, Salim, *The Book of Indian Birds* (Bombay Nat. Hist. Soc., 1946)
Baker, J. N. L., *A History of Geographical Discovery and Exploration* (Harrap, 1937)
Barua, Hem, *The Red River and the Blue Hill* (Lawyers' Book Stall, Assam)
Bower, Ursula Graham, *Naga Path* (Murray, 1950)
       The Hidden Land (Murray, 1953)
Cameron, Roderick, *Time of the Mango Flowers* (Heinemann, 1958)
Corbett, Jim, *Maneaters of Kumaon* (O.U.P., 1946)
Das Gupta, A., *Economic and Commercial Geography* (Mukherjee, 1955)
Davies, C. Collin, *An Historical Atlas of the Indian Peninsula* (O.U.P.)
De Golish, Vitold, *Primitive India* (Harrap)
Foster, W., edited by, *Early Travels in India* 1583–1619 (O.U.P.)
Fuller, J. F. C., *The Generalship of Alexander the Great* (Eyre & Spottiswoode)
Hunt, John, *The Ascent of Everest* (Hodder & Stoughton)
Pant, S. D., *The Social Economy of the Himalayas* (Allen & Unwin)
Prater, S. H. *The Book of Indian Animals* (Arthur Probsthain)
Rambach and others, *Expedition Tortoise* (Thames & Hudson)
Sekelj, Tibor, *Window on Nepal* (Robert Hale)
Seymour, John, *Round about India* (Eyre & Spottiswoode, 1953)
Slater, G., *Some South Indian Villages* (Madras)
       South India (Allen & Unwin)
Somervell, T. H., *Knife and Life in India* (Livingstone Press)
Spate, O. H. K., *India and Pakistan* (Methuen, 1957)
Stamp, L. D., *Intermediate and Commercial Geography* (Longmans, 1949)
Vaidya, Suresh, *Ahead Lies the Jungle* (Robert Hale)
Wadia, D. N., *Geology of India* (Macmillan, 1949)
Williams, Harry, *Ceylon: Pearl of the East* (Robert Hale, 1950)
Williamson, James A., *A Notebook of Commonwealth History* (Macmillan)
Woodruff, Philip, *The Men Who Ruled India: The Founders* (Cape)

Articles from *Canadian Geographical Journal*

1949, Nov., *Magic Land of Assam*, by H. Thompson Rich
1950, Jan., *Nagas of Assam*, by E. O. Hoppé

1951, May, *Scenes from Eastern India*, by William Dunning
    Sept., *The Korku Tribe of Central India*, by G. O. Boast
1952, May, *The Colombo Plan*, by Nik Cavell
    Dec., *Kashmir*, by Hedda Morrison
1958, Aug., *The Land of the Indus*, by Earl Bowser

Articles from *Ceylon Today* (Ceylon Government Information Dept.)

1952, Sept., *The Present Status of the Ceylon Elephant*, by C. W. Nicholas
1953, April, *The Climate of Ceylon*, by D. T. E. Dassanayake
    Salt Manufacture in Ceylon, by Kenneth J. Somanader
    The Sinhalese and Hindu New Year
    May–June, *Buddhism in Ceylon*, by D. T. Devendra
    Gal Oya –The Hub of a Mighty Enterprise
1954, Jan.–Feb., *Turtle-catching in Ceylon*, by K. J. Somanader
    March–Apr., *Irrigation in Ceylon*, by R. L. Brohier
    Work, Home and Leisure, by Mrs. E. C. Fernando
    Aug.–Sept., *The Ceylon Elephant*
    Nov. *Australian Aids for Irrigation Schemes*, by S. Arumugam
1955, Jan.–Feb., *Tamil Customs and Ceremonies Connected with Paddi Cultivation*
    March–Apr., *Sinhalese Customs Connected with Paddi Cultivation*
    May–June, *Harvest Legends of the East Coast*, I, by S. V. O. Somanader
    Huruluwewa Irrigation Reservoir, by S. Arumugam
    July–Aug., *Harvest Customs of the East Coast*, II, by S. V. O. Somanader
    Nov., *Fishing for Pearls in the Gulf of Mannar*, by Alfred Edward
1956, Jan., *Folk-lore and Legends of Ceylon*
    Feb. *Guarding Ceylon's Crops from Ruin*, by S. V. O. Somanader
    March, *Wilpattu National Park*, by Esmé Rankine
    The Walawe Ganga Scheme, by D. W. R. Kahawita
    Rice Cultivation in Ceylon, by Dr. M. F. Chandraratna
    Developing Ceylon's Fisheries
    April, *The Gipsies of Ceylon*, by S. V. O. Somanader
    July, *The Art of the Crab-catcher*, by S. V. O. Somanader
    Aug. *Special Protection for the Elephant*
    Marine Tropical Fish Emigrants from Ceylon, by Rodney Jonklaas
    Sept. *The Kandy Esala Perahera*, by C. B. Nugawela Dissawe
    The Fisherfolk of South Ceylon, by James Goonewardene
    Nov., *The Ceylon Peasant and his Traditional Culture*, by M. D. Raghavan
    The Vanishing Veddhas, by D. S. Abeyagunawardene
    Dec., *Carrying First Fruits to Landlord*, by S. V. O. Somanader
1957, March, *The Buffalo in Village Life*, by S. V. O. Somanader
    May, *The Rebirth of a River Valley*, by Melville Fernando
    Festivals and Fairs in Ceylon, by C. R. Samarasinha
    July, *Noosing Ceylon's Wild Elephants*, by S. V. O. Somanader
    Aug., *The Social Landscape of Ceylon*, by M. D. Raghavan
    Oct., *The Mutwal Fishery Centre*

1955, Jan., *Ceylon's Buddhist Heritage*, by Ralph Keene
Progress in East Pakistan, by Basil Greenhill
July, *Coins on and beyond the Roman Frontiers*, by Prof. Michael Grant
1956, Dec., *The North-West Frontier Agency of India*, by Verrier Elwin
1957, Aug., *Cautley and the Ganges Canal*, by R. M. Panjabi
Pakistan's Natural Gas
The Story of the Survey of India, by Brig. G. F. Heaney
Dec., *The Christian Fishermen of Malabar*, by Ella Maillart

Articles from *Geographical Review of India*

1954, Sept., *Settlements and Habitations in India*, by K. H. Buschmann
1955, June, *Transport in and around Calcutta*, by Meera Guha
1957, March, *Development of a new Port in West Bengal*, by A. K. Deb
June, *Deleisera Revisited*, by Nityananda Patnaik

Articles from *Geography*

1950, June, *A Note on Irrigation in Ceylon*, by E. K. Cook
1952, July, *India's Peoples and their Food*, by Sir E. J. Russell
The Indian Village, by O. H. K. Spate
1955, July, *Aspects of Village Life in Indo-Pakistan*, by A. T. A. and A. M. Learmonth
1958, Apr., *Crop Association Regions in East Pakistan*, by B. L. C. Johnson
July, *The Ganges-Kobadak Irrigation Scheme*, by B. L. C. Johnson
1959, Apr., *Problems of Land-Use Mapping in the Tropics*, by R. Wikkramatileke
July, *Mesta Cultivation in West Bengal*, by B. Banerjee

Articles from *The Oriental Geographer*

1957, Jan., *Govindpur—A Study in Land-use*, by S. H. H. Naqavi
Sui Gas in West Pakistan, by A. H. Siddiqi
July, *Kazikasba, Panam and Joradeul—A Study in Land-use*, by F. K. Khan
Natural Gas in East Pakistan: Sylhet Gas, by S. H. H. Naqavi
Rural Settlement Patterns and House Types in Sind, by M. N. Khan

Articles from *Pakistan Geographical Review*

1949, No. 2, *Cotton Growing in West Pakistan*, by Fakhar B. Mahmud
Jute—The Golden Fibre of Pakistan, by M. K. Elaih
Some Economic Aspects of Fisheries in East Bengal, by A. F. M. Mannan
1950, No. 1, *Jute—The Golden Fibre*, by M. K. Elaih
1951, No. 1, *Cottage Industries of Multan*, by Kaniz Fatma
1952, No. 2, *Climatic Regions of East Pakistan*, by Kazi S. Ahmad
1953, No. 2, *A Study of the Fragmentations of Holdings in West Pakistan*, by A. H. Jafri

302

Articles from *Pakistan Quarterly*

Vol. 3, No. 2, *The Karnafuli*, by Joan Mathewman
Vol. 3, No. 3, *Cloth for Pakistan*, by Qayyum A. Malik
                In the Chittagong Hill Tracts, by Lucien Bernot
Vol. 4, No. 2, *Boat Building in Old Bengal*, by Tofayel Ahmed
                The Sunderbans, by S. Rahmatullah
Vol. 5, No. 1, *Mogh Children*, by Denise Bernot
Vol. 6, No. 2, *The Peasant of East Pakistan*, by S. A. A.
Vol. 7, No. 2, *Pakistan Industrial Development Corporation*, by M. Ayub
Vol. 9, No. 4, *The Powindas Come down*
                The Village Brotherhood of East Pakistan, by Anwar Husain
                Tribal Entertainment, by Sylvia Matheson

PUBLICATIONS OF THE CEYLON GOVERNMENT

Anuradhapura   (1954)
Ceylon, by H. A. J. Hulugalle (1957)
Ceylon: A Tourist Guide (1951)
Ceylon: The Island and its People (1954)
Ceylon Year Book (1960)
Sigiriya (Illustrated travel brochure)
Sri Lanka Annual Progress Report (1958)

PUBLICATIONS OF THE INDIAN GOVERNMENT

Adivasis, The (M.I.B.*, 1955)
Agriculture and Animal Husbandry in India (Ministry of Agriculture)
Assam (Travel brochure)
Banaras (M.T.C.,† 1957)
Bombay State (M.T.C., 1958)
Calcutta (M.T.C., 1957)
Delhi (M.T.C., 1959)
East Indian Resorts (M.T.C., 1959)
Festivals of India (M.T.C., 1957)
5,000 Years of Indian Architecture (M.I.B., 1954)
Guide to Madras (1957)
Handbook of India (M.T.C., 1958)
Handbook of Indian Fisheries (ed. B. N. Chopra)
Hill Stations of North India (M.T.C., 1957)
Hill Stations of South India (M.T.C., 1957)
Improved Fishing (Information sheet)
India 1960 (Reference annual, M.I.B.)
Indian Cotton (Information sheet)
Indian Railways: One Hundred Years 1853–1953 (Ministry of Railways, 1953)
Indian Rivers (Information sheet)
India's Plantation Industry (Information sheet)
Kandla (Information sheet)

Kashmir (Travel brochure)
Kaziranga (Travel brochure)
Kerala (1959)
Madhya Pradesh (M.T.C., 1958)
Mysore and Coorg (M.T.C., 1957)
Orissa (Travel brochure)
Rice (Information sheet)
Romance of Coir, The
Simla (Travel brochure)
South India (M.T.C., 1957)
Temples of South India (M.I.B., 1960)
West Bengal and Assam (M.T.C., 1958)
Wheat (Information sheet)
With Gun and Rod in India (M.T.C.)

OTHER PUBLICATIONS

Ceylon—Her Tea Industry (The Tea Bureau, London, W.1.)
Fabric of Commerce, by Aytoun Ellis
Frontier Speaks, by Mohammad Yunus
How Tea is Grown and Marketed (The Tea Bureau, London, W.1.)
The Indian Jute Industry (Indian Jute Mills Assoc., Calcutta)
The Kolar Gold Field (John Taylor & Sons)
Pakistan (Educational Productions Ltd.)
Your Tea from Ceylon (Ceylon Tea Propaganda Board)

FILMS ISSUED BY INDIA HOUSE, LONDON

Handicrafts of Travancore
Song of the South
Tree of Wealth

*Ministry of Information and Broadcasting.

†Ministry of Transport and Communications.

The photographs were kindly supplied by the following authorities, organisations and individuals, whose assistance is gratefully acknowledged.

Government of India, pages 30, 39, 42, 51, 69
Government of India Tourist Office, pages 81, 199
Information Service of India, pages 27, 43, 44, 52, 75, 79, 87, 88, 99, 101, 107, 113, 115, 116, 133, 151, 155, 157, 159, 163, 166, 167, 179, 182, 190, 195, 197, 198, 215
Government of Pakistan, pages 154, 160, 220, 223, 225, 228, 240, 243, 250
Pakistan High Commission, London, pages 224, 227, 236, 237, 242, 245
Pakistan Quarterly, pages 175, 232, 233
Ceylon Government Information Department, pages 261, 263, 264, 265, 272, 273, 292, 293, 297
Ceylon Fisheries Department, page 280
Ceylon Tea Centre, pages 285, 288
The Mount Everest Foundation, page 201
WHO, photo from Independent Features, pages 64, 65, 66, 78, 139, 140, 141, 142, 143, 144, 145
The National Protrait Gallery, page 12
Independent Features, pages 33, 169, 171
The Geographical Magazine, pages 6, 9, 38
Brigadier G. F. Heaney, C.B.E., page 18
E. O. Hoppé, pages 25, 63, 97, 103, 123, 127, 129, 130, 134, 184, 185
Ella Maillart, reproduced from *The Geographical Magazine*, pages 38, 48, 50, Anand Manker, pages 92, 93, 102, 121, 122, 126, 173, 188, 189, 191, 192, 193, 194
Ram Panjabi, page 148
Oleg Polunin, pages 208, 210
Kenneth J. Somanader, pages 267, 270, 276, 291
S. V. O. Somanader, page 295
John Tyson, page 207
Francis Watson, pages 94, 131

INDEX